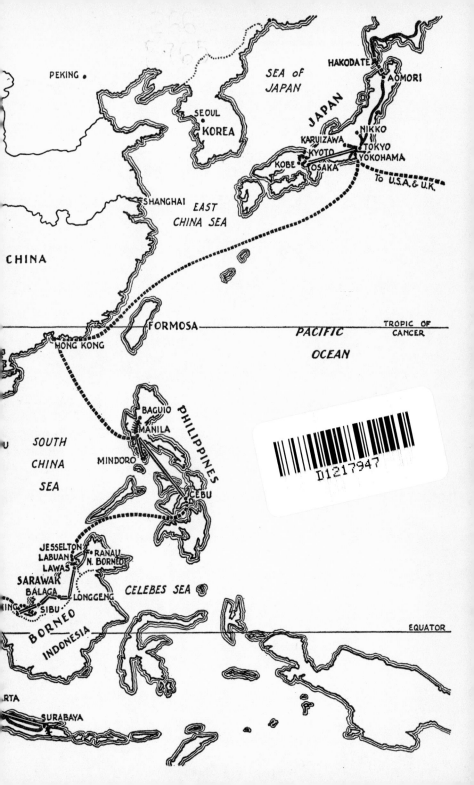

Earth's Remotest End

Photographs by Anne Pollock

Earth's Remotest End

by **J. C. Pollock**

Foreword by Billy Graham

New York
The Macmillan Company
1961

FOREWORD BY BILLY GRAHAM

One of the thrills of my life has been the discovery, during recent evangelistic travels, of the "hidden Church"—warm, devout groups of believers who are active today wherever faithful missionaries have preached the Gospel. Many of these Christians shame us by their lives of prayer, witnessing and sacrifice. Their personal knowledge of Jesus Christ is rich and full-bodied, and something of which the West stands in genuine need.

The Reverend J. C. Pollock, a competent British Christian journalist and former editor of *The Churchman*, here describes his arduous travels into the sections of Asia where unknown and unsung missionaries have been at work for years. His skillful pen has brought to light the increase that God has given. At the same time he has, in this very personal account, managed to bring into focus some of the fantastic difficulties the work of Christ faces in the East.

The conclusions he leaves to us, but to me they are inescapable. The Christians of Asia, like those of America, must learn to live day by day at the foot of the Cross, walking in love in the midst of rising and sometimes antagonistic ideologies.

Furthermore, the work of Christian missions is not over; it has barely begun. Most certainly we are witnessing a revolution in missions. The church is re-thinking the entire approach to such words as "mission," "commitment," and "evangelism." The fact is, Christianity is a shrinking minority in a world of revolt, confusion and tension. One of the definite movings of the Holy Spirit that can be discerned as one travels throughout the world are "little groups" of "called-out ones" meeting here and there, dedicated, disciplined and ready to sacrifice their very lives. I have noticed at various church conferences and retreats that the emphasis is increasing toward the "house church" in many parts of the world. Perhaps the Holy Spirit is getting His Church ready for a trial and tribulation such as the world has never known. One of Europe's greatest theologians recently said: "Within a generation the Church may well be underground." Hopeless? Yes, but also hopeful. To read this book is not only to enjoy a modern-day adventure but to see Jesus Christ, the Man of Asia, crucified and risen for the peoples of that great continent. It is to get a glimpse into the personal experiences of these heroic twentieth century followers of the God-Man from Nazareth.

PREFACE

Throughout Asia so many helped us that it would be impossible for my wife and me to thank them here individually. To the officials of Her Majesty's Foreign Office, Commonwealth Relations Office, Colonial Office, and British Administrators and Representatives abroad I would express gratitude for their assistance. I should also like to thank the Right Reverend the Lord Bishop of Liverpool, Field Marshal Sir Gerald Templer, Major General F. S. G. Piggott, Sir Christopher Summerhayes, and Miss Joy Ridderhof.

J. C. POLLOCK

November 23rd, 1959

CONTENTS

ix

PART THREE   ISLES OF THE SOUTHERN SEA

PART FOUR   FARTHEST EAST

ILLUSTRATIONS

Hindustan Prelude

ONE

Nine Men and a Girl

Mountains in the starlight. I looked, and wondered why Anne and I walked in a lane deep in Nepal in the middle of the night, with a Bengali road engineer, a young Punjabi businessman, and a six-foot-four Communist from South India who had a long gray beard, a black robe, a copper kettle.

I had been there before—or nearly so: overhead, in a plane, thirty-six hours earlier. Anne and I were due at Katmandu, the capital, which had been remote behind its barriers of mountain and political isolation but which now was only an hour by air from India.

On Friday, October 3, 1958, at about 1:30 P.M., we had been flying half an hour. The steward came down the plane. "We are turning back to Patna," he said. "There's a storm in the mountains and we can't get through."

The next day we were in the air again. Saturday in Nepal is reckoned an inauspicious day; as a special concession our plane was allowed to make for Katmandu. And the laugh was on the Hindu astrologers as once more the pilot turned back. He flew through and above the weather, and over the mountains, high enough to make me breathless in the unpressurized cabin. We saw nothing. Twice he circled Katmandu, looking for a break in the clouds; he dared not risk a blind approach, since to come in a little off course would crash us against the hills. In Katmandu it rained all that day; they heard us overhead.

During the descent to Patna, I looked out at the familiar Ganges, broad and muddy and dotted with brown sails, and at the spacious

bungalows of the state capital, and waved sadly to King-Emperor
George V before Government House. In the afternoon heat at the
airport, we extracted a light lunch from the reluctant air line, and
ate it in a small room at the back of the terminal in the company of
a goldfish. I could understand the feelings of the goldfish.

Back at the air-line office in the city the station officer, speaking
animatedly with a waggle of the hand and that confusing affirma-
tive shake of the head which are part of every Indian conversation,
explained that tomorrow's regular flight was already full. If there
were unexpected vacancies they would go to the diplomatic and
United Nations personnel stranded from our flight. An extra flight
was most unlikely, though he would try for one. Days might pass
before we could get to Katmandu.

A Nepalese, a professor of education with a chubby, cheerful face,
turned to me. "Why don't we go overland?" he asked. "There's the
new jeep road over the mountains. You take a train to the border
and on to the foothills and then you hope for a jeep. It may be
rough, and it may take thirty-six hours, but it should cost no more
than the flight." I found that there were five Nepalese, including the
Director-General of the Health Services, a noted radiologist who had
the fair skin, high cheekbones, and slightly Mongoloid eyes of the
Nuwars, the earlier rulers of the Nepal Valley, who were displaced
by the Gurkhas. Three of the others were professors, including one
who had just flown back after a year in the United States. He had a
blue American suit and a Donald Duck badge. He was Donald Duck
in voice and looks, but not in character. Nothing could depress,
annoy, or deflate him.

"Why don't we go overland?" they were all saying. I looked out at
the city street. Fat white-clad Bengalis and Biharis lolled by on the
seats of bicycle-rickshaws pedaled by barefooted coolies, themselves
comfortable in long cotton collarless shirts and dhotis, the garment
which hangs loosely around the legs and which in this area is tucked
up between them. In the office yard rickshaws waited. Sacred cows,
long-legged, heavy and humped, rucked in the garbage. A squatting
coolie unhurriedly placed bricks on his head, pair by pair, until it
seemed the pile must topple, and then with faultless balance rose and
walked away. I love India, but not Patna at the end of the southwest
monsoon.

That night we crossed the Ganges. There were ten of us, Anne and I the only Europeans. With the Director-General and the three professors was a young Nepalese engineering student returning from Delhi who kept assuring us: "You have nothing to worry about. We will entertain you." Three Indians from the stranded plane had joined us. The Bengali, Mr. Bose, fortunately held a high position in the administration of the new road over the mountains. The Punjabi businessman was boisterous and amusing, with a penchant for Agatha Christie and films. His strict vegetarianism and involuntary exclamation of horror at a near collision with a cow showed him to be a Brahman, the highest, most orthodox caste of Hindu. The giant South Indian, the only one in the party not in Western dress, had little English, and his mother tongue, Malayalam, was useless in the North. He said he was a political leader, and since Kerala was then Communist he was darkly suspect. But he had the eyes and smile of an aged saint.

The Ganges crossing took over two hours, upstream against a river full after the rains. We chanced on the best of the two flat-bottomed paddle steamers, the other being a three-storied sardine tin. In the saloon, where a standard fan whirled, insects buzzed round the lights, and a dwarf beggar walking on his knees sought alms, we chatted of Nepal and England. I could sense the pleasure of being, in effect, guests of cultured men from races with a true tradition of hospitality.

In the last minutes of the voyage the ferry listed sharply to port, staggered like a drunken man to the landing stage, and spilled its contents in a seething mass which ran toward a train standing aloof and mysterious in darkness. Before the lights came on, Professor Donald Duck used up most of my torch in settling us all.

The next morning I woke to one of the loveliest sights of India—dawn and sunrise in the countryside. Woods and green crops of sugar cane and rice, and the little villages of tiled or thatched huts, were bathed in freshness. In blue pools small boys scrubbed water buffaloes, patient dark gray beasts absurd with long thrusting heads, swept-back horns, and drooping donkey's ears. They have no sweat pores, and in the heat must be allowed a long daily wallow. Far away under the morning sun, and against a background of blue, rose a superb snow peak of the Himalayas.

At Raxaul, the last town in India, Anne and I got fried eggs, tea, and toast; had I known what lay ahead I would have eaten the meal three times. We crossed a wrought-iron bridge over the line, walked up a garden path, turned a corner, and found most of the others grouped round a toylike train which sat engineless in an open space between the booking office and a row of dirty gray cottages flanked with banana trees. Two children played on a grass-rope swing; a pony covered with sores stood tethered to the booking office; and a man crouched over the line blowing his nose on his fingers.

We all sat on a circular stone seat under a well-trimmed mango tree until the engine appeared, half an hour late, and the day's train crawled over a bridge into Nepal.

I have seen the Nepal Government Railway described as running through "some of the most breath-taking scenery in the world." Actually, it wanders lazily across a plain, drawing deep breaths at tiny stations shared with goats and cows, until it disappears into the belt of forest, the terai, dividing the plain from the hills.

Three and a half hours to cover twenty-nine miles are time enough to tell you why I had come to Nepal.

The story had really begun nearly three years earlier. An ordinary English parson of the younger generation, I had had the opportunity of flying out to India and Pakistan on a two-month visit. Already, like many of my contemporaries, I was disturbed at the ineffectiveness of the churches in Western countries. In England great congregations could be found here and there, and able leaders of all denominations, and the Christian faith received more respect than it had twenty years earlier. Yet millions had no active allegiance; clergy and ministers had a daily treadmill as welfare officers, odd-job men, and masters of ceremonies. And the emphasis was entirely local. Apart from lip service and occasional bursts of interest in other lands, each parish or church was absorbed in its own affairs.

India opened my eyes. Though I had never subscribed to the view that couples old maids and missionaries—pale reflections of pale curates—I was typical enough to consider them as of no concern to myself. India forced a change of outlook. I saw the working conditions of missionaries and their national colleagues, and the problems they faced in a non-Christian land.

The air journey showed how small is the world. It took less time to return to London than to travel between two parishes at opposite ends of England, yet missionaries were treated as if on another planet. Political interaction was accepted as normal; yesterday's events on the other side of the world disturbed the Englishman's digestion at breakfast, and the American Secretary of State might chat with the British Foreign Secretary in Oxfordshire on the way from Formosa to Washington by way of Rome and the North Pole. The church overseas, a factor in world affairs, was almost ignored.

Did this indifference, this condescending detachment while absorbed in local interests, partly result from lack of knowledge?

Should ordinary citizens make conducted tours of the mission field, their indifference would evaporate. Someone must go as their representative, to see and hear (and smell) as they, to experience their reactions and draw their conclusions, and then to put the evidence before them. Travel writers who condescend to notice missionaries portray them as foolishly simple, paving a primrose path with good intentions, or hard-faced bigots. Missionary literature consists largely of specialist volumes out of reach of the general public, or pious works assuming the reader's sympathy and often couched in language of a nineteenth century tract. Even the best normally is limited to one small area. The travel book I wanted must cover a continent.

It turned out that I should be the one to go. In the late summer of 1958, with my wife as secretary, business manager, and photographer, I left England by sea.

This is not a book for the experts. They will find nothing in it they do not know already. It merely records the adventures of an inquisitive man and his wife, thirty-three thousand miles through fifteen countries, to remote areas of mountain and jungle, to great cities and overpopulated plains, by sea and air, rail, car and foot.

I began with the basic belief of any convinced Christian, that Christ is the Saviour of the whole world, the way, the truth, and the life. Beyond that, my mind was open. I wanted to see whether the churches were making good the Christian claim. I was ready to be disillusioned or profoundly impressed; to be constructively critical or frankly admiring. Traveling on behalf of the general reader in Western countries, I sought also to see through Eastern eyes. An

Englishman of the Church of England, my inquiries were not limited to British or to Anglican activity.

After it was all over, however, I had to decide how much to discuss the Roman Catholics. I had talked with one or two of their leaders, a special memory being of the affable, bearded Indo-Irish Archbishop of Delhi-Simla. I had heard also serious criticisms of Roman methods. I have no wish to pass on these secondhand detractions without adequately presenting the other side. But Roman Catholicism in Asia plows its own furrow, and except for cooperation in certain social or political matters it is so completely a separate department that to study it as fully as I did the Protestant churches would have required far more time and money than I could afford. Moreover, though I have no doubt I should have been welcomed, I could hardly have expected, in view of drastic doctrinal divergences, the opportunity for frank assessment. And so I have been compelled to leave the Roman Catholics aside—they have many and admirable writers—until I reach the Philippines, where they are a factor of major importance to the whole political and religious situation, and to confine myself to Protestants.

As I traveled, above all else I wished to find the answer to the question: Is the work of churches and of missionaries in Asia a vital factor in the world today? If it is, we should take urgent notice. Literary critics, whose favor is life to a book, seem to envelop this subject in a conspiracy of silence. Perhaps the spectacle of a parson resigning his parish and its security to write a travel book will interest them.

It was a gamble for an obscure individual to go off on his own through the East. And, as you shall hear, it nearly failed within the first few months.

The little train of dark brown carriages emerged from the forest and dumped us at the railhead, Amlekganj.

The Director-General had already secured the promise of an official jeep for himself and the professors. At Amlekganj he negotiated for a private-hire jeep for the rest of us. This was fortunate, for the only other transport was an ancient yellow and red bus with springless seats. We passed it later in full flight in the rain, bodies bulging from the windows and late comers perched on the roof under umbrellas. Ninety miles over the mountains in that would have been martyrdom.

The Director-General bargained with the jeep driver; the young Punjabi and I scavenged. It was nearly 3:00 P.M., over six hours since the eggs at Raxaul. The others, who would not come for the eggs, had eaten Indian sweetmeats in the train, using leaves as plates and, at the next stop, pouring water into their mouths without touching the brass vessel with their lips. They had pressed sweets on us, but there was little enough between them and we took only a taste.

Amlekganj was truly Nepal—no beggars and no staring—and had rows of booths where cross-legged shopkeepers offered uncooked rice and vegetables, but it had neither fruit nor chapatties nor eggs. The best we could find were two packets of Britannia biscuits, and on these and on glasses of tea we existed until late that night.

At half-past three the jeep moved. At the others' insistence Anne and I had the comfortable front seats, and in the back Bose, the Bengali road engineer, the Punjabi, the young Nepalese, and the South Indian giant sat Eastern fashion on the luggage which had been squeezed in by careful packing. We drove a hundred yards and stopped for gas. We drove two hundred yards more, and the whole jeep was unloaded for customs. At last we were off. For a few miles we drove on the old road through woods and across shallow fords. With the hills, the new road began. It had been built, as Bose told us, by Indian engineers over a period of five years, and opened in 1956. It is called Tribhuban Raj Path, after the King of Nepal who died in 1955, and it is a magnificent feat of engineering. Especially I liked its width; at no time is there a sense of being on the edge of the precipice.

Thick cloud obscured the view of the tops of the hills, and when, after crossing a bridge, we subsided with a puncture in the middle of a village, rain was falling. The driver changed the wheel in ten minutes under the amused eye of a policeman, while goats jostled by, and countrymen almost hidden under loads of hay carried on a pole across the shoulders. Higher up, beyond the rain, a rainbow spanned the hills.

On and up went the jeep, twisting and turning in a rock-and-roll progress round hairpin bends, our bodies swerving in unison over to the left, over to the right, over to the left again. The driver, a silent young man with closely shaved head, and lower lip thrust grimly forward, was one of the best I have ever had. As darkness closed in, the rain stopped and I took a last look back at India, showing red in a sunset we could not share.

The Punjabi businessman was overcome with mountain sickness. He and I changed places. I could not hold up my head in the back, and before many miles I too had to stop the jeep and stagger into the night. By the time we crossed the pass, at 8,500 feet, no one either expected or wanted us to hustle to Katmandu, still over fifty miles away. Bose's own Public Works camp, Palung was now not far, and he proposed that we should all stay overnight.

Palung is in a saucer of hills, and its lights were visible below as the road wound down from the pass. I was sitting in the front, thinking of steak and bacon and eggs and hot soup, none of which I was likely to get, when the jeep turned a corner and drew up sharply behind an unlighted lorry. A line of big trucks, Katmandu's only channel for heavy goods, had been stopped by a roadblock. Bose found that the road was closed until dawn.

We did not carry a senior engineer for nothing. He said he would find the barrier key. We waited, shivering in our thin clothes. Bose suggested we should walk to the camp, for getting the key might take time. The Nepalese stayed to guard the luggage, since he felt the cold least.

And so we walked, a quarter of a mile up the road and then into the lane leading to the camp; the South Indian plodding in his sandals, the Punjabi subdued with fatigue, Bose pleased at being able to offer hospitality, ourselves hungry, cold, and silent, yet curiously elated as we looked around at these hills under the stars, deep in a country which only a few years before had been fast closed to the world.

I shall not forget the kindness of Bose's colleagues, the Indian P.W.D. officers in their Nissen-type huts with flickering hurricane lamps. They made all ten of us welcome, turning out of their bunks, producing blankets, and making the best meal they could, which was painfully slow to come and just chappaties, lentil, and a little cooked and flavored rice—but a feast to stomachs that had gone for over twenty-four hours on two eggs, two pieces of toast, biscuits, and tea. Anne and I were then given a hut to ourselves. The beds were hard boards, but to me seemed soft as down.

Nor shall I forget the splendid panorama of the mountains in the early-morning sun as soon as we crossed over the rim of the saucer, some twenty minutes from Palung. Much of the lower ground was in cloud, but beyond rose snow peaks and plateaus the length of the horizon, stately in shape and symmetry; only the extreme east of the line was blocked by cloud, robbing us of Everest.

The road doubled down the mountain toward the central valley, past woods and rice terraces, and countrymen in their floppy brimless Nepalese hats, carrying black umbrellas. At 8:20 A.M. we met a closed barrier: "This road," it announced, "will remain open only between 5–7 A.M., and 2–4 P.M." We sat in front of it under the sun, munching bananas in lieu of breakfast, until Bose and the Director-General, after fifteen minutes, proved more powerful than regulations. Outside Katmandu was a road tax barrier. Here were Professor Donald Duck's students to garland him in welcome.

We drew up in the Durbar Square of Katmandu, in front of a pair of heraldic lions, a few minutes before 10:00 A.M. on Monday, October 6th, four hours after leaving the Public Works camp at Palung, and seventy hours after the plane had first taken off for its scheduled one-hour flight.

How effortless that experience seemed in the light of later adventures farther East!

TWO ✿ *Katmandu*

Katmandu is not, like Zermatt in Switzerland, steep streets, and the mountains on the doorstep. It lies in the middle of a fertile central valley seventeen miles long and fifteen wide; and, small as it is, gives a sense of spaciousness, though the back streets look as higgledy-piggledy as any Indian bazaar. All around are hills, and away to the north the snow mountains, lovely in the evening light when the clouds cleared and the pink of the sunset rose steadily toward the summit.

Katmandu's temples resemble Chinese pagodas: two or three roofs on top of each other in a pyramid of red tile, supported by gables heavily carved with gods and goddesses. In contrast, the numerous palaces are in the English Georgian or Regency styles—Corinthian columns and white stucco. The palace in the Durbar Square, all proper with balustrades and pillars, might have been an English town hall except for the sentries and black cows dozing below. Most of the city is less than thirty years old, having been devastated by earthquake; but so cleverly had the chief buildings been restored, including the tall tower which I thought must be a minaret but was only a folly, that no one could tell.

Equestrian statues, cast in England and carried over the mountains in the old days by mule or man, dominate the streets. Most of them are of hereditary maharajah prime ministers, of the Shum Shere Jung Bahadur Rana family who, for a hundred years, kept the kings from power, treated the revenues as their own privy purse, and excluded foreigners. The British Ambassador showed me a book which listed every foreigner who entered Nepal between 1881 and 1924. Apart from the British Resident, his staff, the annual inspectors of his escort, and an occasional special envoy, there were only sixty-six in forty-four years. But the latest statue was not that of a Prime Minister. Looking down New Road toward the British Information Room and the American Library stood King Tribhubana, the savior of his country. His dramatic escape to the Indian Embassy on November 6, 1950, was the signal for the rising which overthrew the Ranas, restored the King to his own, and opened Nepal to the world. Since then the nation has been striding out of the Middle Ages and into the twentieth century.

Beyond the river, over the iron bridge brought a hundred years ago from England by the Prime Minister who visited Queen Victoria, is the United Mission Hospital at Shanta Bhawan.

Shanta Bhawan was formerly a palace of one of the Ranas, and the guest room his summer house, a creeper-covered cottage in a little garden. The garden had statuary, and an ornamental pond from which we drew water in kerosene tins to pour down the lavatory, taking care not to catch a fish. It had also chickens, and a white rabbit belonging to the daughter of the American heads of the hospital—Dr. Bethel Fleming, the medical superintendent, and Dr.

Bob Fleming, the administrative. Beyond the garden wall were fields, and in the fields was a charming small house where lived two Norwegians, the Robert Bergsakers.

Bergsaker, who was superintending the building of the new mission hospital at Bhatgaon, a few miles away, could turn his hand to anything. On the walls of their living room hung his oil paintings and his woodcut of a rhino in the terai; on a table lay silver boxes he had wrought; and above the door, holding gaily colored plates, was a rack he had carved. Here, in a room bright with carpets and embroidery, over coffee, waffles, and yak cheese, I heard how the United Mission began.

The Flemings were on the staff of a school in North India, Dr. Bethel as medical officer, Dr. Bob as head of the boys' side. Bob Fleming is also an ornithologist, and it was as such that he was permitted by the prerevolutionary government to lead an expedition in 1949 to West Nepal, where he saw the complete lack of medical facilities, the almost unbroken illiteracy and widespread poverty. He also made a powerful friend in Tansen's Governor Rudra Rana.

At that time Fleming had no thought of missionary work in Nepal, nor did he when he returned in December, 1951, for a second ornithological expedition lasting four months. Dr. Bethel came too, and set up a temporary clinic in Tansen. The revolution was over. The country had opened its doors. American aid was pouring in, and the United States Operations Mission was building public works. And the Jesuit Father Moran, the first foreign missionary to be admitted as a resident, had started a school in Katmandu which now educates the children of most of the leading families.

On his third visit, trekking overland from Tansen to Katmandu, Fleming grew convinced that he and his wife should open a Christian hospital in Nepal if such a thoroughly Hindu state would permit it. He had Tansen in mind, but was persuaded that an application to open in so remote a place would be rejected; the government needed the prestige of a modern hospital in Katmandu. He drew up and presented a formal proposition, accompanied by a private assurance that his hospital would not evangelize and that he would respect the customs and religion of the country, but asking for freedom of worship on his own compound. In the course of 1953 the Nepal Government accepted the proposition—on terms that included the right, after five years, to take over the hospital and everything in it, including expensive equipment brought from abroad.

The mission opened modestly in January, 1954, an American Methodist venture. A few months later Bishop Jarrell W. Pickett, the famous Methodist Bishop of New Delhi, boldly expanded it into a United Mission, interdenominational and international, so that eleven denominations or societies are represented and the missionaries are drawn from nine nationalities: Nepalese from North India, Indians, Americans, British, Canadians, Norwegians and Swedes, Germans and Swiss. It spread. A hospital at Tansen opened in 1954, and schools and clinics at Katmandu and elsewhere. The government has suggested more projects than the mission has as yet funds or members to support.

Nepal, geographically like a step between the plains of India and the high plateau of Tibet, is balanced politically between communism and democracy. Both sides seek to charm her with presents and persuasion, and the issue, when I was there, was by no means certain. The work of the United Mission made an undoubted factor in favor of democracy.

There is, however, a serious criticism that has been leveled by those who have not been to Nepal: that the United Mission absorbs money and men but may not do the first work of a mission—evangelism.

We discussed this criticism during a picnic at the site of a projected leprosy hospital on the edge of the valley, having driven out along a rough road through villages of red-brick houses. Children, recognizing the hospital car, cheered and laughed and held grubby little fingers together before their faces in the ancient greeting of *Namastay*. "Namastay!" they cried, and "Ingrezi! Ingrezi!" Every white man is English to the Nepalese villager. On the street rice was laid out to dry which women in saris with bangles on their arms and gold in their noses threshed and winnowed. Before the houses were poles stacked round with corn on the cob, and the walls were gay with strings of red pepper.

The Flemings know where they stand. Dr. Bethel, gray-haired and motherly, said: "We feel that we are doing Christian work just by being here. Nepalese are seeing the meaning of Christian values.

And we are an encouragement to the little Nepalese church in Katmandu." Dr. Bob, a man thin in body and face, with a pointed chin, small gray mustache and graying hair, a laconic Midwesterner of twinkling eyes and a dry sense of humor, maintained that the hospital played an important part in demolishing prejudice and preparing the way for complete freedom of religion.

From what I learned elsewhere I believe he is right. The situation was delicate. Younger educated Nepalese wished to see democracy a reality. When the codification of the penal code in 1956 had been found to include imprisonment for the propagators or converts of any religion except the Hindu or Buddhist, public reaction was sharp—not through friendship to Christianity but because the clauses were undemocratic. Yet, though these clauses were shelved, during my visit three Nepalese pastors were awaiting trial for public preaching and baptisms in the terai.

I could detect the tension. At Shanta Bhawan the atmosphere of spruce solemnity common to large hospitals, East and West, seemed to spread to mealtimes in the staff dining room, partly because the pressure of work induced exhaustion but mainly because they were there on sufferance. As Western aid they were welcome; as Christians, officially, they were not. Despite the undoubted friendliness and innate courtesy of the educated Nepalese, and the gratitude of the poor, they had to watch their steps.

Four months later, in February, 1959, the King proclaimed parliamentary government. Yet though "fundamental rights" are conferred on the peoples, personal liberty, equality before the law, economic, political, and religious freedom, an article of the new Constitution specifically states that "no person shall be entitled to convert another person to his religion." Freedom extends to practice and to profession but apparently not, as in India, to propagation, unless the new Supreme Court, "to protect the people against the invasion of their fundamental rights," interprets the article more generously.

Looking at the expensive medical equipment given by American churches to the United Mission, I could understand why the ordinary Nepalese, however grateful for skilled attention, regards Shanta Bhawan as foreign, and its religion as foreign.

Fortunately, its staff were not the only Christian missionaries in Katmandu. One afternoon Dr. Bob Fleming took me to the city to meet the Mar Thoma boys.

Some thirty-five years ago a peasant girl in South India heard Sadhu Sundar Singh, that prophetic character who, after making considerable impact on East and West, disappeared in the Himalayas, speaking of Nepal's need of the Christian Gospel. The girl was a member of the Mar Thoma church, a branch of the ancient "Syrian" church in Kerala. When she married she dedicated her first son to missionary service in this country at the other end of her world. Her hopes were fulfilled. While still students, he and a friend made two preaching tours in the terai, the first before the revolution and the second after, and on February 8, 1953, they opened house in Katmandu, nearly a year earlier than the medical mission. Little more than boys then, they have been "the Mar Thoma boys" ever since.

The peasant woman's son was in the United States for further training. I found his original companion and two others, one being a priest of the Mar Thoma church, up ladder-like stairs behind New Road. The street was so narrow I could have poked with a stick the woman in a brown sari sitting in the window opposite. Men in the shirts and Nepalese loose jodhpur-like trousers, their hats at a rakish angle, gossiped noisily below. Flies, that curse of Katmandu, buzzed in the sunlit dust between the houses. Nearby were some of the numerous temples where all day long a trickle of worshipers cast petals and sweets to the idols.

They told me that they had a common purse and discipline, meeting for prayer three times a day. When they arrived in 1953 they found one Nepalese Christian, a member of the dominant Rana family who had been converted over the border. Now they have a roomful, some thirty or forty every Sunday for service, of converts and inquirers. "It is private, as the law demands," they said, "in that it is in our own house. But it is public in that thousands know about it." Inquirers come at all hours every day. One young man had been thrashed by his shopkeeper-father for attending, and was called an atheist when he abandoned worship of the Hindu gods. He dared not be baptized, as some others had, because he would have been expelled from his home.

Round the Mar Thoma boys a church was growing. There was also another group, led by a Nepalese pastor from Kalimpong. I would have met him, but the delay in reaching Katmandu cut short our visit; and much time had to be spent in the Central Secretariat, once the palace of the Maharajah Prime Minister (white stucco and Corinthian pillar mixture as before) but now housing almost all the government departments. Here, from a sea of polite prevarication and genuine Nepalese charm, I extracted at last, in the record time of four days, the necessary pass to the mountains of West Nepal.

THREE   ✻   *A Witch Doctor and Others*

Through the cockpit window I watched green hills and deep narrow valleys slide below. To the right, at eye level, Himalayan peaks emerged from swaths of cloud.

We were nearing Pokhara, a week's trek over a roadless countryside but only thirty-five minutes due west from Katmandu by air. Before I left the cockpit the Sikh pilot pointed out the first sight of the valley, the second largest in Nepal, and banked to starboard to begin the descent. Back in the cabin after the wheels were lowered, I looked out on the grass landing ground and was relieved to see no herd of cattle lining up to charge across the runway as they had one day a few seconds after the touchdown, with disastrous results. The plane landed bumpily and taxied to a halt in front of two bamboo huts.

From the moment that Jean Raddon, Stanley Wall, and the Nepalese pastor waved to us from the little knot of country people meeting the plane until we trudged off into the mountains three days later, the Nepal Evangelistic Band gave us unforgettable hospitality.

It was late afternoon that we went up to the hospital, having spent the day at a cluster of thatched huts above a gorge near the airfield, where Eileen Lodge, a young London nursing sister with fair hair and light blue eyes, and Barbara Best, who had first come to India in 1930 and who had a pleasing touch of empire builder, ran a primitive but effective leprosarium. The walk to the hospital, out on the north road, took us right through the tumbled-down city which boasts of being the third in size in Nepal. Children and adults greeted Jean Raddon with *Namastay*. Little Tibetan terriers lay cozily beside their owners; in the plains of India dogs are mostly pariah, and their characteristics are fleas and the fear of man, but here in the hills many were pedigreed. I saw no jeep or motorcar or wheeled cart in streets where grass grew between the stones. Every load is carried by coolie.

The track led up across an open space to a plateau flanked by modern buildings—the new government school built by American aid, and a row of dazzling aluminum huts, like miniature aircraft hangers, which were the wards of the mission hospital. The land fell away to the river, beyond which deep green hills rose into low clouds.

To the right of the aircraft hangars, past a buffalo pond and through a little gate down to the staff compound, was a group of jungle houses. The straw color of their thatched roofs and dried banana-leaf walls was offset by orange Klondike planted all around. Towering above in white majesty stood the peaks. Not until sunrise on the Sunday morning did the whole range come out of cloud: Fish-tail (Marchha Pucha) in the center, sharp-pointed like the Mat-terhorn; Sitting Elephant and Himal Chuni ("Knobs On") to the east, their names expressive of their shape, forming the Anna-purna range. To the west, a separate mountain, the massive block of Dhauligiri.

These names figure frequently in headlines as climbers come and go. Yet as if to emphasize the loneliness of the place, a woman entered the compound just behind us carrying the first delivery of magazine mail for four months, freighted by air from the plains that afternoon. Letter mail came from Katmandu about once a fortnight. In the rains, when the landing ground was flooded and the hills blacked out by storms, no plane could get through for weeks, and isolation was complete.

In this remote outpost the Nepal Evangelistic Band had created a home. The little huts with their mud floors and leaf walls were gay with check curtains, yellow, red, and green. Each had a name. Our's was Badger's Glory, which took me right back to a keeper's cottage I knew in the Dorset countryside. The others were Bamboo

Hall, Barn House, Bleak House, and Buckingham Palace. The living room had sofa and chairs in the Indian bungalow style (cane and polished wood), and pictures: autumn beeches in England, St. Ives Harbour, and the like; a view of mountains with a text, "Let Christ Rule," superimposed, a colored calendar, plenty of books of all sorts, and a battery wireless presented by the Swiss Dhauligiri Expedition of 1953. It was dead, having once gone to Katmandu for repairs.

Two dogs completed the household. Goley, six, was a Schitzu terrier from Tibet, low on the ground, long in body, round of head, who when given to the hospital by a patient, at the age of six months, was so small that he was christened Goliath—and once got his head stuck in a condensed-milk tin. Stumpy was a mongrel puppy from the bazaar, though believed to be Goley's grandson. He was black with white tips, and in the slipper-eating, trouser-pulling stage.

Food was a perpetual difficulty to the hospital staff. The Brahmans of Pokhara were strong enough to prevent more than an occasional killing of buffalo; the sheep were for wool and not mutton, and as for beef, the staff could only dream of it. That left goat, expensive and unsatisfying, and chicken. Vegetables were scarce, owing to some oddity of the local soil. Dishes were well served and helpings big; no one rose hungry, but all joked about the shortages. In one or two other places, as I scraped up the last of an inadequate plateful, I had to smirk and pretend that I had had quite enough, thank you.

These pioneers did not go around with dedicated looks on their faces, eat off enamel, and wear jumble-sale dresses. There was nothing of wisp and bun about their hair. Yet they were building a solid work in conditions of privation and loneliness. Apart from their innate sense of humor and, on a deeper level, an unwavering faith in a Christ who to them was as real and present as to the first disciples, I ascribed their balance partly to an insistence on regular relaxation. I believe the "sabbatical" principle—one in seven as a day of rest—to be of divine institution, ignored at peril, except in emergencies. Men and women of God seem the quickest to break it. They cannot generally rest on a Sunday, and therefore should take another day. They seldom do. "I've got a

conscience," said one man in India; "I'm supported by the gifts
of people at home. I oughtn't to let up." "We don't know how long we
shall be here," said another; "we cannot miss a moment." "Don't
tell the folks at home," said a third as he painted a toy truck he
had made for his small son. With that attitude goes tension, weari-
ness, low output.

Pokhara hospital was called Shining Hospital. Far up on the
trade route to Tibet, as we saw for ourselves one day, and high on
the slopes of Annapurna, the aluminum wards could be seen shining
in the sun, throwing off the rays, and cool inside. Plans have been
laid to bring up another six or eight huts from Calcutta, expensive
to buy but cheap to maintain, and raise the hospital to a hundred
beds. It is a simple affair, but the first medical aid the district has
known. Patients come from days away. Occasionally a Brahman
objected if he was placed next to a low caste. He would be told:
"This is a Christian hospital and has no caste distinctions. You
must conform or leave." Sometimes a man would hesitate to enter
the outpatients clinic. "I'm very low caste; can I come in?" "We
generally place him next to a Brahman!" said Dr. Gerald Turner.

When they first came, in April, 1952, the land they were given
was haunted, though they did not know it, nor did they know that
the people waited breathlessly to see them destroyed by evil spirits.
The bazaar was hostile, and once they heard of plans for an attack
on the compound. But as men and women were cured or relieved,
acceptance came, and then popularity. Even the Brahmans now
admire the N.E.B. as holy people because they heal sick Brahmans,
thereby gaining merit. Treatment of lower castes is in their eyes an
unnecessary waste.

Now, after six and a half years at Pokhara, the mission hoped
for government leave to survey the northern valleys, steep and
remote but with a considerable population deep in poverty and
the darkness of witchcraft, a shadowy borderland between the
Hinduism of Nepal and the lamaistic Buddhism of Tibet. To open
five or six new clinics they required forty-five recruits, Nepalese
and European.

The N.E.B. has not joined the United Mission, as the latter
hoped and as material considerations might have suggested. "We've

prayed about it," they said, "and we just do not feel led that way. We are alert to any leading in that direction but it hasn't come." I have no wish to dispute that, after studying work astonishingly successful. Organic unity should never be imposed, and could mean less than the present close sympathy. The N.E.B., a small group of twelve or fifteen, with no powerful backing, had been working for Nepal from over the border when the United Mission was not even a dream. It had grown like a family. The family relationship would be jeopardized by absorption in a large combine.

Someday there will be a united church when Christianity in Nepal is stronger. Missions are only temporary.

The Nepalese pastor stood behind a large lectern Bible which he did not use, but fingered a lighter one of his own. Pastor David had fair skin, high cheekbones, large spectacles, a gray mustache, and a thin neck, On his left forearm was a tattoo, relic of the wild oats sown by this son of a Darjeeling Christian before being brought to a living faith.

I was sitting on a mat, my shoes off, on the floor of the first church to be built in Nepal in modern times; in the late eighteenth century the Romans had a mission until expelled. It was a mere jungle shelter—three bamboo poles and two of wood in the center, a thatched roof, and a low bamboo fence round the side—but it was a church, cool and airy, with a cross on the apex of the roof; the cross had fallen askew and had not yet been righted. The men squatted on one side and the women on the other, the missionaries and ourselves at the back. Anne and I were on the outside of our sexes and thus next to each other. The sermon was forty-five minutes of Nepali. I will confess that during long sermons in English churches we have been known to squeeze hands; surreptitious rubbing of big toes was a new game.

Other than missionaries some dozen men and boys were on the left, and fourteen women on the right in white saris. And Stumpy. He had followed the Nepalese nurses, been tied up at the pastor's house, eaten through the rice-grass rope, and now lay at the entrance and quietly nibbled his paws, cocking an eye at the preacher.

Except for one or two who had come from India with Pastor David and the missionaries, the members of the congregation were all local born. They formed about a third of the church membership, drawn from rough country villagers around. They had never so much as heard of Christ until a few years back. Rhoda (they were given Biblical names at baptism) had been searching for peace of mind. An old woman of her village returned after treatment at the hospital and told what she could remember of the Christian message. Rhoda immediately went and heard for herself; she was now training to go into distant villages as nurse and teacher. There was Timothy, a former leper, who had greeted me at the leprosarium where he now worked, a pleasant young man in blue shorts and a dirty white shirt (he had a cleaner one for church) who had stood smiling at us, shyly twisting his hands. His wife Lois had been a water carrier in the early days of the hospital, which Timothy had attended as a leper outpatient. One morning Lois shook Timothy awake as they lay on their sleeping mat on the mud floor. "I have had a dream," she said. "I saw the hospital all lit up. Everywhere around was dark. This village was dark, so dark I was afraid. The town was dark. But light streamed from the hospital. If we want to know the truth, or ever to have light in our lives, we must go and learn it there."

Eventually both Timothy and Lois were baptized, for though baptism was against the law Pastor David was willing to risk prosecution. When the Brahman priest next came to the village, Timothy did not kiss his feet. The priest angrily asked why he had not received his customary salute. Timothy replied: "Why should I kiss your feet? I'll give you a salaam and all respect due to an older man, but not special honor. What do I owe you? You kept us in the dark all these years."

After the last hymn, during which a butterfly flew in and out and an ant scurried across my feet, I was taken to the pastor's house so that three could tell me their stories. I sat on a bed, with Stanley Wall and, as interpreter, a young man called Prem, which means love, as I had realized from frequent repetition in the sermon. Prem, an orphan, had been brought up in Assam with the pastor's sons.

The three men sat on little stools and rose one by one to speak and answer my questions. The eldest was fifty-two, a former Brahman farmer who had given the land for the church and parsonage.

Buddhi Sagar had a strong, open face, heavily mustached. Like many Nepalese he had emigrated, and in Shillong, Assam, in 1938, he met Pastor David. "When I heard of the Gospel," he said, "I gave my heart to God." His brothers, furious, confiscated all his land at Pokhara except a few acres to keep him from destitution. The decision to open at Pokhara in 1952 partly sprang from his offer of land for a church, and his knowledge of the area.

Lucius, in his mid-thirties, stood up next, a small, smiling man in gray shorts and a white shirt not quite Sunday best. "I had no peace from the placating of the gods," he began. "When I was recovering from a bad illness, I felt thirsty in my heart." He talked fast, and the interpreter could give me only the gist: a woman in his village told him that Buddhi Sagar had a book that might help. Lucius called on the farmer, who gave him a Bible. "He told me that Jesus had died to take away my sins so that I would not have to fear any more. And that He could be my Friend." At length Lucius believed, was baptized, and developed an unquench-able zeal to spread his good news. A former Gurkha officer whom I know had him as a porter on trek. When at the end of each day the Englishman was drooping with fatigue, Lucius would ask him to unpack his Nepali Bible and give them teaching; his last waking memories were of Lucius singing little hymns to villagers he had collected.

These were the stuff of which the Pokhara church was made. Its members had the strength and weaknesses of young Christians: enthusiasm, a vivid gratitude for freedom from superstition and fear, a sense of mission. On the other hand, they were semi-illiterate, so that to draw constant invigoration from the Bible was difficult. Little literature was available; as one of the missionaries com-plained, "People were on the border for a hundred years, yet hardly any Nepali Christian books were written or translated." Bickerings broke out occasionally; there were backslidings and failures, but no more and no less than those described in the young churches of the New Testament.

The third convert to tell me his story that morning was Dhun Raj, a heavy dark-skinned man of twenty-eight, with almond eyes and a shock of black hair. He was rather unsmiling, but this was caused by shyness. He was to be our chief porter for the trek to Tansen.

He had been a witch doctor. He lived at a village four hours away and could not often come in to church. Like so many of his race, he had had an aching desire for spiritual satisfaction. He sought it on the Tibetan border by learning witchcraft and sorcery and the worship of evil spirits, yet returned disillusioned, with long hair and wild look. In Lucius' village, which by then had several Christian families, he discovered a little book, a life of Jesus Christ. Slowly he spelled his way through it. "I found," he told me, "peace of God, and friendship, and fellowship with God through reading the whole book." Another booklet clinched his discovery.

Prem was retailing this to me when Dhun Raj cut in: "Tell him I was filled with joy."

I asked Dhun Raj what he would say if the evenings of our trek offered opportunity of talking with villagers. Without hesitation or embarrassment he replied, "If I meet anybody, if I get any chance I shall tell them the story of Jesus—ask if they know Jesus."

FOUR   ✳   *The Mountain Trail*

Twenty-four hours later we stood at the top of the pass. Fishtail peeped from the clouds.

To reach Tansen, chief city of West Nepal, a lazy man could take the plane to the border and walk back in a day. The Nepal Government had given us permission to go direct through the mountains, a three-day trek southward, and an imposing letter as passport.

In the half-light early that morning, Dhun Raj had arranged the suitcase, the bedroll, floppy bag, and picnic basket into two cunningly balanced loads. The other porter was Fish, so called by the mission as the first of Dhun Raj's friends whom he had hooked into the Christian Church, an elderly man—too elderly as it turned out—whose closely shaved head still had a Hindu tuft on the crown. He wore a smock-like garment tucked into a webbed army belt. Below was nothing but a G string revealing bare buttocks that waggled beneath the load.

When all was ready, the mission staff stood round and the doctor commended us in prayer.

A sharp walk of an hour took us to the landing ground to meet Barbara Best and Eileen Lodge, who led us out of the valley and across a swift narrow stream which a few yards higher up disappeared underground in a white boil of foam. Later we forded a wide shallow river to begin the main ascent. Barbara and Eileen plied us with scones and tea in the shade, and pressed their water bottle on us; in Europe we never carry water on the longest walk. We had two Thermos bottles of water now, and thought that would be enough. Fortunately, they overbore our protests, before turning back, leaving with us the Nepalese advice on what to do if you meet a tiger: put your hand in his mouth and pull his tail inside out.

Another hour and a half brought us to the summit where a little village perched and small boys clustered around while we waited for Dhun Raj, by now well behind, and Fish even farther; because the small boys tired of us before he arrived, we ate lunch in peace. After that, it was away into the mountains, and no European face for three days; an elemental, invigorating existence. The track ran along a ridge from which sharp spurs and valleys branched out, a study in green, thick wood or paddy terraces from base to summit merging into fold upon fold of hills. Sometimes the path ran flanked with stone walls well back, reminiscent of the English Lake District; sometimes it zigzagged, but remained clear to the eye for miles ahead, proclaiming itself the main road of West Nepal.

Almost always we were greeted cheerfully by *Namastay* with hand and voice, except from coolies whose heads bent forward under the strap which balanced the tapering basket load. They looked up, the whites of their eyes vivid against dark faces. Trade coolies came in strings of four or five, personal-baggage coolies in ones or twos, laden with yellow or red tin trunks; the owners marched unencumbered in front, barefoot, shading themselves with black umbrellas. A young sadhu, saffron robe slung across shoulder, walked naked except for a loincloth. He had discarded the wooden clogs of his kind, and a shining begging bowl jingled at his side.

Numerous Gurkha soldiers were going on leave for the Dasshera festival. The Indian Army passed unsmiling; the British Army grinned with pleasure at a white face above an Aertex shirt and khaki shorts, with an old army knapsack slung over the shoulder, and a memsahib, and they saluted military fashion with (whatever the time) "Good morning, sir!" They would stop for a chat, and some had a little English. "British officer, sir?" "Well, I was, but not now." "What regiment, sir?" And I would ask who their commanding officer was and how long they had served. One, no longer in uniform but merely a coolie, told me at great length, as we were eating lunch on the third day, that he had been a prisoner nearly four years in Italy and Germany, and how cold it had been.

As afternoon drew on, we passed a large village dominated by a brick-built house, a flagpole, and an ancient cannon—Nuwakot, capital of a province. The track at once descended through a steep jungly gully and through a home-going flock of sheep and goats, so alike that I understood the parable. When the overhanging rocks fell away and the rushing stream became a sedate little river, I felt it time to wait for the porters lest we be benighted alone.

We sat on a *chautra*. All the way along, the pious, to gain merit, had built stone seats where coolies could rest their loads beneath the shade of specially planted trees, one always the sacred bo tree. We sat an hour and a half. Apparently Dhun Raj was waiting for Fish, whose load was really too much for his age. Dhun Raj led on as daylight fast faded, and after twenty minutes turned a corner. There before us lay a wider valley. From its center a brilliant sunset flamed in a victory sign of flaky clouds.

We spent the night in the village at the head of the valley. By Nepalese custom a traveler may sleep without payment in any house, though he is expected to buy a meal; lodging means merely floor space to roll out your bedding. Dhun Raj found a two-storied house for us belonging to a former British Gurkha who gave the whole of his lower room, six feet square, to our party, and placed rugs on the newly washed floor of dried cow dung and mud, and a guttering vegetable-oil lamp above the little fireplace. We duly bought his rice, but had been warned that it would be too coarse. Besides, I prefer to walk on meat; we had brought a supply of tinned Spam, packets of powdered soup, fresh bread, squashy bananas and Nescafé, and Dhun Raj boiled water, some of which we put aside to cool for safe drinking next day. Four men and two boys, one with a rasping cough, squatted on the floor, and watched.

We crossed the street and by torchlight found the way to the river. Sanitation was equally simple. When we returned, Dhun Raj and Fish were back from dinner and swiftly cleared the room of spectators. We went to bed. Fish smoked contentedly, coughing a good deal, and Dhun Raj took from his pack a large Nepali Bible which dwarfed my pocket New Testament and must have added two or three pounds to his ninety-pound load.

At least we had no livestock sharing our stuffy bedroom except one cockerel; it gave a squawk as we went to sleep but was mercifully too lazy to keep first or second cockcrow and came on the air only after we had started to get up at 5:30 A.M.

The village took their places for the morning's entertainment. My clockwork razor and the deflating of the air mattresses lent by the Nepal Evangelistic Band were the hits. Breakfast included two fried eggs each; in the semidarkness I forgot that the plate belonged to our hostess and I sopped up the yoke too thoroughly; some of the dirt got inside.

The mist still had not risen from the hills when we were faced with the alternative of a steep detour or wading half a mile. We chose to wade, guided by a man who had been cutting foliage. At the deepest part, where the river was up to the knees, he made us link arms and splash along so fast that I nearly fell over and Dhun Raj bruised his bare feet; Fish was out of the convoy as usual. I tipped the guide. The country opened and we pressed ahead of Dhun Raj. All that day we walked south along the valley, the track sometimes wide and flat, sometimes a series of steps over bluffs or merely a narrow path through paddy.

The blue of sky and river, and the white of clouds and flecking waves made a gay contrast to the greens of rice, hillside, and forest, and a backcloth to the colorful passing show: women in purple or blue and gold, smoking cigarettes from holders, the long ash drooping; a woman with a chicken sitting on her pack, shaded by an umbrella; another carrying a kid in her baggage; a funeral, the body shrouded, relatives carrying wood for the burning and others in front blowing conch horns to warn Brahmans to keep clear lest they be defiled; and the unending friendly procession of coolies, soldiers, and chokidars in uniforms of businesses as far off as Calcutta, for Nepalese make fine watchmen. I was new enough to the

East to be surprised at the sense of security we felt in so remote a place.

When my watch warned me that the sun would go down soon, the mountains were closing in. I learned later that to keep to schedule we should have been well up into them before the second night, but owing to Fish we had to stop at their foot. The house was smaller and rougher than last night's but the woman in green sari and blouse and a medieval coif was more efficient as a hostess. A crowd of coolies gathered round two or three fires between the stream and the houses, and I wondered after dinner whether Dhun Raj would try a little evangelism. But we had walked him too hard. I could hardly blame him for crawling into bed as soon as we did, in a corner beneath hanging goatskins.

Outside, the coolies chattered. Someone began to play a pipe the sound of which, with the fall of the mountain brook, drifted in and out of my dreams.

So far the trek had not been as grueling as I had been led to expect. The third day was harder—the mountains steeper, the march longer, the day hotter. Incidentally, as we strode along under the midday sun, hatless though wearing dark glasses, I laughed as I thought of the topi. Not many years ago no European dared go in the sun without a topi for even a minute—one of the great examples of the power of mass suggestion; it is still worn, especially in Burma, but hardly ever by Europeans except Roman Catholic priests, for whom it is a kind of uniform.

We passed Dhun Raj and Fish a few steps after starting up the mountain in the thick morning mist, and that was the last we saw of them till noon the following day.

The path rose to get above the mist and then dropped by a little village of banana-leaf huts. Oversized spiders hung in webs from bushes; here and there a red or blue dragonfly flew; travelers were no less than before and kept us sure of the trail except once, when it ran roughly and narrowly down a most unlikely place and I had to shout my Nepali phrase *Tansen-ko Bato?* to an old man chopping branches sixty feet up a tree. Later we lost the trail, and the way became markedly lonely until, directed by hilltop villagers, we regained it, and knew so at once by the hustle of coolies, to say nothing of a pilgrim who walked with a sprig of herbs between his hands, murmuring prayers. I bowed politely and he bowed back.

Also reassuring were telegraph poles, some with wisps of wire, put up for the sole purpose of enabling Ranas to telegraph to India—general public not admitted. Though the new government had no money to maintain so expensive a toy, and most of the wire had long since been stolen, the line of derelict poles ran the whole way to the border.

We were now higher up on a great spur round which, far below, curved the broad Kali Gandhak, making a deep divide. Away beyond the divide we could see the hills of Tansen, and assumed hopefully that the city lay on the near side, for Dhun Raj that morning had said nine miles. Whether he meant nineteen or nine hours or nine as the crow flies, his promise acted like a carrot to a donkey.

The track kept to the southeast side of the spur, the red earth for a short distance becoming sandy-yellow and almost shadeless. We refilled the water bottle from a stream as near the top as possible, using sterlizing pills, and moved on down into a shadier section. I shall not forget the blessed *chautras* nor the succulent Nepalese pears looking like russet brown apples; some months later, on a far more grueling trek, I thought wistfully of those pears. After a tumbledown leprosarium—a mere place of incarceration—we began the descent to the river and crossed it at a magnificent gorge by a narrow swinging suspension bridge two hundred feet above the water where men from the large village beyond were bathing.

The path left the main valley at once and worked steeply up beside a tributary. We bought bananas at a wayside farm, if such a name is not too grand, pleasantly surprised that the woman refused half of what we offered. At the next village we bought mugs of cinnamon tea. It took time and much adjusting of embers and wood and peeping into the large pot before the man had the brew really on the boil, but it was then supremely satisfying. We asked other travelers, by signs, how far it was to Tansen. One replied, "Down a rise and up"; another said, "one hour"; and a third, to general merriment, "Eleven o'clock tomorrow morning."

Passers-by now seemed more than friendly; they smiled broad smiles as of recognition; we were near enough to the Tansen hospital for reflected glory.

The steep trail, always upward, narrowed. At five o'clock we had less than an hour and a half of daylight, and behind us already the views of ridge upon green ridge were superb in the evening sun; if only the Himalayas had come out of cloud. Walking up a path like an English "drain" in company with two coolies, the edge collapsed and I fell into a man-sized ditch; roaring with laughter the coolies pulled me out. Higher up, the road leveled slightly; down to the left boys flew kites, a craze in Nepal at that time of year, running over the hillside at astonishing speed. Above us, the hill disappeared in cloud.

We passed through houses that I hoped were the outskirts of Tansen, but wrongly; my *"Tansen-ko Bato?"* was becoming rather plaintive as the light faded fast. We emerged above a broad valley and at a fork started to descend, but I felt I was wrong and shouted in the twilight to a soldier who saluted and pointed the other way. I said to my wife that I was not going on except in company, as our torch was too low to show the path or scare off leopards. So we kept in with the soldier until he came to a temple bell and turned off, waving us on. Far down in the valley a fire flared in the darkness. Up here a little light remained. A few yards and we came to a fork. The right led into cloud, the left into darkness. Though I knew Tansen was on a hilltop, I did not relish disappearing into a cloud. "We'll go left," I said. "If it starts going down we'll stop and try the other." We had been on the trail eleven hours and twenty minutes.

It did go down, sharply. Suddenly, just below, I saw a shadowy something I recognized as a wind generator. A few steep steps more and a window blazed with unwonted electric light, so abruptly below that we could see the floor but nothing else.

Then, unmistakable, a white woman's legs.

FIVE   *Gas-Can Hospital*

How anyone could live and work in the rickety, rat-infested house that was then the United Mission Hospital at Tansen was a marvel.

The new hospital was going to be excellent, but it would not be ready for another six months. Only two units were completed: the American medical superintendent's house, where Dr. and Mrs. Carl Friedericks had welcomed and fed us, and that of the Norwegian engineer, Od Hofton, in command of the builders, where we spent the night in borrowed things. The new site on the steep hillside beside the town provided a fine view of the snows behind and the distant valley beneath. But the old hospital where they had worked since 1956 was awful. I am glad we stayed there for the rest of our visit not only because of our hostess, the young English woman Dr. Margery Foyle, but also because it gave an insight into conditions.

The house was decrepit: "No one would live in it but us; that's why we got it," they said; and its façade, like those of most of the large houses in Tansen, was, surprisingly, nineteenth century French provincial. An earth closet in the garden did for sanitation, and for bath a small tin tub was brought to the entrance of our bedroom. A bathroom had projected from a landing. It rattled so much when the midday signal gun fired that Margery vowed never to be in it just then; sure enough, it collapsed one day at noon.

Margery's tiny consulting room served as operating theater, X-ray and labor room; Dr. Friederick's was also outpatients' department. The distillery was wedged into a corner of the narrow courtyard and the sister's office into a passage. The beds in the little wards were mostly packing cases, and surgical and medical patients lay side by side. "If we mixed them like this at home," said Margery, "we would get cross-infection, but the Lord seems to give us a special protection." In the women's ward, where relatives sat beside each patient, were six beds in a room of about twelve foot by five: dysentery, starvation, leg amputation—the weight being kept off the stump by a contraption made from a Nescafé tin—maternity, a child with a broken jaw, an infected foot. The starvation case showed something of the pathos of Hinduism: because she was a beggar admitted in this condition, but a Brahman, defiled if she ate in company of low-caste people, she was eating squatting on the floor facing the wall, trying to pretend no one was breathing down her neck.

Everywhere I saw old Caltex gas cans. The place seemed made of them. They were water jugs, washbasins, store places, lampstands.

The heavy medical equipment and the kerosene refrigerator and the construction machinery being used on the new site had all been brought up on the backs of coolies, who took a fortnight to do the day's walk from the roadhead, carrying these deadweight loads a few yards and then resting, and so on day after day up the mountain.

On the first afternoon, we called on the Governor of Tansen.

We walked up the steep narrow street of red bricks and grass and weeds, and caught a glimpse of the governor's garden neat with dark red crotons such as grow in English hothouses, and came to a dirty white gate where a sentry squatted; he had no uniform, but negligently rested an ancient musket between his arms. On his forehead was a large *tilak,* or worship mark. He grinned at Od Hofton's young American assistant as we entered the grounds of the imitation château. At the end of a short avenue stood two blue Victorian street lamps perched on rough wooden poles, and behind them a tumbledown porch and a sentry picking his nose.

We turned right across a lawn into a courtyard crowded with townsfolk dominated by a great gateway of tall wormeaten wooden doors guarded by a policeman carrying a 1914 Lee-Enfield. Beyond was the governor's temple; the protective lions, first cousins to Burmese Chinthes, were covered with blue shirts laid out to dry, and the tilt of their heads had an air of violent protest. Upstairs, past sentries carrying fowling pieces, we came to the governor's anteroom. We were told to take off our shoes.

His Excellency was signing documents of rustling rice paper. "Just two or three minutes," he said in English. At last he pushed the papers aside and graciously asked us where we were from. He made warm if rather platitudinous references to the hospital. "We are modeling our government hospital on the mission one," he said, and discoursed on local development plans. "We could make a jeep road in six months from the plain. . . . But there is so much to do. You are seeing the birth of a new nation."

"Tansen is much harder-hearted than Pokhara. Here they are very proud. And there is much devil worship. Caste, Brahmans, they are very strong. Some people know the truth but they are afraid of the people."

Three of the few local Christians were sitting round the tea table in the pretty and homelike living room at the old hospital. I was on a sofa of packing cases backed by a camp bed, so well covered by cushions and material that I had not realized how it was formed. On my left, between the windows which looked across the valley, was a large map of Nepal and on a little table a small Nepalese flag. The walls had pictures of Norwegian and English scenes and the Twenty-third Psalm on parchment, and the door of the refrigerator (medical as well as household) displayed a transfer of a Dutch boy.

Mrs. Mathews, a young Indian Christian, interpreted for me. Next to her sat the Nepalese from Darjeeling, a small, fair, squat-nosed man who was surgical dresser and unofficial pastor, and a pock-marked young man from East Nepal who had been converted recently through the only missionary in that area, since deceased, and had come to Tansen for medical training. Completing the party was a local girl, Om Shanti, or Ruth, as she had been baptized, less than eighteen months ago.

They told me they had held daily ward services to which they welcomed anyone from the bazaar until the previous governor had forbidden public preaching, so that it must now be for patients and staff only. It was after this order that Ruth at hospital prayers publicly testified to her belief in Christ; the governor was furious. Her reply might have seemed priggish in easier circumstances, but not for a young girl against overwhelming official and public opinion: "He's not my governor," she said; "He's only here." The present governor showed more tolerance, yet while we were at Tansen one of the Hindu staff of the hospital was called to the police to report on its Christian activities. This, in 1958, and on the right side of the iron curtain. . . . But the new Constitution was on its way.

I questioned this group closely. I knew that some people in my own country casually supposed that Hinduism was the "best religion for Indians and Nepalese, so why worry them with ours," and I wanted to discover what had been found wanting. "There's no peace in the Hindu religion," said Ruth. "It was peace I was after, peace of heart." In this she echoed Lucius and Dhun Raj.

Ruth and the young man from East Nepal explained to me that Hinduism offers no assurance of heaven and no certainty on earth, or sense of companionship with God. "They go to the sacred river to bathe and wash away their sins, but it doesn't bring peace, nor does it when they go to the temple to worship the gods and ask for what they want." They must work, work, work for their salvation. There is no certain knowledge that in the ceaseless migration of souls they will rise higher in the next life; each soul must be reborn over eight million times, rising from the lowest to the highest, from animals up to the heavenly scale, put forward or back according to their actions. "If a wife washes her husband's feet each day, and drinks the water she has washed them in, she might be born as a man next time, and that would be wonderful."

On our last night these four were among the congregation in a simple service of Holy Communion that I was asked to conduct. Some of my brethren in the Church of England might have been shocked at this service; only two out of the eighteen present were Anglicans. Presbyterians, Methodist, Baptists, a Mennonite, two Syrian Jacobites from South India, and others were represented, and we followed a modified Church of England rite, leaving out congregational parts which others did not know; the Nepalese could not follow my English anyway. The little chapel was hot from pressure lamps; a squeaky harmonium gave the music. We were a little group of Christians cut off from any others by mile upon mile of mountain and a population hard in its Hinduism. We came from six nations. It seemed to me a moving expression of Christian unity.

As we chatted on the downward trail early next morning, I asked Margery Foyle, who with the Norwegian nursing sister Ingeborg Skjeruheim accompanied us part of the way, about some of the personal difficulties of missionary work. Margery was not an obvious pioneer; Jean Raddon at Pokhara looked the sort who would rap a tiger on the nose, but Margery, frail in build, had endured much ill-health since coming to Nepal, culminating in a big operation for which she had been specially flown back to England. Not that this deters her; she thinks Tansen too comfortable, and hopes one day to get deeper into the mountains.

One remark of her's struck me forcibly: "The greatest difficulty," she said, "is the attack of Satan on your mind. I find it difficult sometimes actually to read the Bible, or to make the mental act of kneeling for prayer." It was not overtiredness, as they had about the right amount of medical work; but, apart from the strain of living among a people of strange tongue and hard heart, if friendly ways, she considered its cause to be the difficulty of getting relaxation, such as concerts, to unwind the mind.

We passed on to discuss the Nepalese church of the future. Nepal, to its advantage, has missed the old "imperial" type of mission based on large stations dominated by missionaries expecting to be obeyed. From the start foreigners have seen themselves the servants of the national church in the making, which in years to come may therefore develop a virility lacking in many parts of Asia. Margery agreed. "The real Nepalese," she said, "people like these porters—are intensely loyal. Witness the Gurkha soldiers. I believe this loyalty can be transferred to Jesus Christ, and will mean a great deal to the Church in the East."

Margery and Ingeborg left us when the path down the precipitous hillside and along a narrow valley began to rise again toward the final pass where, during lunch, we caught a last but inadequate glimpse of Annapurna before starting the descent to the plain. Much of the way now was down a "staircase" built by slave labor but long since fallen into decay; it made for painful walking, especially in the heat hitting up at us from India. This trail seemed suburban, littered with Bat cigarette cartons and with nearly every building an inn—if report be believed, a brothel.

We came to a river about fifty yards wide, and thigh-deep. A knot of men bathed or sat about, waiting for fares, and two carried us over pick-a-back, our legs tucked up so that they hardly got wet. The luggage porters took off their shorts and splashed through in loincloths, arms linked. I paid a rupee each to the ferrymen, only to find that we must be carried farther upstream another twenty-five yards; when the track was reached they laughed and salaamed, making no attempt, as many coolies in India would have done, to extract more. Beyond the river, at a substantial village, we sat at a table waiting for a man with shaved head and a *tilak* to bring his pot to the boil by blowing at the fire through an iron pipe, that we might have *oomale chiya,* or boiling tea. A woman and a baby squatted on a mat; chickens and goats wandered around and a cockerel crowed at my feet, but the water would not *oomale.* The porters drank noisily, wrapping the hot glasses with their shirt-tails before drinking.

After four miles of gorge, and, in fine form about eight and a half hours after leaving Tansen, having dropped nearly 4,500 feet, we marched into Butwol, a ramshackle straggle of houses and bazaars with an excessive population of puppies, baby chicks, and kids.

Because I had heard tales of travelers stranded all night, I wanted to squeeze into an old blue bus just leaving for Nautanwa, the railway station over the border, but fortunately I was dissuaded; it was oozing with humanity, and probably springless. Another bus, a man said, was leaving two hours later at 6:00 P.M., his bus. He put us in, sold us tickets, demanding Indian or, as the Nepalese say, with a sublime disregard of a hundred years of history, Company's money, and tried to charge a rupee for each piece of baggage. I could see by the grins of the crowd that he was trying a fast one, so, guessing he could not read, I knew that the time had come to use my government letter. It had nothing to do with such a case, but it worked.

By five-thirty no one had joined the bus. I feared the worst until the man came back and volunteered that a truck was leaving in a few minutes. As he had no English and we were not to be put upon, he took some time to convince us. He paid back our money and summoned friends to carry our cases, but not for love. Though I let a small boy take the bedroll, I saw no reason to waste annas on the rest, and took the suitcase myself, the crowd not knowing whether to be shocked or amused. "Coolie sahib," I called out to the man as I trotted off.

As night fell, the truck took up a load of faggots and set off, ourselves in front more comfortable than in any Nepalese bus. The road was terrible, and since the driver kept the light in the cab on, all the midges of the district made a meal of us, but he was courteous and helpful, seeing me through the Nepalese customs at the border town, where I was nearly trodden on by an elephant. Once across the border the road changed from cart track to tarmac, and soon we saw again the familiar oxcarts of North India.

At his destination in Nautanwa the truck driver gave me a final taste of Nepalese politeness by taking our fares with a warm hand-shake and gracious *Namastay*. A coolie appeared to carry our load to the railway station. It was 8:30 P.M., and the train did not leave until 3:00 A.M. Carl Friedericks at Tansen, who had been in China and round the world, judged Nautanwa the worst railway station he had ever seen. One look sent us doubling back, coolie and all, to find the old mission house of the Nepal Evangelistic Band. A one-armed Christian took us in, lit a hurricane lamp, boiled water for soup to go with our last tin of meat, and laid mattresses on the beds upstairs. The chokidar promised a call at 1:45 A.M.; he said he had a coolie coming to take our luggage the mile back to the station.

At two-twenty Anne woke, rushed downstairs, shook the chokidar awake, and sent him to get the coolie while I put my boots on. He returned and signed to us that no coolie was about.

There was no time to be lost. Fortunately the chokidar, taking his sandals off, laid aside his dignity and seized the bedroll and floppy bag. Anne took the picnic basket and small things; I shouldered the suitcase; and we set off at speed through the warm night.

"Coolie sahib" with a vengeance.

SIX ✖ *Tibet*

At a little wayside station in West Bengal the crack mail train had dug itself in. Already four hours late, we had stopped again. A perspiring guard was gurgling loudly in English down the telephone in the booking office, where the clerk sat busy at the telegraph, oblivious of the country folk patient beyond the ticket window.

The guard replaced the receiver, and I asked, "What's wrong?" In that singsong Indian English which is as distinctive as an American accent or the King's English, he replied: "A freight-train derailment. A truck off the line. I can't say when we'll get on."

From Nepal we had returned over the Ganges to the Duchess of Teck Hospital at Patna, our temporary base, and after a few days crossed again to catch the mail train for Siliguri, the junction for Darjeeling, the famous hill station and tea-growing center. Before touring the Ganges Plain, the heart of Hinduism, I wanted to see something of the small minority of Buddhists, whose founder had lived and died in India and whose religion, once so powerful there, is confined to the Himalayan hill tracts. And I had heard rumors of stirrings within Tibet, and wished to get as close as I could. This was over four months before the flight of the Dalai Lama. The world knew nothing.

Fortunately, because the Dasshera festival, or Durga Puja as it is called in Bengal and Bihar, had overcrowded the trains, we had settled on the extravagance of traveling "air conditioned" and were comfortable while the train stood sweltering. At last the "up" mail train came through, and the line was ours.

We reached Siliguri after dark too late to catch the miniature train that puffs and circles up into the hills the fifty miles to Darjeeling. I approached a resplendent figure I took for a station official, but saw after I had spoken that he was a police lieutenant; in black peaked cap, smartly pressed khaki, Sam Browne, and fine mustaches he looked like Lord Kitchener in the recruiting posters of the First World War. I apologized for my mistake, but Lord Kitchener was at once at my service. I told my story and he took us across the bridge, followed by the trail of coolies without which no one can move on an Indian station, to apply for a refund on the tickets (a lengthy process—I am still waiting). Just then a puja procession chugged into the station. A cheering crowd sat on railway trucks behind a light engine, banging cymbals and drums in front of the eight-armed benign figure of the goddess Durga. Kitchener's eyes gleamed.

"Now we will go and negotiate for a car to Darjeeling. Memsahib waits here." But I prefer to have Anne in on any negotiation. Kitchener was pained. Having booked places in a car, he took us upstairs, past the tidy restaurant, to an overcrowded, squalid upperclass waiting room. "They will bring your meal here," he said; "this is where sahibs eat." We said thank you, but we would rather sit in the restaurant. Lord Kitchener was shocked.

Just as he was seeing us off at the car, another puja procession came noisily down the road. Kitchener seized my arm. "You must see this before you go, Sahib! Come along quick." A gaily decorated lorry drove by, the goddess in the back, followed by other trucks in which youths stamped their feet and clapped their hands, shouting cheerfully in unison. Some waved incense, others banged drums.

Behind, more young men danced a jiggledy dance with rapture, and others had mock fights with swords and single-sticks. The procession was brought up by a truck of blaring musicians.

"Oh," said this intelligent officer, "isn't it wonderful? We worship the goddess Durga. She gets the victory for us. She is the goddess of protection and treads underfoot the evil gods. At the end of the festival she is immersed in the river with prayers for her return next year."

Of the rest of the journey to Darjeeling the less said, the better. We sat in front of a large car with two Indian men and one woman behind. The driver squealed the tires round the sharp corners as we made the ascent. After fifteen miles he discovered that the bedroll of one of the Indians had fallen off. He turned round and free-wheeled down in the darkness, peering hopefully into most of the ditches, right back to the station, without result. We had now lost an hour and a half and it was nearly 9:00 P.M. We began the ascent again, stopped to inquire whenever a car passed in the other direction, had a puncture, found that since the driver had freewheeled with his headlights he had exhausted the battery and that the only way to start was to push the car precariously downhill until it engaged. At Kurseong, the police headquarters, a fat, bustling police lieutenant whose rimless spectacles and peaked cap gave a Germanic look took endless details from the cringing Indian that had lost the bedroll. "We'll detail him here overnight," the lieutenant announced, as if the poor man were the criminal, "so that we can make further inquiries."

I gave the car a push down the street, and the driver engaged. We screamed round bends, lights growing dimmer, and drew up in Darjeeling at the bottom of a long flight of steps at 1:00 A.M. as the headlights failed. Our Canadian hosts, routed from bed, promptly produced a first-class meal.

A lama in a drab yellow short coat over a yellow robe so faded as to be almost white, and a purple Tibetan hat topped by a little red knob, walked down the hillside path ringing a bell, with his other hand holding a scarf of respect attached to a coffin behind him. In front two more lamas, one in red and one in yellow wearing an ordinary woolen cap, as if to emphasize that he was a gardener in private life, blew clarinet-like instruments called Gye-lings. A boy in shorts and shirt had a conch shell; a young man clanged cymbals softly; and others held bamboos on which red, green, and yellow flags had been tied. Behind the tail of mourners rose the wailing of women left at the house.

This Buddhist funeral to which we had been invited was a funeral with a difference. The dead man, a Nepalese estate worker, though never baptized had asked on his deathbed for a Christian to come and pray with him; he had said he wanted no lamas and, moreover, that a Bible and a cross should be burned with him. All this had been refused by his relatives, and the lamas had been chanting since the previous day. He had died that morning. His eldest son, nearly a Christian, was angry but impotent.

Reaching a narrow space cut into the hillside not far down from the center of sleek, cosmopolitan Darjeeling, the coffin was put to one side while men made ready, rather casually, the pyre of wood. They stuck into the ground a banner of the sort carried by mothers' unions up cathedral aisles, but picturing Buddha and the wheel of life, and a prayer flag such as Tibetans fly everywhere, inscribed with verses of Buddhist scripture for the wind to blow to heaven. Garlands of marigolds lay around. A coolie arrived with oranges, pineapples, milk, and little lumps of cloth containing scriptures: food for the soul. The lama laid out the scriptures beside bowls of holy water a few paces from the pyre, pushed his biretta to the back of his head, scratched himself, and smoothed his large mustache.

They were Nepalese following a debased form of Tibetan Buddhism, itself derivative. The coffin was prized open and the shrouded corpse laid on the pyre and covered over with more wood, including the now broken-up coffin. A man smoking a cigarette looked on, and the two sons, men in their early twenties, set up a violent wailing, beating their heads against their arms.

"Is this part of the proceeding or real emotion?" I asked Al, a tall Canadian of my own age. "It's genuine," he said. "They are not taught to control their emotions as we do."

The sons were led away weeping, but when holy water had been sprinkled with a peacock's feather and the face of the corpse covered with clarified butter called ghee the eldest had to set it alight. He screwed himself to the ordeal.

Thin wisps of smoke drifted up. Drums and cymbals boomed and clashed rhythmically in the background; lamas chanted. The man with the cigarette stepped across for what he supposed would be a last look at the face. Lest the soul should return to the body, passes were made with a kukri and the fire was sanctified by the waving of burning rags attached to sticks. These Nepalese Buddhists believe that the soul hovers until a final ceremony two or more weeks later, when it ascends to Nirvana, which in contrast to pure Buddhism they think of as a heaven of conscious bliss.

I had to leave after an hour and a half. Perhaps it was as well. Al said that the wood burned too slowly. After a while a foot fell off and was shoveled on. He could see the brain exposed. They turned the half-burned body over and he saw the intestines. The sons had to help turn it, but their emotion had dried up. Al stayed to the end and succeeded in not being sick.

The funeral gave a small insight into the way of life on the Tibetan border.

Tibetan monasteries such as Ghum near Darjeeling gave more, but were spoiled by their artificiality as tourist attractions. Buxom women in ample skirts fronted by brightly striped woolen aprons, their hair in pigtails but, unlike Indians and Nepalese, uncovered, walked about carrying little silver prayer wheels (108 turns wipe out one sin) and twirled the large copper prayer wheels beneath the dragon over the monastery door; when not doing that, they seemed to spend most of the time knitting. Inside the monastery, lamas at morning worship chanted the scriptures, but their eyes roved around the tourists. Beside the Buddha were idols eloquent of ancient devil worship which plays much part in Tibetan Buddhism—the idol of eleven heads and a thousand hands, every hand having an eye; the goddess of strength with staring eyes and crown of skulls; she is husband of Shiva, but the lama-guide stoutly denied that she was imported from Hinduism.

Our hosts had arranged for us to visit Sikkim, the Tibetan pocket-handkerchief state, a Buddhist holy land, to stay with the only European resident for the occasion of the Birthday and Fortieth Accession Anniversary of His Highness the Maharajah. So to Gangtok, the capital, by Land-Rover bus accompanied by Al. We went down six thousand feet from Darjeeling to the Teesta River, over the fine concrete bridge which Tibetans have protected with prayer flags, up again four thousand feet to Kalimpong (thirty-two miles from Darjeeling yet only nine as the crow flies) to make a connection; back nearly to the Teesta bridge and turn right, the road running through the forest beside the river to the frontier which is marked by a bridge over a tributary: "One Car or Five Mules Only." Al and I sat at the back with two Nepalese and a small boy who was quietly sick over my suitcase five minutes before we arrived.

The road from the frontier rose gently into the mountains. Only the last ten miles were steep. Then we could see Gangtok scattered over the hillside above, and the rice, still green lower down, drooped yellow-ripe over the terraces. The roofs of small, neat public buildings gleamed with fresh paint, blue, green, and gold, in honor of Mr. Nehru's recent visit. Behind, to the northwest, rose the "Protecting Deity of the Snowy Ranges," Kanchenjunga.

The visit to Sikkim added little to my inquiry. I could describe the reverend abbot of the Palace Monastery blessing the kneeling faithful; I could give a pen picture of our hostess, the New Zealander headmistress of the Girls' High School founded by the Scottish Universities Mission—the whole state her schoolroom. I could describe the comic-opera uniforms of the palace guards. I can tell you no more of lamas and prayer wheels and the strange beliefs and stranger achievements of the religion of the roof of the world.

Yet I would not have missed it.

Apart from our hostess and a sad-looking Oxford scholar, Al and ourselves were the only Westerners to see the ceremonies of the Birthday and Accession Anniversary.

Sikkim was never an integral part of the Indian Empire but a protectorate, and thus not absorbed into the Republic. The Maharajah, of Tibetan stock, is therefore the only prince to exercise sovereignty, which he does under the guidance of an Indian Political Officer. His Dewan, or Prime Minister, a Parsee educated at Cambridge, is seconded from the Indian Civil Service.

As we stood on the Birthday morning in front of the modest palace of cream walls and a maroon tin roof, the officials and landed gentry gathered in their long Sikkimese robes to present scarves of respect. The atmosphere was Tibetan rather than Indian, but the colors were

as vivid: the Dewan in bright yellow with mauve sash, the heir
to the throne in red, the royal grandsons playing about on the lawn
in yellow offset by red sashes, the First Secretary in purple with
his hair parted down the middle and braided over the forehead in
the Tibetan way. When His Highness the Maharajah, accompanied
by the royal party, ambled across the lawn to the durbar in the
Prayer Pavilion he was resplendent, small though he is, in a rich
white silk jacket over an orange robe embroidered with dragons,
and a mandarin hat with a yellow crown and a red bobble.

It was the old Chinese Empire sprung to life from the mists of
the past. One aged landowner who had long jade earrings appeared
to have stepped straight from a Chinese tapestry. When Lepchas
and Bhutias received certificates of merit we saw variations of the
kowtow. A man in Lepcha costume even went down on his face,
rose to attention, down again and up three times; merely a chauffeur
rewarded for good driving. The durbar ended with a blessing from
a line of lamas who faced the Maharajah on his throne and chanted
Buddhist scriptures.

That evening we watched an open-air concert of local songs and
dances—it would have been better had the lights been stronger—
and then moved to the palace grounds for a display of fireworks.
The Dewan invited us to the lower veranda, and Al's democratic
Canadian soul got an immense kick from sitting in the royal arm-
chairs nibbling royal refreshments, the Dewan on the arm of his
chair chatting to him, the Crown Prince a few paces off.

The following day the Maharajah, in a fine embroidered orange
robe and circular Sikkimese hat, attended sports. A monastery band
lined up at the entrance to the ground wearing large red and yellow
hats shaped rather like helmets of ancient Greece. As he passed, they
banged, blew, and walloped: great bass trumpets supported on the
shoulders of lamas in front, great drums slung on the back of
one and beaten by another, cymbals, a triangle, and the clarinet-
style, wide-mouthed Gye-lings. After the parade of the military
might of Sikkim (the police force commanded by a Sikh) and
solemn chanting by the monks' school, sports began.

It was characteristic of this happy little state that the Crown
Prince and the Prime Minister were the referees, the Chief Magis-

trate was the starter, and most of the cabinet (if they call it that) had jobs on the ground.

A new road has been built from Gangtok to the Nathula Pass, frontier of Tibet, with one of the finest views in the world. I asked the Political Officer for permission to go, but only New Delhi could grant it.

So I had to content myself with the Tibetan mule trains trotting into the bazaar. The first and last mule had bells and bright flags, and the men rode ponies. Burly muleteers dwarfing the Sikkimese strode about the streets, their brown woolen robes thrown off their shoulders and tied back round the waist. Soon there would be many fewer, because English engineers were constructing a ropeway to the frontier to carry the trade at reduced cost.

I was no closer to Tibet. At that time the world's press was almost silent, choosing to disbelieve or ignore, except for an occasional halfhearted article, rumors of Tibetan resistance to Red China. Apart from the intrinsic interest, if that is not too callous a phrase, of the death throes of a nation, the upshot related to religious freedom in a part of Asia where it has never been known.

Two interviews, somewhat contradictory, took me almost as near as a foreigner could hope to get to this closed, unhappy land.

The first, back in Darjeeling, was with George Patterson, the young Scots special correspondent and author whose *Tibetan Journey* was a best seller. His later books have been notable for their controversial tone and for slashing attacks on fellow missionaries, some of which, to my mind, were in bad taste; but I forgive him all as one of the few missionary writers of the present day to be read widely by the general public.

Though I had been warned that George was a prickly person, I found him charming and communicative. His wife is doctor to the Planters' Hospital, and it was in the doctor's house high up in Darjeeling, looking across to Kanchenjunga, that the Pattersons had us to tea, in a beautifully furnished drawing room of red sofa and chairs, polished tables, and thick pile carpets, a tea such as no mission house could boast: drop scones, savory sandwiches, bread and a huge round of cheese, cream cakes and fruit cake, served by a faultless Nepalese servant and preceded by an unhurried prayer of blessing. A golden labrador wandered in and out, and a fire was lit in the grate before the end.

Patterson, shorter than his photographs suggest, wore horn-rimmed spectacles and a neat beard. His smart clothes had a dash of Teddy boy. He told me that he spent his time writing and acting as a political agent for the Tibetan nationalists in their struggle against the Chinese. He had been careful to tell the Indian Government that he was no longer a missionary and that his activities were not representative; indeed, he claimed to have their confidence and to be used as a go-between, and was in touch with the British Foreign Office. He gave me fuller details than had been available in England of the Tibetan struggle to overthrow the Chinese, hereditary enemies and now doubly hateful; of high casualties and full-scale battles, of the Communist policy of deliberate annihilation; and of the refusal of the Western powers and India to intervene either directly or indirectly by sending in the ammunition which, he was convinced, was all they needed for victory and independence.

His political activities were a means to an end. George Patterson is nothing if not consistent, and for ten years he has lived for the evangelization of Tibet. "I have had a vision," he said; "I know I am going to get in," and by vision he meant something seen with the eyes and heard with the ears. He believed that his political activities would ensure that on liberation the Dalai Lama would turn to the Pattersons and, reversing the previous policy of exclusion, invite them to choose a team to organize medical and social relief and advancement; it would be the story of Nepal over again. "Tibet is not particularly open to the Gospel, but it will be open to me, and I shall choose Christians. In that way the Gospel will enter."

My other interview gave the impression that George Patterson was overoptimistic. I was received by a very high-ranking member of the former Tibetan cabinet, but in the cloak-and-dagger atmosphere that surrounds Tibetan politics in exile I was told not to say who he was or where I saw him, though if you glance at newspaper files of more recent date your guess would not be far wrong. This man distrusted Patterson, even blanched at the name, for Patterson was closest to the Khambas who originally had cooperated with the Red Chinese and let them enter Tibet, though now they were foremost in fighting them.

The former cabinet minister handed me a copy of the Manifesto lately dispatched to members of the United Nations as a plea for help. On a margin of the day's *Statesman* he scribbled a diagram to show that of the three supply routes from China to Lhasa, two had been cut by the nationalists; until the other could be cut the Chinese would hold Tibet.

I asked him if a liberated Tibet would open fully to the world. "I cannot speak for Tibetans," he replied. "This is a personal opinion; but I say that the whole world is changing, Tibet must change, and welcome foreigners and our people go to foreign lands." I wished to ask if religious freedom would be granted, but my sponsor warned me that the question was unwise.

The former cabinet minister was sadly realistic about victory. "As a Tibetan I hope against hope. Every true Tibetan should. But" —he spread his hands deprecatingly—"we have no ammunition, no helper."

Meanwhile there are missionaries devoted to Tibet who offer the traders Christian literature, and at the caravanserais play records of Christian talks. A pure-blood Tibetan pastor to whom I was introduced seemed more concerned with the activities of the underground movement than with the Gospel; he would argue, with Patterson, that liberation is the prelude to evangelization. Many of the missionaries are Finns and Scandinavians, for a Finnish mission has been on the border for years. I met two old ladies, one of seventy-eight (and never once home to Europe), the other of eighty-two (she had allowed herself one furlough) who are still at it, though officially retired, and who told of reliable evidence that the recently translated Tibetan Bible, an enormous volume, is read in monasteries far up on the high plateau. Far more has been done by one young South Indian than by his foreign predecessors before the area was closed to them, and an Englishman recently toured the Bible schools, urging young men that Tibet was their sphere rather than that of Westerners.

Missionaries were brave in confidence that at any time news of victory would sweep them in. But I remembered the plaintive words of the former cabinet minister: "Tibet is helpless, and there is no one to speak for us."

SEVEN ❧ *Elusive Ind*

The disappointing failure to reach the Tibetan border or (through no fault of our hosts) to dig beneath the surface of lamaism was the prelude to a succession of checks and false casts which dogged my efforts in India.

It may have been that a little knowledge is dangerous. In 1956 I had visited Bombay and Calcutta and some dozen other centers to which I did not return in 1958. Perhaps I should have returned. Or it may have been that in India, alone of the countries covered, we were generally guests of individuals or of institutions, not of widespread missions or dioceses; and the one mission that was host to us could not do all it wished because of the delicacy of local affairs. Certainly the India section was the least intimate of the tour. We met kindness and hospitality, and one man in particular took great pains to assist planning; yet whereas in other lands I seemed to see things just happen, as if I were a lizard on the wall, in India I was never more than a visiting journalist, and seldom got away from the obvious.

These are excuses. The fault lay no doubt in myself. Had I been attempting a survey or encyclopedia of missions, or had this run of misfortune continued once we crossed the Bay of Bengal, I should be in sorry case. But this is a record of personal experience. You must take the rough with the smooth. Meanwhile, I have had to decide whether to trot out conventionalities or to cut this section to a minimum undeserved. Preferring to rely on your charity rather than to try your patience, I choose the latter.

So I give detached memories. Do not look for profound conclusions or exhaustive description. I serve an Indian *hors d'oeuvre*. The main courses are coming. Don't sack the cook.

The North India cold weather had begun, surely one of the finest climates in the world, cloudless skies, warm days, cool nights.

We had come down to the railhead in a bus that did *not* free-wheel. Directly behind our seats beside the driver sat a strong-smelling lama with a cold—at least, in intervals of chanting he expectorated noisily and frequently an inch from my ear. The night railway journey was mercifully without incident except that the air conditioning for which we had paid had been withdrawn, so we were without bedding, for you do not need a bedroll in the A. C. class; the substantial refund reached me in Singapore six months later.

Once more we were back at the Duchess of Teck Hospital in Patna to pick up the rest of our luggage.

A hostess in England asked to lend her chauffeur at 3:30 A.M. would have a fit. India travels round the clock, however, and the Teck Hospital driver took us uncomplainingly through darkened streets to Patna Junction for the train to Banaras. It had left Calcutta about seven yesterday evening, and thirty-six hours later would reach Amritsar on the frontier about seven tomorrow morning.

At almost any hour of day or night an Indian street is alive. Men (and dogs) sleep on the pavement in broad daylight, but the small hours might deceive you into assuming a high proportion of homeless. Most of the bodies are rickshaw coolies by their bicycles. Nearly all have homes, but it is as easy to lie on the floor of a pavement as that of an overcrowded house. At 3:30 A.M. there was not much buying or selling, nor small boys relieving nature in the gutter; otherwise little differed from daylight: cows wandered; men sat, squatted, stood, talked; coolies splashed water in front of their shops or brushed away dust; oxcarts lumbered by. At the station Anne had to step over bodies to reach the booking window. Again, they were not homeless but had walked from distant villages to take the train the following day. What more sensible place to sleep?

No Westerner in India can ever forget the widespread poverty that meets him at every turn, or the dirt, dishonesty, and unceasing begging partly begotten by it. Indian public opinion is somewhat sensitive to Western comments on the subject, but to dissemble would be as wrong as to ignore the active measures which the Government of India is taking, in face of mountainous difficulties, to conquer poverty; moreover the Englishman does well to remember that England even in the late nineteenth century had conditions as bad. Much of the begging would cease had it not the sanction of Hinduism. Begging is not so noticeable farther East because religion does not encourage it. When a man gives in India, the beggar, fawning enough in solicitation, shows no gratitude. Why should he? He has helped the donor acquire merit.

Coolies carried our cases on their heads over the bridge with effortless balance to the "up" platform, which was almost as noisy as in broad daylight. Vendors of bananas, nuts, and sweetmeats cried their wares. Passengers stood or squatted around tin trunks, baskets, cooking pots, and children. A post-office mechanical trolley trundled by, uprooting a few of the coolies asleep on the platform. Pariahs broke into a violent dogfight on the "down" line. At last the Amritsar Mail drew in, thirty minutes late, a searchlight beaming from the powerful engine.

The conductor, always friendly and courteous, walks up, checks our seats from his board, and unlocks the compartment. Ragged blue coolies sweep out the dust, a most necessary process, and ragged red coolies arrange our luggage and are paid off—an art in itself, as they always try for more, and the greater the initial overpaying, the harder they try. Unhurried cheerful bargaining and possibly an extra pittance given with a show of spontaneous reluctance sends them away happy; if they are obstinate the door must be firmly locked in their faces. Never begin to pay until they are outside the carriage. All takes time; there is plenty before the warning bell clangs.

I never lost the fascination of Indian railway travel, once I had geared myself to an Oriental concept of time. Other railways in the East may be faster (on this particular journey the Mail, fastest of trains, took five hours to cover 143 miles), more comfortable, or cleaner, sleeker, or provide towels and toiletpaper; the Indian train is in a class of its own. When we were able to reserve a coupé to ourselves we seemed to have a home again, the world locked out. Indian trains have no corridors, except in certain of the air-conditioned coaches, and are designed for long journeys, each passenger allotted a bunk by night; even in daytime he has plenty of elbow room. That is in the first class, which has a standard of comfort a little lower than English second. Third class must be seen to be believed, preferably at festival time when I have watched entranced a train moved off with bodies packed to suffocation, others hanging out of the windows, clinging to the doors, and sitting on the roof.

Because for this journey we were unable to book a coupé, we could not unroll our bedding. One man did, taking up three people's space, but he was a Member of Parliament and the others dared do no more when the carriage crowded up than push back his toes. Once again we watched the loveliness of dawn and sunrise over the red-tiled village huts and the patchwork of crops and plowland, interspersed with trees, which stretched out flat as a billiard table as far as eye could reach—the Ganges Plain, flatter than any countryside I have known, and every yard cultivated or occupied by teeming millions.

Dotted across the landscape in the morning sun were close-built, tight-packed villages, less substantial than in the prosperous Punjab but more so than in Central India. India of the villages is, and for long years must be, the real India; whatever the extension of industry under Five-Year Plans, by far the most Indians are villagers. And in the North you can travel mile upon mile without meeting a village Christian.

There are exceptions to that, for in the Punjab and in Uttar Pradesh (United Provinces), are the areas of the mass movements. Early in the century, and on into the 1920's and 1930's, a new phenomenon altered the statistics and the outlook of Christianity in the North. Outcaste and low-caste villages, the refuse and offscouring of Hinduism, began to turn to Christianity for the succor and for the recognition of their rights as humans that Hinduism denied. Through the courage and perspicacity of a number of missionaries, of whom Jarrell W. Pickett of the American Methodists was the mouthpiece in *Christ's Way to India's Heart,* these stirrings were directed into the channels of the regular churches, and village after village was baptized en masse, a distant echo of the conversion of the Anglo-Saxons. Pastors and teaching, so far as opportunity allowed, were provided. Undoubtedly many individuals found solace, and some fine characters were molded from the least attractive human material.

To these Christian villages missionaries and national workers have easy access. I recall one village not far from the Ganges, near the bank of a canal. We walked through narrow streets between high walls of baked mud, and sat outside the headman's little house surrounded by small boys and buffaloes, while a sari-clad girl Bible teacher conducted a class for adult illiterates in the shade of a banyan tree beside the village pond.

Mass movements breed problems. A prominent Indian layman told me of his regret, though a close friend of Pickett, that the mass movements had ever occurred. He believed that too many villages had been prompted by mere desire for social or economic betterment. The movement had also mixed Christianity with politics as badly as Hinduism and Islam were mixed, for in the days of communal representation toward the close of British rule a sufficient increase of Christian converts could shift political balance.

That factor has disappeared. Undoubtedly, however, mass movements have burdened the Indian churches with the pressing problem of the nominal Christian whose ethical level, men say, too often is lower than that of his Hindu neighbor.

I came in touch with two Indians who, not only in the mass-movement areas, might hold the solution.

Brother Bakht Singh, one of the most controversial names in Christian India, may yet be one of its chief hopes. More probably he has been permanently deflected into a bypath. I had hoped to meet the man himself—an impressive experience, I believe—but he had left for the United States before I could reach Hyderabad, his headquarters.

Bakht Singh when a young man in beard and turban and other signs of a Sikh, with their pride and independence of spirit, traveled to Canada in the early 1930's for higher education, and was converted to Christ. Returning to Karachi transformed in heart and experience, with a vivid sense of mission, he ran up against a British missionary of the old school who treated him as inferior in status; Bakht Singh (or any other "native") might not enter the mission bungalow without permission, would be kept waiting deliberately, and must suffer petty slights lest he get above his station. Bakht Singh was put off missionaries.

Nevertheless he worked with the Anglicans, and in Karachi and afterward in Lahore brought new life into deadwood churches. "I have never heard anyone who can preach on sin so scathingly or on Christ's power so effectively as Bakht Singh"; words such as these have been said to me by several foreigners and Indians, including some who disapprove of him on almost every other ground. His impatience mounted: impatience with the dependence of Indian churches on the West, with the standards, too frequently low, of Indian Christians. His feelings bubbled up in a denunciation of missionary failings, using as his platform the Annual Convention for the Deepening of Spiritual Life at Sialkot in the Punjab. "Many of the things he said needed to be said," I was told, "but he went too far. The Punjab became too hot for him and about 1940 he moved to South India."

Here too conversions and revival followed. To this day Bakht Singh is a foremost evangelist and preacher in India, farther Asia, and in the United States. A crisis came in his life; to criticize another man's decision made before God is to invite our Lord's "Judge not that ye be not judged," yet it is hard not to feel that Bakht Singh's was a grievous blow to the church in India. When we were discussing him, the Bishop in Madras, David Chelappa, remarked: "Every pulpit in the city was open to him once. Now there's scarcely one."

Bakht Singh's crisis arose from serious concern at the number of his converts—Hindus, Moslems, and nominal Christians—whose faith afterward fossilized. He ascribed the failure to the unhealthy condition of many of the churches of all denominations to which these converts were linked. A conflict developed in his mind and conscience. "If you bring children to birth should you leave them to die in a ditch?" He heard God calling him to form new congregations on which his converts could be grafted, coming out of the old churches or coming in fresh from Hinduism or Islam. He foresaw the antagonism such a policy would arouse, but the conviction grew so strong that he yielded, and founded his first "Assemblies." A storm beat about his head as it had about Wesley's in somewhat similar circumstances.

Bakht Singh went further. He worked himself into the belief that the Assembly was the only truly apostolic "ark of salvation." It *was* the church; the rest were outside. On this point one of his closest associates, a friend of mine, broke with him. Bakht Singh had reached the position of the Roman Catholics—this and this only is the church of God—and thereby had merely formed another denomination. He himself refuses to accept that his assemblies are a denomination; they are *the* church.

DAWN IN WEST NEPAL
The view of Annapurna from Shining Hospital

CENTRAL INDIA
A beggar waving a peacock-feather blessing

SOUTH INDIA
Fishermen near Trivandrum

The power, the urgency, the apostolic vision combined with an indigenous approach which might have brought a blood transfusion to the Indian churches have been deflected and circumscribed. The assemblies will cooperate with no one. On the other hand, from what I have heard, the love they show to individuals regardless of personal attitude is quite remarkable.

I wanted to see for myself. One Sunday we went to the Assembly on the outskirts of a North Indian city. The service had been on for two hours already when we arrived, and was to last another three, a truly Indian conception of time; also, people came and went freely, either having had their fill or to visit the latrines behind an unkempt banana plot visible through the door beyond the preacher.

The chapel, below the house of the pastor was a low white building well kept within and without. On the walls were painted texts in English, Hindi and Nepali: "Surely the Lord is in this place" announced the outer wall; "Christ is Lord of all" proclaimed the wall behind the preaching desk; the center beam: "Holy and Reverend is His Name."

About thirty-five of each sex and a number of remarkably well behaved children sat on mats. They use no benches, for they owe nothing to the West—perhaps a trifle affected for these days. I recall a bishop of one of the ancient indigenous churches of South India saying that his people were beginning to put in chairs because so many now used them at home: "Just because Father sat on the floor in church, why should we?" The congregation of El Shaddai were grouped according to the sexes—anything different would scarcely be expected in India—and the women were all covered.

The pastor wore a brown suit, a blue shirt done up at the collar, but no tie. As we entered he was preaching on Samson. Beside him a local businessman in a light blue suit and open-neck shirt interpreted into English (not very well), swaying as he spoke, announcing almost every phrase with "This brother he say . . ." The interpretation was not for our benefit but for one old English lady who came regularly, a touching consideration on the part of the Assembly. Both men held large Bibles.

After half an hour the pastor was replaced by a young former carpenter with tousled black hair who had been sent by the As-

sembly on a 150-mile three-week preaching tour and who now reported, with engaging modesty and humor, the conversions from
Hinduism (most of the congregation now present were converts,
though a few had "come out" from the regular denominations), the
opposition of some nominal Christians and of Hindus. He had
supplied himself through the charity of friends made on the way.
He spoke, with interpretation, an hour. They sang a hymn, a
thoroughly Indian hymn accompanied by a drum, a floor harmonium, and tambourines, and during the singing we all filed up, row
by row, to hand in our collection. Then we prayed.

It was a prayer meeting rather than a liturgy. We knelt with
legs tucked under knees, sometimes leaning forward with heads
on the ground. Everyone, including women, might pray aloud, ex-
tempore, and occasionally someone struck up a song and all joined
in unaccompanied. Shortly before three-thirty the Lord's Supper
began, quite short and very informal. For wine, orange juice, for
bread the common bread of the people, chappati. The pastor brought
the elements round while the congregation remained at prayer;
anyone not ready to receive was sharply rapped on the head. Oddly
enough, people continued to withdraw to the latrines during this
most sacred part of the service.

When it was over, the chapel became a social hall; we had a
cup of sweetened milky tea preceded by a long grace, and I was introduced to the pastor and elders.

The Assembly membership in this city was some two hundred. An
English woman missionary told me more about it as we walked
home. "They are very dear brethren but they do love long meetings!"
she said. More seriously: "They seek to be truly simple and apostolic.
They are very aggressive and are always on the go—a really strong
sense of mission. Nearly every night there are meetings for evangelism or building up. But they are very suspicious of the older
denominations and doubt if any who are in them are 'born again.'"

This pattern would be repeated in any of the several hundred assemblies founded by or in connection with Bakht Singh in various
parts of India. Undoubtedly they have burning faith and a supreme
sense of the omnipotence of God and a vivid experience of redemption. How much more significant for India if Bakht Singh,
who cooperates warmly with other Christians when out of his

own country, could demolish the dam of exclusiveness which keeps the waters of his movement from irrigating parched areas!

I met the other man of the future in the guest room of an important Methodist city church where he was conducting a mission. Sitting on his bed while I sat on the only chair was a man of thirty-eight in a gray check suit, red waistcoat, and a blue tie pinned by an enamel brooch decorated with the picture of a coach. His black hair was swept back; he had the light-brown skin of a Punjabi, a Douglas Fairbanks mustache and, curiously for an Indian, a slight American accent.

Dr. Akbar Haqq, a man of brilliant scholarship and son of a notable convert from Islam, had been head of the Henry Martyn School of Islamics until Dr. Billy Graham came to India in 1956. Dr. Haqq told what had happened: "I had been aware of the dire need of spiritual awakening in the Indian Church, but I did not believe in the need of evangelization or of decisions for Christ among nominal Christians. I was intensely disturbed by the state of the Church—you grafted a Muslim convert to a local church; they saw the sort of life being lived, and they went back. All our worst opponents have been apostates or near converts. I was dismayed, too, by the spiritual condition of many mission compounds. I saw the need of a man to bring revival. When Billy Graham came, I thought he was the man."

Dr. Haqq was interpreter at Dr. Graham's meetings in Delhi in February, 1956. They had long talks together. "Billy Graham," continued Haqq, "said: 'I am not the man to be used for a spiritual awakening here. It has to be an Asian. I think you are the man.' I was overwhelmed at the vision, and doubted. When, later in 1956, I returned from taking part in the Louisville Crusade I thought I would give God a chance. I had been invited to be evangelist in a city-wide campaign in Kanpur sponsored by the Evangelical Fellowship of India. 'If it's your will I should do this work,' I prayed, 'Let me know in the context of this campaign.' When on the first night I gave the invitation I closed my eyes; I didn't want to see failure. But scores came up! And our audiences grew from four hundred on the first night to over five thousand before the end.

"Since then God has never failed me, all over India. Wherever God has taken me He has honored His contract." Dr. Haqq's preaching is, as he puts it, "more of divine than of emotional reasoning," and when he gives the invitation he seeks to discourage all but the spiritually hungry. His follow-up system is similar to Dr. Graham's, and as church-centered. His message is firmly based on Biblical theology, and he preaches either in Hindu or in English. "God's pattern in these campaigns is so wonderful," he said. "It includes both non-Christians coming as well as nominal Christians. In my three years at the School of Islamics I had no convert. Since beginning this ministry I have had scores."

Dr. Akbar Haqq has now conducted campaigns in several cities of India, and in Ceylon from one of the Anglican bishops I heard warmest commendation of the campaign which had concluded shortly before this Delhi interview. "A splendid job!" said the Bishop of Karunegula, "especially among intellectuals and university students. He got a lot of half-baked Christians warmed up! Because he is one of us he can do what Billy Graham never could have done. He can do such a great job in Asia."

In that little guest room in Old Delhi words poured out from Dr. Haqq which will be proved the shrewder as the years pass: "Missions were designed to lean heavily on support from abroad," he said. "We have got to get to the position of self-support, in the context of spiritual awakening. Therefore we ought to talk less of 'self-support' and more of the Spirit of God. . . . Revival in the Indian Church must not be an end in itself. If it is it will go wrong, will stagnate! Revival must be seen as a means to change the face of Asia—'Ye shall receive power . . . and ye shall be witnesses unto me . . . unto the uttermost part of the earth.'" . . . When I go to the West it is a demonstration of the fact that Jesus Christ is a universal Saviour. Hitherto it has been too much a one-way traffic, West to East. Yet we need fellow Christians from the West out here, called of God, to prove the universality of Christ, though the actual evangelizing now has to be done mostly by Indians."

Dr. Haqq rose from the bed he had been sitting on. "We must get out of the old idea of sending missionaries to pagans. The whole world is a missionary field, and we Christians have to band together to confront the East and the West with God."

EIGHT 🌿 *Way of Obscurity*

They were burning her a few feet off. We sat in a boat on the Ganges soon after sunrise in company of a Christian sadhu whose saffron robe, young face, and black beard were faintly suggestive of John the Baptist.

She had died in Banaras (or Varanasi, as it is now officially called), in that part of the city beside the waterfront called Kashi. In popular Hindu belief by dying there her soul was freed from any further migration and would be absorbed into Brahma, the Spirit of Life: she had gained salvation—by the place of her death.

The corpse in its pink shroud (a man's would have been white) had already been dipped in the river. The husband, dressed in white, his head newly shaved except for the little tuft on the crown, walked round the pyre holding a bunch of long twigs. A few other men stood about, but the wailing and the women had been left behind. A temple official took the twigs from the husband and kindled them from a fire burning night and day and placed them under the pyre.

As our boat drifted away the pyre was burning strongly, and the husband would not need to wait long before the half-burned body could be raised to a sitting position so that he, as nearest relative, might break a hole in the skull to prevent it bursting: If the skull bursts the spirit has not been released. When the body was burned the ashes would be thrown into the river.

Every day a succession of corpses are carried down through the narrow *gullis* between the houses and temples to the river. To die at Banaras, or at least to be burned there, is the hope of every devout Hindu, though the climate imposes a strict time limit on the distance a corpse can be carried.

A few quiet strokes of the boatmen's oars brought us to the bathing ghats from which arose chatter and prayer. I watched one of the many pilgrims, in loincloth, step into the river to his knees, scoop a little water, and throw it in the direction of the "sun god," now well risen over the south bank. He scooped another handful and

drank it, murmuring a ritual prayer toward the sun. The Ganges is itself a goddess; a woman cast flowers on the water; another was
filling a brass vessel to carry home and place on the household altar
of the one- or two-roomed hut in a village perhaps hundreds of miles
away.

Bathers also thoroughly washed themselves (someone irreverently
described Hinduism as a mixture of devotion and laundry) or had
a short swim. A few young men did physical jerks on a stone platform
above the ghat; others sat cross-legged in the position of medi-
tation, soles turned upward, which is difficult for an Easterner and
almost impossible for a European. A launch of American tourists
chugged by.

We landed and walked up to one of the pundits under his large
umbrella with whom, for a fee, the pilgrim leaves his outer clothes
and after bathing returns to be ritually marked on the forehead, for
a further fee, with the *tilak* of colored ash according to the god or
goddess worshiped. And so to the temples where the pilgrim must
next go. The temples vary in shape and size, for nearly every Hindu
divinity, sect, and caste has its own. The general pattern is the same:
a conical roof set about with lesser cones to denote that the many
(gods and goddesses) are the manifestation of the one (Brahma):
a sublime conception which those who know India best emphatically
believe to mean nothing to the illiterate villager; the idol is all.

At the top of steps by the entrance to the narrow *gulli* leading
to the Golden Temple a man threw bananas from a sack into the
cups of beggars, male and female, adult, adolescent, and small,
who are liberally sprinkled all over the temple area to provide the
devout with opportunity of merit: the man was mobbed by a clamoring crowd, and tempers rose on both sides before he walked off annoyed. Sacred cows and brahmani bulls do not wait for alms:
they take them from the vegetable stalls. Nor need they push their
way through the *gullis* as we must; the crowd makes way and they
plod in godlike superiority.

It is a fashion among some Western writers to applaud the mys-
tical atmosphere of Banaras. To me it seemed pathetic, lacking in
awe of the Divine or in the beauty of holiness. The noise and shouting, the clang of bell as worshipers bade the god listen, the slush
where sacred water had been sprinkled on the image, the chattering

of devotees bringing petals and sweetmeats to the idols made me think of the prophets of Baal rather than of Elijah. And behind it all lie the distinctions of caste, in some ways still rigid despite government attempts to ease them—caste, that age-old domination by the accident of birth, a status, high or low, which cannot be changed by achievement or failure, poverty or wealth; a negation of the Christian belief that all men are created equal and are brothers. To the question "Who is my neighbor?" Hinduism answers, "One of my caste."

The worship of Banaras is the worship of the mass of India. The large Muslim minorities, especially around Lucknow and Hyderabad, the minority religions, such as the Parsees, and what might be termed the reformed Hindu sects, such as the Sikhs, whose refreshingly austere temple at Amritsar in the Punjab we had visited on our way through to Patna, are few compared to the millions upon millions who with local variations worship the Banaras way.

This immense religious devotion which should put most Christians to shame and which should be neither despised nor condemned represents a deep-seated hunger for peace of soul. Again and again converts from Hinduism told of this search for peace. Sadhus will travel for years all over India from shrine to shrine, temple to temple, preaching and teaching, but essentially searching for peace and for that ecstasy of union with God to be attained, they believe, only by prolonged asceticism, unwearying pilgrimage, and the cultivation of virtue. Hinduism knows nothing of salvation as the gift of God.

With hunger goes a widespread reverence for the holy, though holiness often has a different connotation from the Christian's: in Banaras cantonment, the residential and military area laid out by the British on the outskirts, in the dusk one evening we saw a full grown man walking stark naked, his hands folded in prayer. Such are considered highly holy, and it was when pressing to see a group of naked fakirs that a vast crowd got out of control with fatal result at an Allahabad puja some years ago.

With reverence goes prejudice, ignorance, and a deep-seated fear of angering the gods.

Village Hinduism appears quite different from that of philosophers, and from that of the highly educated and cultured men and women

of affairs, politicians, businessmen, and army officers whose friendship is to be prized and whose company is delightful.

Of the many conversations which I had with Hindus and former
Hindus as we traveled round India, I would recall three.

The first was at Kanpur (the Cawnpore of history). We were
staying a few days with a British businessman and his wife, Kenneth and Pat Willcox, old friends of ours, in their spacious bungalow.
The British business community in Kanpur, though dwindling, is one
of the largest outside Calcutta and Bombay. The Willcoxes took
us to several parties at the bungalows of Indian colleagues or neighbors, and as I munched chicken curry and other good things, now
chatting to an Indian manufacturer, now to an Englishwoman, and
next to a government official, I reflected on what a long way the
world had come since the frigid separations of E. M. Forster's *A
Passage to India.*

One evening we went to a Dewali party at the home of a charming well-read woman whose father is a notable Indian diplomat.
Dewali is the festival of lights in honor of the goddess of wealth.
Wicks set in little bowls of vegetable oil were alight all down the
drive, on the roof, on window ledges, so that with every Hindu
house lit up Kanpur was enchanting. Kenneth's small sons William
and Stephen were thoroughly enjoying themselves as their host
popped off fireworks in the garden. Dewali provides Hindus with the
presents and jollifications of the Christians' Christmas and is especially a children's festival; when they have gone to bed their elders
gamble through the night, testing their luck to see whether the
goddess is smiling.

As soon as our hostess, in a very pretty sari of red, the Dewali
color, heard why I was in India she drew me aside and, while the fireworks whooshed and banged and servants handed round sweets, out-
lined higher Hinduism. "It is essentially a philosophy, not a creed,"
she reminded me. "We believe that all religions are manifestations of
the truth of God. We revere Jesus as having been an incarnation of
Brahma, and accept His teaching of the Sermon on the Mount.
Buddha too was an Incarnation." She might have added that many
modern Hindus consider Gandhi to have been another. And an Indian Christian showed me a Home Science textbook in which Bud-

dha, Christ, and Radhakrishnan, the modern philosopher, were mentioned in one breath.

This philosophy seems remote from the ceaseless idolatry of the poor, I suggested. "You must remember," she said, "that many of them live as animals, poor things. But the more I have studied the so-called 'higher' philosophical streams, the more tolerant have I become of the so-called 'lower' ones. This is not to suggest that I consider blind idolatry on a par with the kind of religious consciousness which is always seeking to broaden its vision, and awareness of the multitude of ways in which God chooses to manifest Himself. But taken in the context of certain physical circumstances, including accidents of birth, I think blind idolatry no worse, in its own place, than other more aesthetic forms of worship." This is an attitude typical of the thoughtful, cultivated Hindu, those men and women who move with such gracious ease in the conference halls of the United Nations or the drawing rooms of London and Washington—that religion is a matter of endeavor and that any form of belief or action is valid if it is sincere.

I asked why Hinduism, so tolerant philosophically of other religions, is in practice grievously intolerant: a Hindu seeking baptism may suffer not only social stigma but physical hurt. She had begun her answer when her principal guest, the Canadian High Commissioner, arrived and our conversation ceased.

This point I took up a month later in South India with a distinguished Hindu philosopher, Dr. K. Sheshadri, in his modest almost bare house in Trivandrum. I had hoped in New Delhi to meet the greatest of them all, Radhakrishnan, now Vice President of India, but he was in Paris for the UNESCO meeting. Dr. Sheshadri is a loving, humble, and friendly man in his mid-fifties, a follower of the Visishta Advaita based on the teaching of the eleventh century Tamil saint Ramanujam. I told him of a young South Indian I had seen recently at a seminary whose story was certainly not unusual. While away from his village he had become a Christian, and his hitherto affectionate father had tried everything from tears to witchcraft and attempted murder, and now had renounced him as a son.

"The father must have been more of a father than a Hindu," said Sheshadri, cryptically. If a son of his, he said, began to believe in Christianity, he would show him that everything Christianity offered was already in the Gita, the Hindu sacred books. He would let him absorb all the Bible but saw no need of outward rite. "You Christians would have far more influence if you did not insist on conversion" —by which he meant baptism. It puzzled him that Christ should demand exclusive, open allegiance.

I widened the discussion by asking whether he would agree that Hinduism "absorbed" truth from other religions—Radhakrishnan is continually quoting the Bible. "No," he replied, "but other religions have helped us to see more clearly what was already in Hinduism."

"What would you say of the malpractices of Hinduism which so revolted Europeans early in the last century? Widow burning, hook swinging, and the rest of it. You know the saying: 'Whereas Christianity has crept steadily into the statute book, Hinduism has been steadily edged out.' Were these things mere accretions?"

"That wasn't the only bad period of Hinduism," he replied. "There have been many others."

Sheshadri was satisfied with his philosophy, certainly one of the finer of the many teachings which are all Hindu, however they differ. Each aspect of Christianity to which I referred he capped with a Hindu quotation, and yet there was always a subtle miss of the point. We were discussing the Atonement. I had said that Christians believe that because we are sinners salvation lies not in what we do but in what Christ has done for us; Hinduism has no such sense of sin and thus its way is not by atonement but attainment. " 'Nothing in my hand I bring' is an unknown attitude to a Hindu," I suggested. Sheshadri went to his desk and took out a typescript of English translations from the Alwars, the twelve Tamil Saivite saints. *"Twelve,"* he murmured; "there's a parallel there, too. . . ." But he did not press it. He read a passage which began, "I am not of high caste and have no power. . . ." "There you have it," he said: "resourcelessness, helplessness."

"But not *guilt*," I replied.

Geoffrey Paul, a Church Missionary Society missionary and an able theologian who had brought me to Sheshadri, tried to make the point plain. "Hindu philosophy teaches that salvation lies within you, doesn't it? That it consists in discovering the true self, the atman, the center of your being, and that that is pure? The real center core of your being, if you can find it, is pure?" Sheshadri agreed. "Then," continued Geoffrey, "may I put it like this? I find that the deepest level in my being is *not* pure. It is sinful, corrupt. That is why I need a Saviour."

"Ah," said Sheshadri, "but you have *not* understood your real center!"

And so he would have us search on for a divinity within, instead of humbly accepting the forgiveness of sins as the gift of a personal God releasing us for untrammeled service.

Sheshadri himself goes on searching. "If I could see that Christianity offered what I have not got already," he said, "I would change. But so far I cannot see that it does." As Geoffrey and I left this sterling character, we agreed that the Christianity which is to win such a man must be utterly in the Spirit of Christ.

The third conversation took place over a New Delhi luncheon table.

In New Delhi we stayed with the Dennis Clarkes, opposite the old Hindu astronomical observatory, Jantar Mantar. Though Dennis and I are poles apart ecclesiastically, we have close sympathies and especially a common interest in Christian literature. He has founded with great success a Christian Literature Institute (Masihi Sahitya Sanstha) for production and distribution in Hindi. Hindi covers already over a third of the population of India and is being promoted as the national language. There is therefore more than enough need for M.S.S., the Society for the Promotion of Christian Knowledge, and other mission publishers, since literacy leaps ahead.

When the Bible Society ran a nation-wide campaign printing the Gospel of St. Mark in vernacular newspapers, M.S.S. was given as the address for inquiry by readers of the principal Hindi paper. One of Dennis Clarke's assistants is a man who in his youth was a militant Hindu, then a communist, and now a strong Christian. His correspondence with many hundreds of these inquirers gave him good understanding of the middle-class Hindu in North India.

He and Dennis had been acquainting me with the three principal organized strands of modern Hinduism: the Brahma Somaj, which accepts Christianity as one of the world's great religions, and seeks to absorb it in a syncretion in many ways more dangerous than open antagonism, but which reacts sharply to Christianity's claim to uniqueness; the Arya Somaj, which is militant against Christianity and even promotes campaigns of reconversion; and the Maha Sabha and the Jam Sangh of politico-religious extremists who equate Hinduism with India, who wish to see India as a Hindu state, and who claim that Christianity is anti-Indian.

In contrast the educated middle classes display a growing interest in Christianity. "There are three reasons," said Dennis' assistant. "The first is *disillusion*. They had hoped that the new India would be a better place as a result of freedom and all the application of new knowledge. It is not. They know there is, for instance, corruption in all but the highest levels." Gladys Clarke interposed that the government lately had made a determined effort to improve the ethics of the people by emphasizing the great virtues, clothing Christian qualities in Hindu dress. Perhaps too, I thought, men sense that beneath the Indian assertion to be a people of peace and nonviolence in contrast to the warlike West lies the violence which broke out so terribly in 1947.

He continued: "The second reason is *uncertainty*. There is no certainty about anything. Partition is partly responsible. They feel a sense of instability—spiritual, not political. The foundations are being shaken. Religion might give a sense of security.

"The third is that Hinduism has provided no answer."

Some of the dissatisfied turned to the Buddhists of Ceylon, and many to communism. But increasing numbers ask about Christianity. I was shown translations of some of the letters received from educated Hindus who often collect their neighbors and friends to read and discuss the Bible and Christian literature. "Many have said," ran one from a man lately Hindu, "that they are the incarnation of God, or angels, but only the Lord Jesus claims to have brought salvation to man. With the help of science man can do many things, but no man can change the stricken nature, only through Jesus Christ can we get a new nature and a new birth."

"The real trouble," said the Clarkes, "is the large number of Christians who cannot give any answer when asked about their faith, though they would rather die than throw it over. Look at Delhi— 1,000,000 population, 18,000 Christians: if all went and *told* others, think of the effect!"

NINE   🦋   *Seats of the Mighty*

The Prime Minister's anteroom clock showed twenty minutes after the hour of appointment. The day previous had been Mr. Nehru's birthday. To judge from newspaper photographs he was now delayed at his home by a Sikh sadhu ceremonially garlanding him with a live snake.

As I sat on the comfortable yellow sofa, idly turning pages of glossy official propaganda, my feet on a green carpet opposite a handsome and solemn private secretary, I recalled that Pandit Jawaharlal Nehru has been termed the missionary's best friend. His own beliefs no one knows. A Hindu by name, a Christian in ethics, an agnostic at heart? When Hindu extremists introduced into the Lok Sabha an Anticonversion bill, Mr. Nehru's personal intervention demolished it. From the start he has done more than anyone to uphold the freedom of all religions to believe, to practice, and to propagate that is enshrined in the Constitution.

Forty minutes late, the Prime Minister entered his room by another door and I was invited in. He stood, slender, short, fair-skinned behind the wide desk of polished wood so shaped that four men may have a side and yet face him. He was dressed in a brown *achan* buttoned to the neck, and his customary boutonniere was a red rose. He smoked a cigarette in a holder and did not look so tired as when I had formerly seen him, having lately taken his first holiday in ten years.

Mr. Nehru is reputed a man of moods. A distinguished American told me that the Prime Minister hardly said a word until the last minutes of the interview. Perhaps because many of my family have been lawyers and because I too was at Trinity College, Cambridge, he very kindly spoke freely.

After the usual courtesies the Prime Minister sat waiting for me to open the conversation. I reminded him that my previous interview, in 1956, had taken place soon after a scare in the British press that missionaries would be shortly expelled or prevented from returning after leave. His assurances then had not been vain, and there now seemed less uneasiness. He agreed. I had sensed, however, a wide-spread belief that the government's policy was to cut down the number of foreign missionaries. "That is not correct," said the Prime Minister. "The government has no such policy. India still welcomes missionaries provided they have some qualification—doctors, nurses, teachers, so on. They must not be just evangelists. Indeed it is in their own interests that direct evangelical work should be done by Indians." He told me a story of a foreigner who read out to a village audience some strictures written by a Hindu against errors in Hinduism. "They gave him a beating. Now if it had been an Indian, that wouldn't have happened. And they must be invited by recognized bodies. We don't want people just wandering about."

I referred to the criticism that few recruits from non-Commonwealth countries were given visas whereas non-Commonwealth technicians came in freely. The Prime Minister answered: "Technicians come and go. They enter to do a job and then leave the country after two or three years. The missionary wants to settle down."

"A very clever answer," commented an Indian Christian to whom I told this. The denial of visas to Americans and Continentals—only seven of the language students at Landour in 1958 were non-Commonwealth—shows that the government's admission of missionaries is closely bound to the principle of reciprocity: if India wants her people admitted freely to other Commonwealth countries she must not discriminate herself. It is not surprising that a South African would find entry impossible. Commonwealth missionaries must have a "Special Endorsement" which is not needed by businessmen, and a "no objection to return" when they go on furlough. This is discrimination, though so far merely a formality. The Prime Minister ascribed it to the need to keep check on numbers; it certainly gives missionaries a feeling of insecurity.

Our talk broadened to the general attitude of the government. Mr. Nehru pointed out that in one respect missionaries were less restricted than in British days, for several of the former Native States now merged in the Republic, and therefore open, had then excluded them. "But you must remember that the States of the Republic are semi-independent and vary in their treatment of the question. . . ." Frontier districts? Missionaries were excluded from the Inner Line not because they were missionaries but because they are foreigners. "An Indian Christian can go where he pleases. No nation can tolerate foreigners on its frontiers." And to this all sensible people will assent, especially since the Chinese aggressions; though it was a typically Indian experience of one man who was held in jail thirteen days because the Inner Line was moved behind his house without anyone telling him, he being then arrested for living on the wrong side.

Undoubtedly the Indian Government is hypersensitive about "political interference" by missionaries. I have often tried to trace the source of this myth. Had the Prime Minister real evidence? "We have some, but not very much." That was as far as he would go. "Political interference" remains a myth except for the case of an American who in early days of independence unwisely encouraged the Nagas.

I asked the Prime Minister if I might be permitted to visit the Nagas. In the Naga Hills the Indian Army is operating against the only active rebels in the Republic. The Nagas are mostly Christian.

"No, I am afraid not," he replied. "White faces up there are an embarrassment—even United Nations personnel. Ideas are built up round them which are not helpful. Besides, there is your own safety. . . ." He went on to say that the government did not blame the missionaries, though the leader of the hostiles was a Christian. "These primitive tribes are inclined to slip back to whatever they were."

The Nagas of Assam, fierce head-hunters turned to Christ by American Baptists in one of the most spectacular advances of Christianity, had not taken kindly to the ending of British rule, and after five years rose in a revolt still not fully suppressed. An official who ought to know assured me that the rebellion certainly was not the fault of American missionaries except that they had built themselves up as fathers and mothers of the people rather than training responsible leaders. The government had withdrawn missionaries from the Naga Hills too abruptly.

Mr. Nehru, having politely turned me from the Nagas, was now discussing the famous Nyogi Report.

This report was issued recently by a commission of the Madhya Pradesh government. The commission's composition and its methods of securing evidence scarcely entitled it to be termed unbiased, and its pages bristle with explosive extravagances: "Evangelization in

India appears to be part of the uniform world policy to revive Christendom for re-establishing western supremacy and is not prompted by spiritual motives. . . . A vile propaganda against the religion of the majority community is being systematically and deliberately carried on so as to create an apprehension of breach of public peace." The report recommended an absolute prohibition of any attempt, direct or indirect, successful or not, to "penetrate into the religious conscience of persons, whether of age or under age, for the purpose of consciously altering their religious conscience or faith."

"It went too far," the Prime Minister said. "It was against the spirit of the Constitution. It rebounded on its own head." In fact, it encouraged more men and women of intelligence to investigate Christianity. And, ironically enough, Nyogi, the exponent of "absolute prohibition" on change of religion has himself switched from Hinduism to Buddhism.

As the interview drew to a close I asked the Prime Minister whether, quoting a favorite phrase of his, he considered that Christians contributed to the "emotional unity of India." "In the North, no; in the South, yes," he replied. Christianity is reckoned to have been in South India for two thousand years, and is one of the ancient religions of the land. "In the North, however, it came in with the British. The Church of England before Independence, remember, was an arm of the Imperial Government. Christianity in the North is still too much in the pattern of the West, not fully integrated in the life of India."

TEN ✨ *South India*

The Church of South India is probably the most written about of all. I touched only the fringe. For in a way which occurred nowhere else my plans were thwarted. Some Indians who, I had hoped, would take me out on their excellent evangelism among children were too busy the one week I could come. Bishop Lesslie Newbigin of Madura, who was enthusiastic to show me his diocese of the C.S.I., was on furlough. A man of influence in another important diocese, though no longer resident, had promised valuable introductions but did nothing. To cap it all, a hammer-and-tongs argument with the Minister of Education of the then Communist Government of Kerala became dead mutton when the Communists were deservedly dismissed by presidential action some months afterward.

Because rail communications in South India are slower than in any other part of the Republic, the traveler with limited time must be selective. Looking back on the ruin of my intentions, I have at least no regrets that I chose to go to Kerala, an eye-opener to a Western Christian.

In the second week of December we awoke one morning in a train below rugged hills east of Coimbatore, over eighteen hundred miles from Delhi. It ran on beside a river of wide sandbanks, shallows, and frequent busy fords. At the stations beggars were more insistent, more dirty. Vivid against the dark faces of irrepressible small boys who darted about the platform were their white teeth, not yet blotched and reddened by betel nut. An elderly, bearded, hook-nosed munshi in a white and gold fez, yellow scarf, and cotton clothes sat patiently on a bedroll.

The Cochin Express, which crosses South India, turned deep into Kerala, "land of the coconuts," the old name revived when Travancore, Cochin, and Malabar were reorganized into one state: a fantasy of green—banana plants, their great leaves frayed in the wind; coconuts in all stages from prodding bushes to graceful palms shooting up slender and bare to spill over in waving fans; paddy fields under water as if red-brown inland seas; palm-fringed lagoons; red earth and a background of hills in the heat haze. The train whistled interminably past level crossings where on tarmac roads unexpected lines of cars gave evidence of the high development of this land of tea, coffee, and rubber.

How the Malayalas stride! They have athletic bodies, square heads of high cheekbones, thick lips, heavy foreheads, and dark wavy hair, and pace along in starched white or yellow shirts, dhotis tucked up to hide their shirttails, black umbrellas hooked over their shoulders. The familiar soiled look is missing; even the peasants in the fields appeared clean as the sun shone on chocolate skins. How inquisitive the Malayalas are! At one station I counted forty-three adults beyond the fence, quietly watching.

Whistle full blast, the train hurried through village after village and then idled away its gains at each town. Every village and town had its Christian church. In contrast to the North and Central Indian countryside, a church is part of the Kerala landscape. Kottayam, where we were guests of Mr. A. V. George, a banker, newspaper, and plantation owner who is reputed a rupee millionaire and who is Lay Secretary of the Diocesan Council, has more churches than most English towns and more bishops of varying ecclesiastical hues than anywhere outside Rome.

Mr. George sent us in his car to tour his plantations. After a huge lunch of typically fiery curry with his brother, we were driven deeper into the hills to reach Ashley Estate at Peermade, a famous hill station. The road led through strings of houses. Every so often we saw a church, Roman, Syrian, Mar Thoma, or Church of South India, or a Christian shrine; we passed trucks displaying names such as "St. George," "St. Mary," "The Good Shepherd." To Ashley, where most of the workers are Christians, though labor troubles are by no means thereby removed, we came in the early evening and said we would like to climb the hill above the estate. Good Mr. Kurien, the manager, gave a distinct "mad dogs and Englishmen" look but put us on the track. We climbed. The scenery was reminiscent of Wester Ross. Out over the Malabar coast the sun dropped steeply in a glorious blaze to be extinguished by the sea.

Beside us, from the summit of the hill, rose a tall wooden cross.

His Holiness the Catholicos of the East leaned on the arm of a monk at the entrance to the Catholicate Aramana in Kottayam. Eighty-five years of age, forty-six a bishop and twenty-four head of the Orthodox Syrian Church, Moran Mar Baselius' ancestors were worshiping Christ in South India when mine were dancing round Stonehenge or sacrificing to some dark druidic god. He was a patriarchal sight with his long white beard, a red robe which buttoned down the middle like a shirt, a gold cross and chain, and on his head a cap of St. Anthony, the Syrian monastic order, dark blue with little white crosses. The whole effect was slightly spoiled by brown shoes worn at the toes.

He was toothless, had a humorous face, and when we were seated in a room hung with portraits of his predecessors he lay back with his head aslant and mouth hanging open; a charming interpreter with a cold in one eye rendered my opening remarks into Malayalam, a language which sounds like water down a bath drain and looks like the letter *m* run riot. Priests (bearded), deacons (beardless), and even house servants peeped over screens or round doors.

As we talked, the names of ancient councils and theological battles long ago were bandied back and forth: Chalcedon, Nicaea, Monophysite controversy, *filioque* clause. The "Syrian" Christians (who are as Indian as anyone else) claim descent from the converts of St. Thomas the Apostle, whom they believe to have landed in India in A.D. 52; his supposed grave is shown at Madras. The evidence that St. Thomas came to India is only circumstantial; irrefutably in the year 345 several hundred Christian immigrants from Syria took up residence on the Malabar coast and found others already established; since the fourth century the records of Christianity in South India are unbroken.

I was shown copper plates dating from 1325 renewing, in the name of the local King, high privileges awarded the Christians a thousand years earlier. The plates were a clue to the tragedy of Syrian Christianity in South India: the Christians became just another caste, below the Brahmans but above the caste of the Kings. They fell into the attitudes of a caste, exclusiveness and pride. Instead of evangelizing in farther provinces and among the Hindus around, they guarded jealously their caste position. They fossilized in their little corner of India behind its hills.

In the sixteenth century the Portuguese attempted to subjugate the Syrians to the pope, concentrating all missionary energy to the questionable task of forcing an ancient, independent tradition into a foreign strait-jacket. After lengthy wrangles they secured a superficial success until the authority of Rome was repudiated by the majority in 1653. The Syrians have maintained their independence ever since, and, as the Communist Chief Minister admitted, are among the foremost citizens of Kerala in commerce, education, and wealth.

I have met Orthodox Syrians (or Jacobites, as some prefer to be called) active in other parts of India where they have gone as professional men or as missionaries. They work closely with Protestants, and one was chairman of the Billy Graham Committee in Delhi. I attended a service of Holy Qurbana, massive in its ancient ritual, among a large congregation in St. James by the Kashmir Gate, an Anglican church in Delhi which is lent each Sunday. Corporately, the Syrians of the old tradition have never exerted the weight they might. Their energies have been dissipated in legal disputes between two sections, which have subdivisions too entangled to unravel. After fifty years the Catholicos had won the final legal decision a few weeks earlier. With unconscious irony he said, "Now that we have won, we shall get down to work in other parts of India."

In the early nineteenth century the Church Missionary Society, at the suggestion of the British Resident at the Court of Travancore, sent a Mission of Help to the Syrian Christians which was designed to strengthen and awaken without destroying the traditional structure of their church. In 1836 the Mission of Help ended in apparent failure. Yet numbers of Syrians were not content to abandon the light which, they believed, the C.M.S. had brought. Some, finding the church of their fathers obdurate in what they now conceived as error, threw in their lot with the Anglican missionaries. The diocese of Central Travancore, since 1947 part of the Church of South India, resulted.

Bishop M. M. John, a comparatively young man, had been elected to step into the very large shoes left by the late Bishop C. K. Jacob, who had known the Bible like the back of his hand and was one of those men whom you never forget. Bishop John had moved into the house on the hill which looks across to Kottayam C.S.I. Cathedral. Pictures of Ireland and of a castle in England remain from the days of the English bishops, above garlands, scrolls of greeting, and processional photographs of his recent consecration, and a Teddy bear, "a gift from Canada to our youngest," said Mrs. John. Like the Catholicos and our host, Mr. George, they had a reproduction of Hofmann's "Christ in Gethsemane."

I had wondered whether the Church of South India, over twelve years after its inauguration in 1947, would prove merely a loose federation of different traditions, each keeping to its own ways in its own area. The late Bishop Jacob, Bishop John, and others assured me that this is not so. The ordinary untraveled parishioner may not sense much difference, for he will worship in the old way, but a true sense of unity pervades the higher reaches of church life.

Certainly there are tensions remaining. In Trivandrum, where Bishop Legg in South Travancore and most of his clergy are former Congregationalists, the people of the former Anglican Christ Church insist on remaining under the jurisdiction of the Bishop in Central Travancore. This, however, is not so much because of ecclesiastical scruple as on the more reprehensible ground of social snobbery: they are Syrians, of ancient Christian lineage, come to Trivandrum on business. And they do not like to mix with the Trivandrum Christians, who are mostly of low-caste origin, products of the London Missionary Society's work. Another, more understandable tension, was resolved at Trivandrum while I happened to be there. The mainly former Congregationalist diocese had been reluctant to give full support to the C.S.I.'s women's order which seemed to them to savor of "high church." At length this hesitation had been overcome, and in the Kerala United Theological Seminary chapel, that Saturday afternoon, at a service which included celebration of the C.S.I.'s own liturgy of the Holy Communion, a girl was received into the order.

A sign of the C.S.I.'s spiritual health has been seen in its elections. I heard much talk about a recent episcopal election where the right man, it was felt, had emerged despite attempts by interested parties to press by doubtful means the claims of another: if not to rig the election yet to press members of the synod to cast votes for the wrong reasons. "Again and again," a C.S.I. presbyter said, "our elections have thrown up the man who seems to prove to have been God's choice."

The C.S.I. has had undoubted effect beyond its own borders. There is no need to refer to the changed attitude of most of those in the Church of England at home who, having opposed the union for doctrinal reasons, now give nearly unqualified support. I feel that any still opposed cannot have visited India and seen the absurdity of keeping the East permanently in the divisions of the West. One bishop of the C.S.I. told me he had been born an Anglican "simply because my great-grandfather went to bed a Lutheran and woke up S.P.G.—the missions had changed their boundaries!" The success of the C.S.I. has been an important factor in the progress of the reunion schemes in Ceylon and North India, both rapidly nearing fulfillment. The Anglican Bishop of Delhi, an Irishman and one of the few non-Indians still on the bench, had given me the latest news of the North Indian scheme. It will include the Baptists; in the South they did not enter. And equally notable is the fact that whereas the Anglicans of the South were predominantly evangelical, and thus more at home with non-Episcopalians, in the North many are Anglo-Catholic; and it had been the Anglo-Catholics in England who opposed the creation of the C.S.I. As another Anglican said, "In these lands you cannot afford to hate your brother."

"There has been a great increase of spiritual power since Reunion," Bishop Jacob had said in 1956, and in support stressed the widening part played by the laity. "Kerala holds the key to the evangelization of India," he maintained, and his son has told me that it was a favorite thought. Certainly Travancore is the only state in India with a substantial reservoir of Christian manpower, apart from Assam. The church in Assam is a recent church with a missionary framework; but the Church of South India, especially in Kerala, is indigenous, with a handful of missionaries.

The Bishop in Madras, David Chelappa, said, "Depend upon it, Mr. Pollock, the Church in India will never get on until all pre-1947 missionaries are withdrawn." He is noted for provocative remarks, not to be taken too seriously, for they are aimed to make people think. I understand he has difficulties with certain older American missionaries who insist that they and not the bishop should have the last word in the allocation of their money and men. Most missionaries, old and young, have adjusted their outlook to the new age. I asked a South Indian layman, prominent in the educational world, if a place remained for foreign missionaries. "Undoubtedly," he replied, "but they must be men of very definite Christian character." An Englishman said, "India wants from the West saints, men of Christlike life—this more than experts." A South Indian lady said, "Send us people who can show us how to live." Her Christian ancestry stretches into dim, forgotten centuries.

South and North the Indian Church still needs Westerners of tact, unending patience, and complete absense of personal ambition. Though the missionary in India may not need to be so tough physically as in some of the countries we visited, he needs to be seasoned in character and spirit, displaying the attitude of an American who had been out since the mid-1920's: "When people ask me what I do, I reply that I am a servant of the Church—in St. Paul's sense: a *slave*."

Not all the dissatisfied Syrians of Travancore joined the Church of England on the failure of the Mission of Help in 1836.

The Right Reverend Philipose Mar Chrysostom, over coffee in his little house at the seminary on Zion Hill at Kottayam, told me the story of the reformation which led to an exciting development of Indian Christianity too little known in the West: the Mar Thoma Syrian Church. The bishop, like the Catholicos, wore a cap of St. Anthony. His beard was black, with a few gray hairs, for he is in early middle age. He is tall, and has a pair of the brightest, most smiling eyes. He was not in episcopal dress that morning but a plain white cotton robe. He had spent a period at St. Augustine's, Canterbury; present at our conversation was a part-time lecturer who is also incumbent of a parish, who had attended Westcott House, Cambridge. Several bishops have had theological training in America.

"We do not talk of the founding of the Mar Thoma church," said the bishop, "but of the Reformation, just over a hundred years ago. We believe that we returned to the teaching brought by St. Thomas." A Syrian priest called Abraham Malpan had contrasted the biblical teaching of the C.M.S. with the current beliefs of the Orthodox church to which he belonged, and on the withdrawal of the Mission of Help took a stand for which his metropolitan excommunicated him. He and his people had no desire to abandon their traditional forms and be Westernized, yet they could not be blind to the light they had received. Abraham became the Luther of the Syrians. In southwest India the story of the Protestant Reformation in Europe was repeated, not without some of its more unsavory touches, until from small beginnings and through much opposition the Mar Thoma Syrian church has grown into a vigorous force. Their episcopal and priestly orders are as valid as the highest churchman could desire. Their liturgy is essentially Syrian. Like the early Protestants, they threw over practices and ideas which they believed to conflict with primitive Christianity: prayers for the dead and to the Virgin, the sacrificial view of Holy Communion, intercession of the saints, auri-

cular confession, a mediatory priesthood, all of which are tenets of
the Orthodox Syrians. They brought much in. "A true church," said
Bishop Philipose, "must be a biblical church and a witnessing
church. Evangelism must be church-centered, but a church which is
not witnessing is not true."

While still small and despised, as far back as 1888 they founded
an Evangelistic Association. Their annual conventions at Marama
for the deepening of spiritual life are famous throughout India, and
draw great preachers from the West. Their Sunday-school organization is second to none. In Singapore and Malaya are Mar Thoma
missionaries. I met a Mar Thoma at Djakarta returning from training in Australia; four are teaching at an Anglican school in Borneo.
The "Mar Thoma boys" in Katmandu and Brother George on the
Tibetan border are not officially sponsored, though by the way the
church authorities speak it might seem so; much of their support
comes from their own and neighboring parishes in Kerala. The Mar
Thoma church encourages young men to follow their lead.

Bishop Philipose did not talk in quite such Billy Graham language
as one of his episcopal colleagues whom I have met, but the effect
was the same: a church clothed in Eastern dress speaking with a
strongly evangelical voice.

That the Mar Thomas have not joined the Church of South India
is a trifle strange. "We felt that by not being in we could form a
bridge between the Orthodox and the C.S.I.," said the bishop. Many
of the younger clergy are anxious to join. Practical relationships are
close; in interdenominational concerns, such as the Kerala Band of
the Children's Special Service Mission, or the Bible Society, C.S.I.
and Mar Thoma work side by side.

The venerable Catholicos, I am afraid, is bitter against the Mar
Thomas. "It was all because of a court case," he complained. "They
failed, and so became schismatic, but pretended it was because they
wanted to be more evangelical. There are two kinds of faith. Theirs
is hypocrisy and superstition." It took me some time to ease him
away from a diatribe which seemed as out of keeping with the facts
as with the kindly old gentleman's character.

I had hoped to attend a Mar Thoma Communion Service, their
reformed Holy Qurbana. The only celebration on the Sunday when
I could go was in the local prison. The general opinion was that
though I would be let in easily enough I might never emerge!

We left for Ceylon by ferry on December 16, 1958. Adam's Bridge, the distance between Dover and Calais, is where the monkeys tied their tails together so that Rama could cross to rescue his wife from the demon-king of Lanka.

The sandspit behind Dhanushkodi Pier reflected the gold of a splendid sunset. From the kaleidoscope of memories one was with me: Mount Everest at dawn and sunrise, from Tiger Hill above Darjeeling. A great mountain dominated the scene, not Everest but Kanchenjunga, a thousand feet lower, less than a quarter of the distance. I at length discovered Everest over on the western horizon, center of three peaks peeping above a nearer range. Everest did not appear the tallest of the three. Because of my stance the highest mountain in the world looked trivial.

The Indian Church may look trivial beside the Kanchenjunga of Hinduism. Nothing can alter its postion in the sight of God.

two

Lands of the Yellow Robe

ELEVEN

No Murders on Christmas Day

We joined the *Worcestershire* at Colombo after a Christmas holiday in the hills of Ceylon.

The few days in Ceylon made an unexpectedly depressing introduction to the lands of the yellow robe where—such is the cleverness of Buddhist propaganda—I had expected to find a contender for spiritual supremacy of the religion of Christ but instead discovered an island of economic, racial, and political strife apparently justifying the casual insult of Bishop Heber when, in "From Greenland's icy mountains," he wanted a rhyme to "spicy breezes blow soft o'er Ceylon's isle, Though every prospect pleases, and only . . ."

The memory of those few days is of blue seas and waving palms, shops stuffed with British goods, secondhand London buses which, as you hear that unmistakable change of gear, exhort you still to go to "Ireland Overnight" or learn at the British School of Motoring; of rain at Newara Eliya where arum lilies bloom all the year, cows look English, cups of tea smell like tea factories and tea factories like cups of tea, and among British businessmen on vacation and a dash of American tourists a party of Russians, so unbelievably bearish and shoddy that I wondered they had been let out of the cage. And a wet Christmas night at Kandy, which still stinks as in 1945.

Strikes—dockers' strikes, busmen's strikes, strikes of gasoline workers, shop assistants and bank clerks, all in those brief ten days. And murders. The *Ceylon Daily News* on Tuesday, the 23rd, reported the fiftieth homicide of December. No murders on Christmas Day, but before we sailed, on December 28th, the score had risen by six to bring the year's total to 666. A prelude to the tragedy ten months later, when the Prime Minister was murdered by a Buddhist monk.

As I watched yellow-robed priests with shaved heads taking their places of privilege in trains or buses I could not banish what I had just heard from trustworthy authorities: how in the riots of April and May, 1958, when Sinhalis tried to bludgeon Tamils and the Tamils retaliated, some Buddhist priests pushed their way into a hospital staffed by Roman Catholic nuns and inspected the riot casualties: "That man is a Tamil—let him die. And he, and he; don't tend them. This one is a Sinhali; save him." "The year 1958 ought to be cut out of Ceylon's calendar," I heard in a Sinhali pastor's sermon. "It is a year we should be ashamed of." An influential Ceylonese whom I had met in London exclaimed: "Look at my country! Twelve killed in yesterday's papers, nine in today's, and twenty or thirty last week. And the Buddhists think that their's is the way of peace in contrast to the Christian West!" Not surprisingly, little is now heard of the Buddhist Missionary Society to Darkest Europe which was launched in Colombo with a flourish of notables a year or two ago.

Buddhism and nationalism are intertwined. The Portuguese, first colonial settlers, achieved genuine conversions among the fishers. The Dutch who followed allowed only Christians to enter public service or receive the advantages of registration: headmen would line up whole villages and the predikant sprinkle the water of baptism. The British when they came showed their customary official aloofness from the beliefs of their subjects; wholesale defections from skin-deep Christianity reduced the Christian percentage (it is only 9 per cent now), though many from higher classes, anxious to keep up with the "Burghers" of mixed European and Sinhali blood, remained in the Church. Since Independence the pressure is the other way. Without parading change of faith a man ceases to attend church or call himself Christian, and registers his children as Buddhist. The then Prime Minister and several of his colleagues in Her Majesty's Government were born Christians. "They all were," said, with pardonable exaggeration, a Buddhist district officer who gave us a lift, "but now a good politician has to be a good Buddhist. And Buddhist priests are interfering in politics. In colonial times they felt they were underdogs, so now they are pushing hard. They forget that Ceylon is a secular state."

On the other hand a Christian leader claimed that the Buddhist resurgence was not so marked as propagandists suggest: in a recent census his own church learned that it had five thousand more adherents than were listed, people who could have lapsed with ease had they wished. This was Jacob Lakdasa de Mel, Anglican Bishop of Karunegula, a scintillating personality who lunched with us at Kandy.

The bishop had told me of the negotiations soon to lead to the union of churches in Ceylon. Over the turkey—or was it roast lamb? —he made a remark so close to a conviction I had already formed that over coffee I asked him to expand and clarify and let me write it down. He did, pausing now and again to give ecclesiastical grins to numerous acquaintances who passed close to where we sat in Queen's Hotel.

The statement of this Ceylonese churchman provides a counterpoint to the unfolding melody of our experience eastward across Asia: "The small Christian churches in Asia have a great part to play in these days of strong nationalism. First, in showing that in the last instance we must obey God rather than man. And secondly that in spite our very real loyalty to our own land and culture we can allow nothing to break our fellowship with Christians in other lands—in other words we stand for Religious Liberty, and Internationalism."

TWELVE   ✻   *Into Burma*

The *Worcestershire* moved slowly up the Rangoon River. The fresh green countryside, wooded here and there, seemed through a lifting mist like those translucent landscapes of the lower Thames before the days of steam. The comparison was spoiled, but the picture enhanced, by glittering pagodas stabbing gold fingers to the sky.

The Union of Burma had lately been handed to the military administration of General Ne Win. Former Prime Minister U Nu, to

his credit, had recognized that government had, as an English businessman put it, "reached a point where inefficiency could go no
farther" and that the only men in Burma with real skill in management, as contrasted with politics, were senior officers of the army.
So, with a small cabinet of nonpoliticals, General Ne Win was clean-
ing up the country, physically and morally, through a team of
colonels. It was not dictatorship but superbureaucracy, and though
half the time had passed, its extension into semipermanence was
ardently hoped for.

The new broom was evident: teams of "volunteers" on Sunday
mornings scouring garbage from roads which had been too offensive
to walk down; army engineers widening streets, surfacing a particularly slushy market, building public conveniences (but because these
were not to be free, probably no one has used them) and planning
the rehousing of squatters. They were also repairing the pavements,
but not fast enough: I walked across to tea at the bishop's in my best
pair of shoes. . . .

Rangoon is steamy, smelly, and dreary with decay and a black
preservative to prevent decay which gives the houses funeral shut-
ters and verandas. It had washed its face somewhat for Independence
Day, January 4th, and at night the floodlit Shwe Dagon pagoda,
over three hundred feet high, and the fairy lights in the trees made
a charming prelude to the remarkably smart parade of troops with
Japanese war-reparation helmets and small arms. The B.A.F. Dakotas droning overhead suggested a last-war air raid; they had four
jets too—or eight? It depends upon whether they flew round twice.

On the same Sunday evening we went to the cathedral. Fans
whirred, city noises came in at the open windows, and a mangy
black dog in the aisle gave tongue at the precise moment that the
choir began the anthem. Later, rather tactlessly for Independence
Day, we sang Chesterton's "Our Earthly Rulers Falter."

In Burma we were guests of the Bible Churchmen's Missionary
Society. The oldest, most extensive mission is the American Baptist,
beginning with the great Adoniram Judson in the early nineteenth
century before any part of the land came under the British flag. I
met several of their missionaries and national workers, saw much of
their influence and had time and money permitted should have

UPPER BURMA

Demon altars in a Jinghpaw village

THAILAND

Literature from the launch
(Author on left, John Casto on right)

visited upcountry Baptist centers. An invitation had come from Anglicans. In view of the generosity of their committee in London and the patient chaperonage and the superlative warmth of the hospitality of their people in Burma I have no regrets; very much the reverse.

The whole episode made a study of some of the tensions on the mission field today.

At the Bible Churchmen's Deaf School we stayed in Rangoon as the guests of Miss Winifred Lemon, a senior missionary and a born hostess. She came from the West Country and had our local paper: I took impish pleasure in reading how the most eminent of my former parishioners had been fined for speeding when late for royalty. John Hobson, the medical superintendent of the B.C.M.S. mission hospital at Mohnyin in the Kachin State, our first destination, had returned from furlough on the *Worcestershire*. We traveled north together. John is a tall, quiet doctor of about my age who had served as M.O. in my own regiment, which accounts for his exquisite Coldstreamer manners.

The express to Upper Burma now ran again at night; ours was the fifth night express since 1948. And nearly the last. While we were sleeping peacefully in the maroon-and-cream German upper-class carriage (foam-rubber seats, but several light bulbs missing or broken, and inner doors difficult to slide back), with a pilot train of guns and soldiers a mile or so ahead, an armed guard in the first carriage, and patrols along the line, a goods train far behind was attacked by rebels who damaged a bridge, so that though we drew into Mandalay, from Rangoon the exact distance from London to Glasgow, dead on time at 8:20 A.M. after a seventeen-hour run, the next night's express was nine hours late.

Mandalay had always fascinated me since an uncle had been stationed there when I had a boy's delight in Kipling. It disappoints. King Thebaw's wooden palace, together with everything in the fort behind its square mile of thick moated walls, had been destroyed in the war, and the streets, laid out symmetrically like an American township, and the famous covered bazaar where birds of prey sat on the roof were pocked with bullet marks. Burma was the one country in which the war seemed only the day before yesterday: the stark, derelict tank in the middle of a paddy field was symbolic.

Many of the twisted girders in river bottoms by railway bridges and the burned-out carriages chucked beside the line were probably relics of more recent scraps.

Pagoda Hill had been restored. We took off our shoes, passed in by the protective chinthes, mythical beasts sitting like confident chows to ward off evil spirits, and climbed the hundreds of steps past gold-leafed Buddhas, some sitting, some standing, one of them huge with finger outstretched toward the site of the palace. Here yellow-robed priests and faithful laity knelt to pay their respects while a man tolled a bell to spread the merit to all in earshot. A notice gave the cost of the lamps which every night make a pagoda a fairy palace; merit is gained according to the length of time and the number of lamps paid for. From under the golden "umbrella" which, like an outsized papal triple crown is placed with much ceremony on the top of these characteristic memorials of Buddhist piety, we had a magnificent view of the winding Irrawaddy, the barrier of the Shan Plateau, and the hills to the north.

Pagoda Hill is over five hundred feet, and can be climbed up and down in half an hour in a hurry in bare feet: I know, because after a leisurely descent I found I had left my pen on the seat at the very top.

The exigencies of what is left of the rebellion determine the times of train departures. It was before dawn that John Hobson and we were inserted into the northbound train after a day and three-quarters of a night at Mandalay. I say "inserted," for advance booking is a lottery in Burma—the army has a habit of requiring your seat. We were over the famous Ava Bridge at first light, and ambled, as the day grew, past a large lake in which cranes waded, and up into a more hilly and empty countryside of thickening jungle, sometimes bamboo, sometimes the smooth-trunked broad-leaved teak. At a long halt for lunch beside an alfresco station replacing one burned by Japs or rebels, passengers bought curry and rice which they ate squatting, hand to mouth with concentrated, noisy speed under the gaze of country people in wide hats of straw or sweet-smelling cane, and all the pye-dogs of the district.

Bonchaung Gorge, famous from Bernard Fergusson's *Beyond the Chindwin,* we crossed in the afternoon and soon left Burma proper for the Kachin State, one of the most loyal in British days, and free of insurgents despite Kachin repugnance to the establishment of Burmese rule. Mohnyin is 634 miles from Rangoon. From Colombo we had doubled back from latitude 6° to the 23rd parallel, the latitude of Karachi, Medina, Nassau in the Bahamas, and the Florida Keys.

Mohnyin is a few hundred feet above sea level. I do not think I had ever realized how cold the East can be until we alighted there that January night, wearing woollies and met by our hosts, Dr. Peter Thompson and his wife, Rachel, wrapped in scarves, gloves, and tweed.

The little town of Mohnyin is connected to the outside world by the thin artery of the railway, hemmed in to left and right by the contour and color of the Kachin hill tracts. It straddles a modest river, and the bazaar displays the mingling of races in Burma. A dull town of timber or bamboo weave, a symphony of brown, but the people wear bright, distinctive clothes. The Burman townsfolk are in skirt-like *longyis*, the women in transparent nylon blouses over white bodices, and hatless, the men in shirt and collarless cutaway jacket. Tribal Jinghpaws from the hills are in dark blue or purple, Shans from the valley villages wear loose trousers, almost bell-bottomed, and bath towels round their heads. Many of the shopkeepers are Chinese.

These meet in the bazaar but lead separate lives in separate areas, speaking their own tongues and seldom intermarrying.

The majority in the Kachin State are the Jinghpaws, not Buddhist but animist, the first animists we had been among; and many of them have become Christians in the past quarter of a century. Every four years they and the other Kachin tribes get together in a Grand Manau at Myitkyina, to sacrifice to the *nats* or spirits, perform ritual dances, meet their sisters and their cousins and their aunts, and generally have a good time as guests of government. Such a Manau coincided with our visit, and our hosts packed us off there in company with Mr. Cushing Hla, a middle-aged schoolmaster training for ordination.

The northbound train arrived an hour late. We squeezed in to make twenty-one in a lower-class compartment designed for seventeen. I spent the five hours of the sixty-mile journey through the small hours sitting on a bedroll surrounded by dusky film stars and technicians in various stages of sleepiness. One of them offered me hot toddy. Another, who had annexed the luggage rack to sleep on, I took for the funny man, as he looked like the comedian George Formby, and cracked jokes.

Mr. Cushing Hla is a Karen, of the race which counts the most Christians in Burma though 50 per cent are Buddhists. He was named for a famous American missionary. When the American Baptists turned to the animist Karens in the last century, they discovered a tradition that a white man with a book would come from across the seas to teach the truth, and they had phenomenal success, so that you do not need to scratch a Karen to find a vigorous, hymn-singing Christian, generally Baptist. Many Karen soldiers in the war put to shame the religion of their brothers-in-arms of the West. Mr. Cushing Hla had arranged for us to stay with his cousin Mr. Saw Rainbow (called after the bow of the Covenant in Genesis), Public Works engineer of Myitkyina, whose wife was a niece of the President of the Union of Burma, who is a Karen and once nominally Christian. The President must by law be Buddhist.

When Mr. Rainbow's driver brought us to his house at 3:45 A.M. two or three Poor Relations were asleep on stagskins on the floor of the living room by a burned-out brazier. Saw Rainbow gave Poor Relations a home in return for housework. In the evenings they sat round the brazier in company of a tame pigeon, making desultory conversation and occasionally using the spittoon. Upstairs was a room occupied by two wooden bedsteads waiting for our bedrolls, which we had brought as normal among Burmese; a large table, a chair, and a drying line. Two film stars, a family group with Uncle President, and a text, "Take Your Troubles All to Jesus," graced the walls. Beyond a curtain was another room in which snored the parents-in-law. The Rainbows' room opened out of that. There were no doors, and when, in the succeeding days, a Poor Relation needed to come through when Anne was changing and had no clothes on, he just came.

Mr. Rainbow, who had very kindly taken us at short notice, was a large, jovial man. He had spent a year in England and had a hearty Manchester laugh. He bounced in next morning to greet us while Anne was still in bed. Over breakfast he regaled us with exciting stories of the wartime Resistance. We were manfully putting down lukewarm, sugary, milky tea (neither of us normally takes much milk or any sugar, and we like tea to be hot). Another pot came in. "Ah," said Mr. Rainbow, "this is for Cushing and me. *Really* milky and *really* sugary."

After that he drove us to the Manau ground where were drawn up the tribes in their finery: Jinghpaw women in crimson skirts with yellow woven design, and dark blue blouses decorated with rows of silver discs and bangles; the blue trousers and long dahs of the Zi, the green and red stripes of the Lisu, all the local organizations in distinctive dress or uniform, waiting for the President.

I shall not weary you with processions and ceremonies. In some ways the Manau ground reminded me of an agricultural show except that in the ring men and women dancing formally took the place of livestock. The only outside evidence of animist origins, since the sacrifices took place in the early morning, were totem poles round which the dancers jogged, the men with long, sharp Kachin dahs in their hands, the women with waving handkerchiefs, led by animist priests in feathered headdress. Some of the steps were complicated but most of the dances were slow "crocodiles" to a monotonous, haunting rhythm of drum, cymbal, and gong. At the end the President and his party were invited to join, and he circled round, dah in hand, a half-smile on his round face, looking sheepish. Behind was a backcloth of hills, the frontier between the Union of Burma and Communist China.

The Manau provided a colorful and entertaining introduction to the Jinghpaws. After return to Mohnyin, more comfortably but again in the small hours, we were able to stay in their villages and, through David Darlington, one of the Mohnyin missionaries, learn something of animism and of the grip of the *nats,* and why they lose ground to Christianity.

David Darlington has a remarkable history. He had come out to the B.C.M.S. shortly before the war. When the Japs invaded Burma he had been on leave walking to India with the party surveying the future Ledo Road. They all returned to help luckless civilians in their ghastly trek through the passes. Darlington was asked to remain as a political officer guarding the open frontier and, after General Slim's army had swept back to Myitkyina, helping the Jinghpaw tribesmen in the remote "Triangle" to the north. He had left the mission. The war over, he went back, courageously, independent of mission or other support, to the area which had known him as a political officer and not, he felt, as an unequivocal Christian. His success as an evangelist had been remarkable, but it stirred the jealousy of certain Baptist Jinghpaws who lacked the charity of the American missionaries. He was in country technically theirs but untouched. He had promised to teach nothing not common to all Christians, yet they reported him as a troublemaker to the Burmese Government, which expelled him from the hill tracts. He can now work only in the valley where, once again a member of B.C.M.S., he lives with his Jinghpaw wife.

Darlington sent us in company with two Christian Jinghpaw high-school boys one of whom drove a local cart carrying our bedroll and bag, drawn by two oxen, one gray, one brown. It had well constructed steel-rimmed wheels and was lighter and more finished in style than an Indian oxcart. A walk of eight miles along sandy tracks through thick bamboo jungle and across watercourses brought us to a clearing where were scattered rough long huts of thatched roof and bamboo walls, on stilts three or four feet high. Dogs, puppies, pigs, goats, chickens, and children ran under and around. The longest and most substantial house had a thatched roof projecting some distance forward to give shade. At each side hung a decoration of suspended bamboos like some jungle chandelier, and the main crossbeam was painted with wavy lines and figures of a man and a cockerel, the sign of a chief's house.

A young woman, fresh and pretty, dressed in a dark blue skirt with broad mauve stripes, a blue blouse with red facings decorated with silver rupees, an everyday version of the Manau ornaments, and a dark turban, came down the notched tree trunk and took my hand in hers. We were not expected, but no Jinghpaw will turn away a traveler. He may stay two days without payment and without question.

THIRTEEN ✖ *Jinghpaw Jangle*

She led us up the tree trunk, which had an even number of notches as the *nats* like, past animal skulls and horns from former sacrifices, and into the house, dark although it was only late afternoon.

Taking care not to step over anything, since this would "degrade" the owner and upset his *nat,* we walked along the bamboo floor, past the first fireplace, for women, and past doors leading to little rooms, and sat down at the second fire, for men and men guests (a European woman seemed to count as a man). The fire was formed of three large logs pointing inwards like spokes of a wheel with smaller logs and bamboos in the center. A draft came up from below, smoke curled into the rafters and sometimes our eyes, and round the four sides were deerskins and reed mats on which to squat or sprawl and take one's ease.

Behind us stood the demon shelf: a wooden contraption, shoulder-high, cluttered with the remains of offerings.

The *nats,* evil spirits or demons, must be constantly bribed and appeased by offerings. The heavenly *nats,* such as the sun and moon, will have no truck with anyone but a chief, who is priest as well, so that the ordinary household is mainly concerned with its domestic *nats* or the many other lesser ones. To these are sacrificed buffalos and pigs, and the offerings placed on tall bamboo altars, platforms some eight or nine feet high with what looks like an upturned broom at each corner. Several were in front of the house, others in the village and out at the paddy clearings. "They haven't any real *dread* of the *nats,*" David Darlington had said. "It's more like a very superstitious Englishman's fears. For instance, if a guest when leaving doesn't go out of the *front* door, the domestic *nat* will get into a whirl and "bite" someone—cause sickness. And this religion hasn't anything to do with morals. That's a matter of tribal custom. If you commit adultery you must pay a heavy recompense, not because of religion but because you have broken tribal custom. Religion is all a matter of physical health and well-being."

A. T. Houghton, founder of the Mohnyin mission, who but for the war would have been consecrated Assistant Bishop of Rangoon and who is now General Secretary of B.C.M.S., challenged the view that "they haven't any real dread of the *nats*." "David Darlington ought to know," he wrote to me from London, "but it is clean contrary to my own experience. We have known a great many, men and women, boys and girls who have literally lived in fear of the *nats*. 'Why do you give to the *nats?*' we used to ask. The almost invariable answer, 'Because we are *afraid*.'" The factor reconciling the two views, as both men admit, is that the Jinghpaws we were visiting were in the foothills and affected by the town, education, and comparative wealth. Far up in the mountains the *nats* hold unquestioned sway. Darlington once arrived at a Jinghpaw house late; the guests' fireplace being full, he was put a little farther off, and when he had unrolled his bedding he knelt to pray. "I found I just couldn't. Something seemed to be dragging me away as I tried." Three times he failed, and so went to sleep. Next morning he saw, immediately above, a demon shelf piled with an immense offering, as the chief's mother had died. I asked him his theological conclusion, if he believed the *nats* to be "evil spirits" in the New Testament sense— personal evil powers. "Yes, I do," he replied; "up there where they have a real hold, I think that demons in our Lord's sense really are at work." I have not yet met a Western Christian living among primitive animists, as contrasted with some who study the matter from university chairs, who seriously doubts the reality of spirit possession.

Anne and I sat on the floor by the fire. The sun set in a blaze of red behind the hills, darkness crept down, and they shut the door to keep out the cold which at that time of year is in such contrast to the midday heat, and we wrapped ourselves in blankets. Farther from the door, the other side of the fire was warm enough; one man took off his shirt.

They handed us rice beer in strong bamboo containers. To sip it is to show that you do not come on a feud. The chicken we had specially asked for was carried squawking to the other fire to be killed, plucked and popped in, probably to a separate pot. In the other might be anything, vegetables, leaves, bamboo shoots, or on a big day some pig or buffalo. They abstain from cats and rats and boldly assert that, unlike the Nagas, no Jinghpaw has ever eaten bits of another. Everything is so overloaded with chilies that it is tasteless and too "hot," at least for us. Currying here is a sign of poverty, to hide the inadequacy of the diet.

Each dish came wrapped neatly in large fresh leaves, placed together in a basket, one per person, with the usual enormous heap of boiled rice, and mustard water in a cunningly contrived banana-leaf holder which I spilled; it went through the floor to the ground below like the men's spit. The chicken, broken up in little pieces, seemed mostly bones. We were given spoons, but it was easier to eat with fingers in their normal way. Guests are fed first. As we ate, the men prepared opium to smoke in heavy wooden pipes, using a metal spoon over the fire, boiling extra strong bitter tea to counteract the intense dryness of mouth.

We slept on the floor of a little square house across the village, for in the main house men guests sleep at one end and women at the other. The back stairs collapsed next morning under our breakfast. We slept well, for we had brought mattresses. Not being fully inured, we would, I think, have been surprised had we known how many nights we would sleep soundly enough direct on hard floors before leaving the East. The worst of that village was its paucity of water for washing, a mere trickle from a spring or mountain brook channeled into a bamboo pipe, the briefest splash until the Philippines.

This household was prosperous. The chief had sugar cane and a fish pond and an orange grove. One of his men wore a wrist watch; another had a bicycle. But the time might be when a *nat* bit the family into sickness. A diviner must then be called who "pops" bamboo over a fire or unravels fiber to read the signs. They showed us how, and fortunately announced that the signs were good. When the *nat* is biting, these signs indicate what sacrifice should be made to appease it, or how to bribe another to go to the sun country for medicine.

Only an accredited religious butcher may kill, cut up, and cook the sacrifice and place the *nat's* portion on the bamboo altar. A *dumsa*, or intercessor, sitting on a tall bamboo platform calls loudly to the *nats*, and intones incantations in ancient Jinghpaw. Diviner, butcher, intercessor must be paid, usually in opium. If the patient gets worse, the process is repeated with higher fees and more expensive offerings.

Death involves costly redemptions depending, not on the character of the dead—nor may he pile up merit as the Buddhists believe—but solely on how death came. Death in childbirth requires one of the heaviest redemptions, and those who die mad are enslaved unredeemedly to the terrible mad *nat*. We saw the strange structures in the jungle where the final feast takes place to send the *minla,* or immortal human spirit, on its long, dangerous journey through the northern mountains to join his ancestors in Katsan Ga, the distant land. And we saw the scattered graves, half smothered by creeper.

When sickness and deaths assault a prosperous family, payments to the *nats* and their "clergy" may induce poverty. Then, today, they turn to Christianity. I had hoped that while we were at Mohnyin a call might come, as it often does, for an evangelist or catechist to hold a service during which the family pull up the altars, cut down the demon shelf and its offerings, and burn the lot in front of their house.

Not only poverty but education turns them, for many of the younger men are ashamed to be animists, and seek baptism. Broken with animism and its expensive demands, they begin to prosper once more. Relatives see this, and they too turn. Darlington told me that "large numbers who have received practically no Christian teaching have given up animism and become Christians—in order to be better off materially. Their motives may be wrong but they come under instruction if there are sufficient clergy and evangelists." And now and again some fine genuine Christians result.

The houses in a Jinghpaw Christian village are square-built. First impressions of the village we visited were not favorable except for the government school and dispensary, run by Christians for the whole area. The older people seemed as dirty as the animists, and I saw two betel-nut chewers, their teeth rotted and red. The houses did not look so substantial, though the women had an improved way of pounding rice and there was a wooden pram or two. But the atmosphere grew on us. The headman's house where we stayed stood in a little enclosure fringed with small banana trees. In a byre by the ladder (not a notched trunk—a distinction between animists and Christians that I met nowhere else in Asia) to the front door was a cow and its calf, and upstairs beside the fire a large pile of unpounded rice, haunt of fleas, close to where we slept. Our hostess was elderly, beaming, and grubby. After dinner, similar in style and serving to the animists', placed on a low table with a guttering oil lamp, the younger of the two village schoolmasters, a neatly dressed man who leads the services on Sunday, brought the young people to sing hymns.

They squatted round a lamp, hymnbooks open, on the bamboo floor and sang in part song, some of the men indulging in a strange falsetto. Listening near me was a piratical old fellow with what appeared to be burned-cork side whiskers. The Lord has some strange sheep. The Jinghpaw hymn tunes are all adaptations of English or American, but I wouldn't have known. As one of the B.C.M.S. said afterward, "They get it wrong, and the wrong sticks." A drum and a cymbal were heard outside, and they asked if we would come to see the old Kachin dances. A little later a fire had been lit in the courtyard, two old deck chairs were brought out, and while we sat under the starlight in blankets the village "crocodiled" round us, first the men and then the women, in slow steps to the rhythm, as at Myitkyina, of a long drum slung under the arm, cymbals, and a little gong.

I had seen that opium, that character-deforming drug, and rice beer were cut out; that was negative. Here was positive friendship, as they laughed and chattered making the steps, a few of them with skill but most in just an amble.

When it was over they walked into the night, some with electric torches, others with flaming sticks from the fire, except several of the younger who came back for a last sing upstairs. Then we prayed the Lord's Prayer, each in his own tongue.

The background to our time around Mohnyin may be summed up in the two words Hospitality and Hospital. In conditions that would make suburbia wince, John Hobson and Peter and Rachel Thompson laid themselves out to entertain us royally in their houses of bamboo weave plastered with whitewashed cow dung. The comparative comfort of India and its well trained servants had been left behind. There was a refreshing amount, not too much, of your own chores, though they had brought in a Chinese cook and had a Burmese boy, hunched with cold morning and evening despite several pullovers. You bathed in Indian style, pouring water over yourself from a bucket, and at that time of year needed, and obtained, ample hot water heated on an open fire in a shed beside the kitchen.

Meals by Western standards were at odd hours, which scarcely surprised us, since on the tour we had already experienced evening mealtimes ranging from 5:00 P.M. (Tansen Hospital) to 10:00 P.M. (a dinner party at Kanpur). Our digestions survive. At Mohnyin the dinner was a normal 7:30 P.M., but after an early breakfast of porridge, fruit, toast, and at least for us an egg, the main meal, called breakfast or lunch or "brunch," as you felt inclined, was served at 10:30 or 11:00 A.M., generally a substantial curry. The time is supposed to originate in the habits of the pioneers who would march from dawn through the cool until about ten-thirty, as we were to do in Laos, and then lie up and eat.

The Mohnyin staff had the same difficulty in obtaining meat that we had met in India. They were careful to have a diet as balanced as circumstances allowed, recognizing that lack of protein is as dangerous as lack of vitamins. One of their colleagues away up in the Hukawng Valley not only lived entirely on the country when he was on tour but preferred native food in his home; however, he spent part of each year teaching at the Bible School in Mohnyin with its more normal diet. He seemed to thrive. A missionary doctor in another part expressed himself vehemently on those who run themselves down by bad feeding: "And then we have to waste time nursing them. If you don't feed properly you get weary and then you can't work well."

The hospital at Mohnyin was far removed from the Ludhiana style: no Shan or Jinghpaw would venture near a strictly regimented, highly polished institution where his relatives could not squat outside and sleep nearby. A nursing sister who tried to polish the Jinghpaw nurses to the methodical efficiency of a British teaching hospital returned to Europe in despair. This rougher style is natural to an upcountry missionary hospital, as also a home-trained nursing staff, limited equipment, uncertain supplies, the need to turn a hand to any ache or pain, surgical or medical, in an astonishingly varied succession of cases. They say it is most satisfying medically, and I used to notice the gleam in John's eye as he returned from extracting bits from one patient, sewing up another, or treating a third.

When I asked Peter what direct spiritual result there was, he said, "Practically none."

In old days many of the patients were animist Jinghpaws (Kachins), often coming great distances, and A. T. Houghton has since told me that "before the war, when there had been near eight hundred adult baptisms in the mission, the vast majority being among the Kachins in the north, a very large number were converts directly through the medical work, and the policy of 'medical evangelism' which we pursued both on an amateur and professional scale was producing notable results. I could point to scores of cases where the first contact with the Gospel was through medical treatment in hospital or dispensary." Today the patients are mostly Shan or Burmese Buddhists. Therefore it is not too surprising that Peter should say "Practically none."

"The hospital gives the mission a good name," he then said. "We have a name for honesty which is a big example to the civil hospital; here you get hospital treatment with just that difference. We are well known for eyes too. People come hundreds of miles for eye treatment. And Christians are helped and encouraged by having us here, and nurses get medical and spiritual training. Many of them know nothing spiritually, though baptized, when they come. We aim to get them to know the Bible, know the Lord."

Peter said that the attitude of local Jinghpaw church leaders to the hospital was not right. "They want to use the hospital to finance the church. That's all wrong; we mustn't bleed the hospital. The church members won't rally round to do jobs for the hospital either. They look on it as their special rest home. If we tell them there isn't a bed free when they come with a tummy ache, they say: 'No bed? But I'm a *Christian!* Isn't this *my* hospital?'"

Apparently there were too few leaders of sharp spiritual insight—too few leaders of any sort. This seemed puzzling also, for I knew that the prewar mission had aimed at building a self-governing, self-propagating, self-supporting church. What had gone wrong? "The war caught us before we were ready," one of the senior missionaries in the neighborhood said. The younger members of the mission lay blame on lack of schools: the mission had been so concerned to avoid spending money and time in mere educational uplift that they failed to produce educated leaders. This is too facile. Though reacting from the contemporary (1920's) doctrine of "Christianizing through education," they planned to make schools as soon as there should be sufficient Christians to benefit: when they began work there were no Christians. Houghton at first could not even take one on his strenuous treks in the hills; he had to make do with a pagan. By 1939 they had founded a school at Mohnyin; they had, Houghton has told me, "the beginnings of an indigenous ministry and were about to embark on a larger program to ensure that the church was literate and able to benefit from education."

The year 1942 swept it away. The Japanese fell hard on the Kachins for their loyalty to the British, as the main source of recruitment for the Burma Rifles. Jinghpaw leaders were scattered and killed, and no missionaries were seen in Mohnyin until May Stileman came down the line on a road-rail jeep in 1945 in the guise of a Red Cross nurse.

And whereas the Church in Lower Burma had the start of a hundred years, and survived better, in this area all had to be begun again. Not, at first, entirely wisely, for the place was flooded with missionaries waiting for their own stations to be rebuilt.

Except that both have dark hair and are much of an age, John and Peter are entirely different. John is tall, quiet, gentle, a man of few words and an unpretentious, deep sense of humor. Peter is short and slight, volatile and expressive; his words tumble out; he knows his mind and lets you know it.

One evening this couple, contrasting but close-knit, opened their minds as we sat in John's living room. I had asked them to define their purpose. Why were they there? "To give all I can give at every possible moment," said Peter, who answered first. "To reflect as much as possible of the character of God with the gifts He has given me," said John. This was rather general. I wanted their detailed intentions. Peter had already said, when showing me over the hospital: "We are aiming to get out of here as soon as possible. As soon as we could get a Burmese Christian doctor I would go." He wanted to see Burmese Christians take over the hospital and free him for what he called "clinical evangelism" in the hill tracts. I mentioned this, and John said: "Until recently my aim, too, was to make myself redundant. But now I am not so sure. I have been reading Stephen Neill's *The Unfinished Task,* especially his piece about the Oneness of the Body of Christ and the artificiality of any distinction between missionary and national. I'm not so keen to go. I want to carry on just as a Christian."

"That distinction," said Peter, "is one of our great troubles." With this we went to the heart of the difficulties in the Jinghpaw church, and I was brought against problems of relationship between foreign missionaries and national Christians. "Until missionaries," Peter continued, "are considered on an equality with nationals they cannot do all they might." At Mohnyin the old inequality, by which missionaries were considered, by themselves as much as by anyone else, superior persons, had been reversed. John and Peter felt regarded as flies in the ointment, foreigners to be mistrusted and hindered lest they should dominate; whose duty it was to pay the piper but be pecked at and harried lest they should call the tune. "They resent us. They won't take us as we are, Christians who have certain gifts; and we wouldn't have come all this way if we had not—and want only to use them to the full."

The trouble focused on a Jinghpaw layman who had been trained as a political agitator, and reflected a trend too prevalent in the Christianity of Burma—a desire to extend the Church numerically as an organization rather than as a Kingdom "not of this world." A church should not withdraw from its social or political environment into narrow otherwordliness; but to desire extension at the expense of spiritual depth is a false desire, if understandable in Burma, where the Buddhists pick the political plums and Christians are tempted to seek safety in numbers.

Eight months later the situation much improved on the setting up of a Deanery Council under the Burmese Assistant Bishop, thus breaking the dominance of the layman. That particular tension between foreigners and nationals has receded into history. It is one which may arise in the transitional stage wherever missionaries are genuinely anxious to see (in that hackneyed phrase) a "self-governing, self-propagating, self-supporting church." John and Peter stressed that the Mohnyin situation was not typical of all their mission's operations in Burma, mentioning another place where the missionaries were still in close control. "At least it means they are appreciated—father and mother of all, and so on. Everyone may be happier, but they haven't advanced so far."

These two English doctors in their unobtrusive way were cutting as strenuous a trail as those pioneers in the actual jungle whom we met later in less developed lands.

FOURTEEN ❧ *Shans, Irish, and Sawbwas*

A little stream barred the approach. We had begun to jump or wade it when a young Shan woman appeared and led us to a plank specially put down. "Her husband has just started at the Bible School," remarked May Stileman, "but she is a Buddhist. It's a pity, but what can you do? There are no Christian girls around. It may be a bar to his ordination, though."

At Mohnyin, as usual, Anne and I walked considerable distances, out through the teak forest on the western edge of the valley to the Christian village below the hill, where we were entertained with oranges by the headman; up on to the eastern ridge, where you are supposed to be able to glimpse the distant Irrawaddy; and now today we had walked out a brisk five miles before the morning mist had lifted, and the dogs were still curled on the ashes of last night's fires, along the northwest track fringed with a flowered weed, like Michaelmas daisy, called Germany Plant because it first spread in the 1914 war. At the end, now under a strong sun, stood an ancient temple: a monastery and school connected by a covered way to a pagoda tipped with tarnished gold, beautiful against the nearby hill.

At a bungalow in the village beyond, we collected the veteran May Stileman, an admiral's daughter and for over thirty years missionary to the Shans. She was to take us to "breakfast" with two of the very few Shan converts (they were first) in the area. Shans are Buddhists, and those of this neighborhood were of a strict sect; the Shan-Burmese were Buddhists of a more usual sort. For both, the impersonal, rarefied philosophy of Buddhism had been diluted so that they called the little alabaster Buddha in their family shrines "the god."

We continued a further mile through paddy fields to the hamlet of which U Aw, the convert, was headman. It was his daughter-in-law who had come to meet us. Over the stream we came to Aw's house, the most substantial in the hamlet, though he was once desperately poor. It stood on low stilts. Strong wooden steps led to a veranda where mustard was drying on the rail, and pots and pans, a fly-blown pile of rice, vegetables and a relation queer in the head were on the floor, she vigorously eating her rice. U Aw's wife, Daw Ee, an elderly woman with the usual Shan headgear of a bathtowel, gave us water to pour over dusty feet before entering the living room of bamboo-strip walls with reed mats. Facing me were an assortment of family photographs, pictures of all the royal family back to George V and Queen Mary in coronation robes, a large array of prewar cigarette cards, and certificates of proficiency in Bible courses. An old deck chair, two uprights, a low round table, a Singer treadle sewing machine and, suspended from the roof, a cradle chockablock with materials showed it was the house of a prosperous man.

U Aw sat in a denim suit on a mattress in the corner, one knee up and the other tucked under, an old face well-chiseled below gray hair, and a mustache bushing out like a Victorian colonel's.

Guests are served separately before the hosts eat. A bowl of vegetable soup with floating mustard leaves held the center of the table, and round it were bowls of curried fish, chicken, and vegetables. The daughter-in-law placed an enormous pile of rice on each guest's plate, and on to this you spooned soup and a little of what you fancied, enough for a few mouthfuls at a time. To stretch was good manners, and as for using licked spoons in common dishes Sir Alexander Fleming is said to have pronounced that women gossiping over teacups are in more danger of germs.

U Aw while we ate told his story through Miss Stileman's interpretation. He had first heard the Christian Gospel at the hospital in the early thirties. "I heard, but I did not understand." Meanwhile his wife, doubly bereaved of small sons, had poured out her troubles to Miss Stileman, had believed, renounced Buddhism and been baptized. Shans are highly group-minded. It required not only deep conviction to abandon Buddhism in the face of overwhelming public opinion but strong courage. It was a trifle easier when the missionary was, as then, of the ruling race, but the few baptisms and the many deathbed confessions of hidden faith which Miss Stileman could recall point to the contrary. And Ee (though Aw did not tell us) felt the force of her Buddhist husband's wrath. He beat her, taunted her, tried to make her recant—until her indomitable patience wore him down. He began to wonder whether Christ might be the only true Saviour of the world.

Curious incidents, he said, undermined his faith in Buddha. Once he was taking down pails of water to "wash the god" in an annual ceremony at the temple; the strong yoke over his shoulder unaccountably broke and spilled the water. Taking food to offer to the god, it disappeared as he walked. Probably a bird stole it, but in both instances he said to himself: "If the god can't take care of his own things, things I'm bringing for his own use, he cannot be much of a god." Aw's Buddhist theology was awry, typical of folk belief in Burma.

He was baptized two years after his wife. Immediately trials assailed. His neighbors ostracized him: "I was not physically maltreated, but they sought to hurt me in every way they could." The social life of a Shan centers upon religious ceremonies, and thus he had cut himself off from normal intercourse with his fellows. Furthermore those were lean years; he mortgaged his rice before it was harvested, as most of them did, and could not free himself of debt.

Persecution continued but he never retaliated. The war came, and general poverty and distress brought Aw opportunities to help his neighbors. To strangers fleeing from other parts of Burma he gave livelihood; he organized his village so that the best should be made of the little they had. Those who had railed at him were now paid back in practical love. He said also that several Japanese soldiers privately made themselves known to him as Christians, though concealing their faith from their unit.

The war wiped out debts. After it, Aw began to prosper, and as principal farmer and the most trusted of the place was elected headman. Those who once abused him say you won't find a man like him for hundreds of miles. I asked whether any neighbors had accepted Christ too. "No," he said. "Many have heard, and may respect the Christian way, but cannot bring themselves to make the break."

I liked the Aw household. Aw was as genuine as his oranges, some of the sweetest, juiciest I have tasted.

Aw and Ee were a prelude to life among the Shans. Placed like a question mark round Burma proper are the other components of the Union. The Southern Shan States form the eastward bulge.

Our destination was the B.C.M.S. hospital at Panglong, the burned-out site of which was used for the postwar conferences between the British, the Burmans, and the minorities to settle the future of the country. We spent forty-three hours on the journey: the southbound mail from Mohnyin at 2:30 A.M., all day, and for a short distance with soldiers in battle order who stopped the train out in the jungle near the area of anti-insurgent operations; across Ava Bridge "When the mist was on the rice-fields an' the sun was droppin' slow"; a night at Mandalay, again with the Dennis Reeds of the English Methodists, whose fine work is principally on the Upper Chindwin; a long, hungry wait for an overdue plane made more tedious because I had been told, wrongly, that it would be unsafe to drive through dacoit-infested hills after dark and I foresaw having to lie up over-night; a flight, fortunately short, in a cheerless Dakota over a browned-off countryside, paddy stubble in the Irrawaddy Valley and the forbidding trackless edge of the Shan Plateau, as an alternative to a day-long roundabout journey on indifferent roads. And finally ninety miles by Land-Rover with our new hosts, Dr. and Mrs. Walter Barr Johnston. A journey memorable for their flow of talk (the Johnston brothers have an international reputation for quantity, speed, and quality of talk) and for the beauty of wild hills in last light, a pastel-blue western sky, the black silhouette of hilltops edged with pink, and Venus solitary above. Far ahead in the darkness were controlled jungle fires in a great square of twinkling points, as if Napoleon's Grand Army lay in camp.

When a travel-worn couple, after a hot bath, and dinner eaten in their hosts' thick winter dressing gowns by a fire, were sent to bed with blankets and hot water bottles it was none too soon.

The Barr Johnstons, who opened the Panglong Hospital in 1938 and had the buildings completed in time for the Japanese to burn, are Irish and their fathers were both regular army colonels.

The atmosphere was that of an Irish country house. At meals, which were at European times and had no shortage of meat, con-versation sparkled with good stories, though inclined to relapse into a duet until Mrs. J. would rap the table and say, "Walter, you're talking too much. Get on with your food," in a way that took me straight back to my own home. Intimate details of gory medical cases were related with unselfconscious relish. Twice after dinner they went off to emergency operations, with hurricane lamps because the town electricity, Irish fashion, did not come till ten. Burma, after all, is called the Ireland of the East. Once the doctor brought back the proceeds to display the wonders of creation in a three-month miscarriage. The hot bath was Irish too. A relic of British days, a little chipped but a long bath still, it had been picked up for a song and attached by a short narrow pipe from the hot tap to a tar or kerosene barrel outside, built into an earth oven. Fill the barrel by hose, light the fire, and in due time your guests could wallow—most welcome when we came back covered in red dust from Mong Hsu or in red mud from Wan Yung. The water was running red too by then, after the storm.

The bungalow is of timber, unplastered inside or out. Not having then been in Borneo, I thought it rather primitive for a British-style house. Because rats made their home in the rafters, these were taken down and now you look straight up to the aluminum roof, the whole effect being that of a mountain chalet. During the storm the noise of rain upon roof, accompanied by thunder, was deafening, but a more gentle rain later percolated through my dreams like the falling brook in the mountain village of Nepal. The bungalow, on a steep hillside, stood in a small garden with rose trees, coffee bushes, strawberries just coming on, and across the hedge and the tops of trees immediately below lay the red-brown valley, a dash of blue water, and the more distant green hills.

The hospital was a glorious improvisation which the Johnstons ran singlehanded except for indigenous subordinate staff, mostly home trained. The nurses and all Shan women carry themselves well but have "either bun faces or horse faces," in Mrs. Johnston's phrase. The more elderly looked like dowager duchesses, but as Mrs. Johnston talked like an English duchess this was appropriate. The place was littered with patients' relatives. "The government hospital won't allow them," said Mrs. J., "so people won't go. We even let them have beds if any are free. If not, they sleep on the floor. You have to let them come, or the patients won't either, and anyway it means they hear the Gospel too. In the Hukawng Valley before the war we used to allow dogs and hens, which they brought in at night. But I drew the line at goats or pigs." Taking us round, she broke off twice to separate fighting geese, her own.

We passed a convalescent, a man attacked in the hills by bandits who had sliced off his left hand at the wrist, three fingers off his right hand, and severely gashed his head. He was sitting in the sun, and at our approach he put on the expression used by village widows in England when they see the parson come. Mrs. Johnston said: "He is very near the Kingdom now, if not already there. What can we do with him? We can't just turn him out like that. That's our problem." I was also interested in an opium case in the men's ward. He was a Chinese Christian in his early forties who had recently confessed to having been an addict for twenty years, smoking heavily. "It requires great courage to ask us to cure him at that stage," Dr. Johnston told me. "He thought he would die if he gave it up. The course takes ten to fourteen days, and is agony. You stop the opium at once and put them on Largactil and bromides, increasing the dose till you get over the maximum sufferings, and then tailing it off."

My eye caught a Chinese notice outside a little hut on the path back to the bungalow: "Anybody can sleep here provided they join in prayer and read the Bible." Apparently an opium addict's story lay behind. The hut belonged to Simon, an old Chinese whom I had seen at Mohnyin poring over his books at the Bible School. Simon had been brought in unconscious from opium. He had gone home believing himself cured, but lacked moral strength to resist the habit and before long was again carried in unconscious. This time he received and read a Chinese New Testament. The effect was electric. "Why, this is just what I need," he said. "I've never heard this before. I want to be baptized." He soon had other patients aware of his discovery, inviting new arrivals to his bedside to be told the Gospel story. Three months after his baptism, in September, 1954, he saw his first convert baptized, and when he was confirmed by the Bishop of Rangoon a year later no less than eighteen of his converts were confirmed with him. His son, Hla Aung, a young man in his early twenties, had come to the Johnstons saying that he wanted to be a Christian. "My father was a bad man. Now he is a good man.

This must be for me too." Later he left a secure job to work as hospital dispenser at a far lower salary, and is ambitious to follow his father to Bible School.

A trip from Panglong showed how thinly Christianity is spread in the Southern Shan States and what immense areas of responsibility may fall to the individual missionary.

At Mong Hsu, 110 miles northeast, the Johnstons had an outstation, not so much medical as pastoral, though the Karen Christian male nurse, the government's provision for the health of the place, whom Dr. Johnston had discovered there depressed, isolated, and discouraged, was now the mainspring of the local church.

We drove through an autumn parkland splattered incongruously with cherry blossom on trees large as oaks, and wild wood apple trees as spreading as chestnuts, and clumps of planted bamboo. In the back of the Land-Rover were a retired Shan schoolmaster then engaged on the translation of the New Testament into a local tribal tongue; his wife, a senior nurse; a returning Shan patient (and small son) who, the wife of a Chinese Christian at Mong Hsu, hoped to be baptized when we arrived; and one duck. A trailer containing bedrolls and luggage bumped and rattled behind as we ran steadily down twin strips of tarmac (nobody bothered to tar the crown of the road) until at a small city we turned on to an untarred metaled road and were soon covered in a red sand which plastered hair, got into ears and eyes, and down inside clothing.

Mong Nawng, the next place, was also by courtesy a city because the seat of a sawbwa, hereditary prince of a Shan State—the Southern Shan States being a checkerboard of these minute principalities; in this journey we were in four. Here we had a puncture, and a late lunch at a Chinese cookshop: our first attempt at chopsticks. We took a road more wooded, more hilly, more dusty. Occasionally I saw Shans in bullock carts or on foot in baggy ankle-length trousers and straw coolie hats perched on bathtowel turbans, but their habit of building villages away from a road gave the country a deserted air. We crossed the turquoise Nam Pang, a tributary of the Upper Salween, and as the day faded drew into the yard of Chinese Christians who run a trading combine at Mong Hsu, sending strings of mules into the mountains to sell goods from Mandalay and fetch back the small farmers' tea crop. The Land-Rover promptly got a punctured tire again. And again before starting next morning.

Dr. Johnston held a baptismal instruction in the combine warehouse by the light of a pressure lamp. On the bamboo-weave walls were a white cross, a decorated notice in Shan and another in English: HAPPY CHRRST (*sic*) MONG HSU. From one of the timber support posts hung shoulder bags and an umbrella upside down suspended by a nail through its point and a Burmese gong. In the rafters lay brooms past which the smoke curled up from a brazier on the floor.

Next to the doctor on the low platform intended for sacks sat the old schoolmaster, his kind, wrinkled smiling mustached face sandwiched between a bathtowel and a thick blue jacket. Beyond him was Hla Aung, the young hospital dispenser, Simon's son. The journey had dirtied his smart red-and-yellow shirt under a corduroy windbreaker, but his face was alert and quick to smile. The Shans being of western Chinese origin, there seemed little facial difference between the races.

A middle-aged Chinese whom the local church leader reported as a recent arrival, three years a Christian but without opportunity of baptism, passed his catechumen's test. The Shan woman from hospital failed. Her husband was away in the mountains, as he had had no means of knowing when she would return. To baptize her without him was unsatisfactory and so were her answers. The question "Why do you want to be baptized?" produced the reply, "Because my husband is a Christian." "Suppose he died tomorrow, would you still want to be?" "Oh, yes," she said vaguely. Dr. Johnston examined her on doctrine. When he asked, to lead her to some expression of man's need of redemption, "Have you any sin?" she replied brightly, "Oh, no, I've got no sin." Thinking his mind was on the red-light district, she relapsed into bashful giggles.

Dinner was announced. We sat round a table in the shop. When the schoolmaster had finished a long Shan grace which appeared to include much of his evening devotions, we assaulted bowls placed on the center of the table: rice as a basis, pork and cauliflower, chicken, mutton, potatoes, biscuits of dried milk, plying chopsticks in conversational silence but a lip-smacking determination which properly showed your appreciation, until a glow of satisfaction began to steal over you and pair by pair chopsticks were laid down as each guest felt he could eat no more: a pleasing sensation which, owing to the Western custom of separate courses, I had scarcely had since the jam tarts of school days.

The dozen Christians of the sawbwa city of Mong Hsu had now gathered, mostly Chinese. We held a meeting.

Early next morning a baptismal service took place behind the shop. The font was the millstream, for they prefer to dip, as the rubric allows, rather than pour water upon the candidate, to make a more emphatic witness. Though at that hour the water was cruel to a middle-aged Chinese, his baptism was open and obvious to passers-by or curious neighbors, some of them bleary eyed from all-night gambling in the big fair. I picked out a woman stooping from the weight of a three-year-old child on her back, his nose running; two women smoking cheroots; a policeman in gray with a slouch hat, and a man, across the road, stock still in a white blanket.

After the baptism and a score of medical cases we drove back to Mong Nawng and arrived at midday, three hours late and ravenous, for breakfast with the sawbwa. Instantly his staff produced a superb English breakfast which showed no trace of having been kept so long.

The "Lord of the Heavens" was a charming small man with tattoos on forearms and ankles, which showed beneath a green check *longyi*. His black hair was close-cropped. He wore glasses. His lower teeth were complete; he had three uppers, two on the left front and one at the back. His house had been burned down not long before, and he was in a modest temporary dwelling, the recent fire giving point to buckets of water perched comically on the roof of this and every other place by government order, and long poles to pull down burning thatch before flames could spread.

There was poignancy in our visit, for the sawbwas were about to lose the last of their powers after a thousand years. They had ceded paramountcy to the British in 1885. The Union Government had taken over, and after prolonged negotiations had at last set a date when the sawbwas should surrender their offices and receive a pension. The Sawbwa of Mong Nawng was sending his son to

Australia "to get wisdom" and a profession, since now he would not inherit.

I should like to have seen a sawbwa funeral. When a sawbwa dies his body is embalmed in a great bath of honey until the family can afford a sufficiently sumptuous ceremony. The honey is then sold. . . . The funeral is Buddhist with undertones of animism. Three coffins are carried in the great procession, the first being highly ornate and the last plain, for in it lies the body, thereby foxing the Devil. A man dressed as the Devil walks last in the funeral, and at the burning place he must hammer the coffin well down and run for his life into the jungle, chased by a crowd of roughs. He throws off his Devil's clothes and joins in his own chase. The man who acts the Devil is highly paid. But it is not a post much sought after. Always within two years, mysteriously its holder is dead.

FIFTEEN ❦ *Jungle Dodg'ems*

We conceived a warm affection and admiration for the Barr Johnstons. Yet I could not banish from my mind the words of the French general as he watched the Light Brigade using the methods of Waterloo against the guns of Balaclava: *"C'est magnifique mais ce n'est pas la guerre."*

The whole mission revolved around the Johnstons, who ran the place with loquacious gusto and an energy and devotion almost overpowering. The one was full-time doctor, and the other, matron, anesthetist, and hospital sister. Both were also in effect pastors to the Shan Church and, in intention, evangelists to the surrounding hill tribes.

Ecclesiastically the situation was Gilbertian. Many thousands of square miles had been ceded by the American Baptists in 1937 when, having translated the Bible and a hymnbook into Shan, they found it necessary to shorten their front and invited the B.C.M.S. into the Southern Shan States. The B.C.M.S. started two medical centers where no mission previously existed. At Panglong a small nucleus of baptized Shans formed, by 1941, a church which the

Japanese destroyed as completely as the buildings—destroyed it by slaughter and exile. Not one believer remained when the Johnstons returned. Certain Baptists volunteered to come up from their own area farther south to help the Anglicans, including an excellent pastor called Aaron whose father was the first Karen to enter the Southern Shan States with the Americans. Aaron in 1949–1952, when imprisoned in Mandalay jail with other Karens at the time of the Karen Rebellion, was one of those responsible for no less than 137 jailbird baptisms (they used the criminals' washtub) and a situation which caused the deputy commissioner to exclaim: "What's come over the prison? It is like a chapel—singing all day." Pastor Aaron takes the Anglican services, ranking as a lay reader. His son, at present a Baptist, is likely to be ordained the first Anglican parson.

A Baptist in Anglican clothing—metaphorically, for he does not wear robes—is an example of the close unity that prevails. This circumstance, however, increases the dependence of the local church upon the Johnstons. "I'm trying to do the work of three people," said Dr. Johnston one night as we sat by the light of a kerosene lamp (the electricity gave up all pretense for twenty-four hours after a heavy storm). "I'm turning fifty and I find I just cannot do it and must revert to one person." He cannot be doctor, parson, and itinerant evangelist at once; because of medical responsibilities he certainly cannot tour the hills, and though there is a vigorous youth group the people do not seem to venture out as they might. An American told me that in default, rather to the Johnstons' distress, Shan Baptists are fishing in Anglican waters and that their leaders can hardly be expected to stop them.

The Panglong people do not evangelize widely because initiative is unwittingly smothered; it lies squarely with the missionaries despite their expressed conviction that indigenization is essential. The intention is to prod the church into action. "We are Deborah to their Barak," said Mrs. Johnston, but the people display less energy than Barak in the Book of Judges and make decisions as they think the Johnstons wish, although some resent the leading strings more than would appear.

The supreme difficulty is of personality. Two older missionaries who have founded and built a work, are loved and appreciated, vigorous and almost untiring, cannot easily let converts make their own mistakes. "After all," Mrs. Johnston said, "we brought most of them into the work and many of the younger into the world." Dr. Johnston felt that there would be "a place for the missionary in Burma for a long time, provided we take the position of the father of a man of twenty-three or twenty-four. In other words, to say: 'You're an adult now. You just need a senior person to guide.' " Perhaps Panglong Christians are treated more like children.

The Johnstons are imbued with a prewar paternalism, and it is magnificent. Paternalism still exists widely on the mission field, and much is deplorable. Not that of the Johnstons. I salute them as the finest of the old guard. And when I asked a man who knew them well whether Panglong would collapse on their departure, he said, "No, they have worked too deep." Their personal popularity in the Southern Shan States is tremendous. Bandits who held up the Land-Rover in broad daylight not long before our visit let it pass unscathed the instant they recognized the Johnstons, and local opinion was so furious at their being stopped that the authorities were forced to liquidate the gang.

Nor is the problem of Panglong straightforward. "Look at some of the difficulties," said Dr. Johnston. "Take finance. The local church has only twenty-five or thirty households to raise funds. If they support the pastor only, I think they have done well. In fact the B.C.M.S. now pays half the pastor's salary. Then there is the question of getting indigenous doctors. It's almost impossible. I went down to Rangoon for a conference of Christian medicos, and found that almost all were under obligation to serve the government or whoever paid for their training. Or they must get a good job to pay back their parents. Of the few free ones you must find a very deep Christian who will be ready to come at the salary we can offer. Medicine in this country is not a vocation but a lucrative business. The only way is for us to pay for a man to be trained, and that means for ten years—the three last years at school and seven at college."

Rain had fallen all night. The village of Wan Yung where two members of the Panglong Church, a former hospital nurse and her former policeman husband, kept a small school and dispensary, depending on the village people for support and not on the mission, was a mere twenty-five miles away, twelve miles up the same main road we had taken for Mong Hsu and thirteen along a jungle track.

Six of us made this comic expedition which, though we spent only two and a quarter hours at Wan Yung, took no less than eleven hours. Dr. Johnston drove. With him in front sat Mrs. Johnston and I. In the back with Anne were old Moung Moung, the retired schoolmaster, as a substitute for Pastor Aaron, who was not available, and Moung Tai, the Johnstons' mali, taking a day off digging borders to dig out the Land-Rover.

Leaving the main road, we stopped to lower pressure in the tires. Around was a Buddhist holy place, a forest of flags on the skyline and scores of little beehive piles of white stones that commemorated money paid in the belief that the donors at death would go straight to heaven. A holy man had lived here not long since, attracting crowds of disciples. Mrs. Johnston said: "People used to tell us with awe, 'He is so holy he hasn't passed urine or opened his bowels for months.'"

Almost at once we began a steep, winding descent. The rain had stopped at last, and the sun shone fitfully on a bright red new track of loose sticky mud which Dr. Johnston negotiated with the four-wheel drive, trying to balance the Land-Rover by ordering us as if in a speedboat: "Lean to the left! Lean to the right! Lean to the right again." The new track was abominable. We got out and the doctor tried the old track, with his wife ahead to guide him like the proverbial taxicab passenger walking in front through a London peasouper. The Land-Rover began to slither. Yells came from inside. "Look out! Get out of the way, Kitty! Kitty, I shall run you down, I shall run you down!"

The hill was mercifully short—when you were descending. At the bottom we piled in and made reasonable progress for about a mile to a stream. The new track sheering away to the right looked treacherous, and we tried a rickety old bridge, unshipping both ourselves and everything heavy. The ladies and the old schoolmaster walked on. The bridge was easy—it groaned a little—but beyond rose a sharp bank which the Land-Rover refused. The mali and I pushed; wheels whirred, the engine whined, mud flew. We put brushwood under the wheels without effect. I ran down the stream and thought I had found a ford when the Land-Rover appeared through the scrub to my right, cutting across to the new track. When I was in again we drove a quarter of a mile, still on the same side of the stream, until the track cut into a hillside and we found ourselves perched over a minor precipice, the surface becoming so loose that a slight skid would bring the Land-Rover on to the edge which, after the rain, would cave in; and though a Land-Rover keeps balance where a jeep turns turtle, nothing then could have saved us. Dr. Johnston reversed gingerly to safety by my shouted directions from behind. We found a way below, and emerged beside a ford which brought the old track back the same side, so that crossing the stream was unnecessary. Here the ladies were waiting, and we had coffee at 11:50 A.M., an hour and a half since we had turned off the road three miles back.

After that it was a simple slither. Once we even touched eighteen miles an hour. The woodland on either side was splashed with pink and mauve cherry blossom, and here and there trees were losing their leaves or turning golden brown. There were barking deer about, shy little creatures we failed to sight. The sun had surrendered to clouds and occasional bursts of rain, so that the driving reduced the doctor almost to silence and left the field clear for Mrs. Johnston, who kept us in fits of laughter. "We took the Land-Rover to a bazaar three miles beyond where we are going now. There were Tunghtu tribespeople down from the hills who had never seen a car before. They crowded round and I heard a woman exclaim to her neighbors: 'Look, they just sit in it and it walks.' Walter tooted to get them out of the way. And one of them said, 'Why, doesn't it call nicely!'"

With a thunderstorm we reached the village at 1:15 P.M., three and a half hours for the twenty-five miles from Panglong, and went to the little raised bamboo house of the teacher-nurse. She was a shy, small woman of worried expression in a maroon skirt and a thick brown cardigan, buttoned so close that only the brooch on her blouse showed below. Her husband, who taught the school drill and did odd jobs about the house, had on a red check *longyi* and a blue jacket over a faded red shirt and thick woolen vest. He had a strong, kindly face. Mrs. Johnston unpacked the cooking things and food, sitting on the skins and watched by a puppy beside the fire in the center of the main room; the other was bedroom and dispensary. We walked through the rain to the square schoolhouse, a bamboo hut only forty feet by twenty-five, containing nearly sixty solemn girls and boys ranging from five to sixteen, erect on the most uncomfortable circular bamboos I have ever tried. In front of each boy lay a minute trilby hat, the latest rage. The uprights of the room were festooned with black umbrellas.

The children, coming from several villages, were Buddhists but sang a Christmas hymn, recited the verse "God so loved the world . . ." in Shan, displayed their progress in Burmese, which the government insists they should learn, and answered simple questions. I was not allowed to ask who the Prime Minister of Burma was: "Much too difficult."

Squelching back to the house, we ate lunch and went into conference with the teacher-nurse. She had cause to be gloomy. The people, glad enough to send their children to school and receive medical aid, declined to pay or even give rice. They promised, then heard that the government planned schools, a plan which in present circumstances hardly could be carried out, and so said they would not, because soon school would be free. Meanwhile the couple had not enough to live on. Dr. Johnston said the hospital would tide her over until the people realized that no government school could come, and Moung Moung strengthened her oratorically with the reminder that Satan was trying to wreck her service but that Christ was stronger. She smiled wanly. Her position was further embarrassed because the military had announced that government-appointed nurses only might practice, yet sent no nurse or doctor. Dr. Johnston wrote a certificate saying that she was his authorized representative.

They had been talking in Shan. As he put away his notebook he said in English: "It takes a Christian motive to stay in this place. The government cannot get people to teach or nurse; it's lonely; and there are dacoits about." Before we left we prayed with the couple. Two months or more might pass before the Johnstons could visit them again, and they had no Christian companionship.

At 3:30 P.M. we came down the steps of the cottage. Cows splashed through a ford beyond a clump of bamboo. Rain blotted out the wide paddy plain that begins here, and the hills beyond. Irish weather.

The homeward track was hard to trace from the outskirts of the village, and the mali's jungle sense temporarily deserted him; he got us lost in the wood. "Everyone watch out for *daws*," shouted Dr. Johnston, fearful of those unyielding stumps, camouflaged by undergrowth, which work havoc on a Land-Rover's bottom. After a hundred yards of indifferent progress the Land-Rover took control out of the doctor's hands, wove a drunken pattern across the mud, and buried its nose in a bank. We put brushwood under the wheels, dug away the earth, and eventually reached the main track, which no longer deserved the name, for cows, carts, and the rain had carved alternative channels to an extent that made necessary not only a driver, glued to a wheel now thoroughly insubordinate, but a navigator. Mrs. Johnston and I, noses to the glass, would call out, not always in unison: "Keep to the right! Left here! Make for that puddle!" Following a specially bad bog-down and dig, we all walked and watched the Land-Rover waltz down the track. We overtook it hesitating before a shallow gorge, tested the bridge by jumping, and waved the Land-Rover on.

Only an hour of daylight was left. We voted against stopping overnight in the halfway village, and hardened our hearts as the inhabitants came out for treatment. The Johnstons said that they could always go to the dispensary we had left or come into the hospital.

We pushed on, sometimes literally, and when the going was good enough for speech Mrs. Johnston kept our spirits high by her comments: "Just like a caterpillar, first one end then the other. . . . Wish the committee could see this. . . . Isn't it amazing what a Land-Rover can do?" Four potholes in a row played ball with us between the roof and the seat. "Are the 'ooks of your 'eart and liver giving way yet? It's like that sideshow at the Wembley Exhibition of 1924," she remarked when the Land-Rover was sliding from side to side, " 'Witching waves,' it was then. What do you call them now?"

" 'Dodg'ems'," we said.

"Then that's what it is," we agreed in chorus—"Jungle Dodg'ems."

Just before the final hill, in thick darkness and a light rain, after crossing the ford to avoid the precipice and more or less manhandling the car up the slope, we bogged down fair and square. "It's the tenth," murmured the mali as he jumped out. He was a splendid fellow, short, with a mustache, and his trousers, rolled up to the knee, displayed football-stocking tops of tattooing above legs red with mud. As a child, bereft of his parents through cholera, he had been adopted by a Christian and was now as fine a lay preacher as he was gardener and handyman. He dug, and I cut brushwood with his dah, and we were out in twenty minutes. The hill itself took three-quarters of an hour. The lights of the Buddhist holy place twinkled comfortingly above as the Land-Rover roared for a few yards, stuck, was given a jungle carpet and a push until it made another thirty or forty yards, stuck, was given a jungle carpet and a push . . .

We reached the top—four hours after leaving Wan Yung. The rain suddenly cascaded into a storm which would have made the hill impassable. We drove across a field between the stone "beehives." We hit something. "Is that a *daw?*" cried Dr. Johnston in an agonized voice. "No," shouted his wife above the storm, "only a bit of somebody's way to heaven!"

SIXTEEN 🐾 *Pooh-bah and U Nu*

There was an Irish touch in getting away from Panglong. By six-fifteen on a misty morning we were motoring south. At Taunggyi, the capital of the Southern Shan States, where we stopped for some household shopping, I was walking alone through the bazaar when I was greeted by a polite man in Western clothes who in conversation cleverly extracted considerable information about my comings and goings before I realized he was a detective. His job was to check up on foreigners, and he shadowed me to the cookshop to prove that I was really in the hands of the Johnstons. Had he not seen them, Anne and I would have been held there, the enforced guests of an English spinster missionary, until Rangoon vouched for us. These precautions were for our safety, not because we might be spies.

We drove onward to reach the airport at eleven-thirty. The experience at Mandalay had led me to suppose that if you speak of "catching" a plane in Burma you are thinking in terms of catching fish rather than trains. This was one that got away—half an hour before the time given by the agent in Taunggyi.

The Johnstons took us a further twenty-four miles to Kalaw, and dropped us on the headmistress of the American Methodist Girls School, Miss Cavett from Iowa, who received us for the night without turning a hair—even the spare-room beds were already made up. British officials used to retire to Kalaw. The houses are pure Esher or Cheam, small suburban pseudo-Tudor, and as the trees are fir I had to pinch myself on waking that I was not in the Surrey Hills. Miss Cavett had sixteen elephants of graded sizes, each of a different wood, and, if I may be so indelicate as to mention it, bright pink toilet paper.

The heat in Rangoon was not so trying as I had feared after the cool air of the hills, and worth while for the conversations with leaders in Church and State.

I asked one of the American Baptist missionaries why the A.B.M. work among the Karens of Burma, as also in Assam, should be undoubtedly some of the most evidently successful in the world.

He stressed as a very important factor the animism of the people —the mission had no Great Religion contending. Next was the emphasis from first days on education. The Baptists erected a school system from primary to theological, and thus bred leaders. Another American, one of several who followed their fathers in Burma, admitted that for a period between the wars education suffered from the disease to which every missionary institution is liable—of becoming an end in itself; it was particularly noticeable, he said, when nationals first became headmasters. Even then there was a credit side, for the multitude of prominent Burmese who received their education at Baptist schools retain, though Buddhists, an affectionate respect for missions and for Christian ethics which has had effect on the policies of independent Burma.

Adoniram Judson commissioned his earliest converts to go out on their own. Ever since, the Baptists had worked for an indigenous church. "We were prepared," said my informant, "to put nationals into positions at the price of second-rate leadership for a while, when other missions waited until their Christians were more polished." This long and admirable tradition of indigenous leadership means that for over twenty years the Burma Baptist Convention, and not the mission, has ruled the roost—outwardly. The con-vention negotiates with the government, invites and posts the sixty or so Americans, and in one instance refused to have back a mis-sionary in whom the A.B.M. had not lost confidence; it was rumored that he was too frank in his opinions. Yet certain non-Baptists are convinced that indigenization is more theory than fact, since the bulk of the money comes from America; and although the convention settles its use, the power behind the throne, I was assured, was an American. He was away from Rangoon. His colleagues, maintaining that indigenization is as real as it appears, admit that he is a strong personality with an able brain who speaks only when he has mastered his facts.

The Anglican Church is an undoubted asset in Burma, though Church Union such as grows in India is remote, hankered for neither by Baptists nor diocesan authorities. I have always been catholic in sympathies: many of my friends are not Anglican, I owe much to inspiration from non-Anglican sources, and anyone who after travel-ing the mission field continues to assume that Anglicanism has a monopoly of the good things of God must have a small mind indeed. It was not mere loyalty that made me a better Anglican the farther our tour continued. As never before I appreciated the way of the Church of England when faithful to itself in the spirit of the Ref-ormation: truly biblical, evangelical, and pastoral.

Its liturgy: I have yet to find a more thoroughly congregational service. I will admit that Mattins in Shan sounded rather comic. Shan is such a long-winded language that we using English had finished the Lord's Prayer while they were still forgiving trespasses, and as for setting the Venite in Shan to an English chant, you have to rattle off ten or a dozen words to every note to fit a twofold chant to each two verses. I shall treasure the memory of their reading aloud the Apostles' Creed from an immense wall roller unfolded clause by clause. An Anglican congregation has a full part in the service, not only in the singing.

Its balance: The Baptists in Burma have a high code of Christian behavior but are prone to legalism, erecting secondary matters into primary, as in the Baptist "Ten Commandments" ("Thou shalt not smoke tobacco, Thou shalt not smoke opium," and so on), which if a man keep he may be honored in certain Baptist circles even if judgment, mercy, and faith are lacking. The Panglong bungalow has no hot water on Sundays because local Christians think it wicked. The Johnstons refused to accept the ban on a hot Sunday lunch. Incidentally, as we were excused early prayers in Shan, our breakfast was sent to our room, and since the mornings were cold we generally ate it in bed. After a few days a servant (whose matrimonial morals left much to be desired) voiced her disapproval to our hostess. Mrs. Johnston on our behalf gallantly sacrificed the British Empire. "Don't you know," she said, "that *all* English people who are not missionaries have breakfast in bed?"

Its interdependency: Each local Baptist church is a law to itself and esteems very highly its independency. A leading Anglican said that as far as he could see the Baptists had little sense of a wide church structure, though they might deny it, pointing to their convention, and lacked that vivid sense of belonging to a world-wide body which is one of Anglicanism's greatest treasures.

Another Anglican of long experience said to me: "Any organization when it is old and successful is in danger of patting itself on the back. The Baptists are resting on their oars. They are the big organization. In my part of the country they have a very good missionary inheritance—all the ones we have known have been first class. But the nationals pat themselves on the back. Therefore it is good for them to have the Church of England come in, younger and fresher so far as the Burma mission field is concerned."

The Deputy Prime Minister of the Union of Burma, the Foreign Minister, the Minister for Religious Affairs, the President of the Buddha Sasana Council and the former Chief Justice sat in an office at the Secretariat so small as scarcely to have space for a desk and two chairs. There was room for me, however, because all these exalted persons were one kindly Pooh-Bah, the Honorable U Thein Maung. Like each member of General Ne Win's caretaker cabinet, U Thein Maung was not a politician but a very distinguished public man, and he was renowned also for his Buddhist piety.

He looked younger than I expected. He wore the traditional Burmese silk headdress called a *gaung baung,* which fits closely on the head like a snood, with a large bow over the right ear. Beneath a black silk blouse peeped the narrow collar of his white shirt. He was very friendly, had a ready smile and a quick laugh.

In answer to my first question he said: "No problem at all. Relations between the government and the missions are excellent." (A leading Christian—how I wish discretion permitted the use of names—snorted when I retailed that.) "We are very grateful for all they have done for us." He spoke of educational work especially, and mentioned that in certain instances subventions were made to missionary educational institutions.

"But what about conversions? How do you, as a convinced Buddhist, feel about people trying to convert your countrymen to another faith?"

He laughed. "Ah, to be frank with you, no, I don't like that. I think my religion a very good one and of course I don't like losing people. But *Government* does not interfere." He referred to a conscience clause regarding education, but it dated from British times. He stressed that there was no deliberate anticonversion policy, for freedom of religion was enshrined in the Constitution.

Soon we were talking of the Karens. "They had no real religion," he said. "You always get successes where there is no real religion. . . . The Karen Rebellion? There *were* American missionaries involved, a few black sheep. We did not think it was general. Yes, they have gone now. They were not the best, not typical." From other sources I was led to doubt whether Americans had any part in encouraging rebellion. The editor of the *Nation*, Rangoon's leading English daily, a Roman Catholic of mixed Kachin and Chinese parentage, said that some American missionaries spread the legend that it was a Christian movement although as many Buddhist Karens as Baptists were fighting. The only missionary actively involved was an Englishman, Baldwin, who has since disappeared and may be dead.

On my referring to the Kachins and mentioning that missionaries seem to be admitted freely to frontier areas in contrast to Indian policy, the Minister for Religious Affairs simply said: "In British days British missionaries were allowed into the hill tracts. We were not. Now we go, and are doing very well. We'll catch up." This is optimistic. The Kachins do not favor Buddhism partly because it is brought by Burmese, mainly because, as they know it, Buddhism is too streaked with the animism from which they are turning.

I brought up one of the thorniest problems of missions in Burma—the strangulating slowness with which the government grants visas for residence. A mission was permitted to bring replacements to the scale of prewar figures, a rule which bore more hardly on Roman Catholics than on Protestants, but the years which might pass between an application and the granting of a visa made nonsense of the ruling, and caused intense difficulties. U Thein Maung said: "To be frank, I have not been in office long and have not been able to get right down to the question. I can tell you this. When China expelled missionaries we did not wish to do that. But what with the rebellion and other complications we have to make many inquiries about each applicant. It takes a long time. We have to be very careful. I assure you, there is no deliberate policy to keep people out by holding up their visas."

When I passed this on to someone who is at the receiving end of that particular stick, he let out a long, low whistle. The situation has since slightly improved. The matter was transferred from the Foreign Office to the Controller of Immigration. Missionaries are to be admitted only for philanthropic work or to train indigenous leaders to replace them in the churches, but visas, though uncertain, have been granted a little faster. The government refused to permit, as contrary to the Constitution, discussion of a measure to expel foreign missionaries; in the newspapers Buddhists as well as Christians sprang to the defense of missions.

At my request as we talked, the Foreign Minister having disposed of the visa question, the President of the Buddhist Sasana Council told me of the council's activities. Formed in 1951, it has worked on the revision of the Buddhist Scriptures, pruning them of many noncanonical accretions with help from Ceylon, Thailand, Laos, and Cambodia, and on translation into Burmese. It has sent missionaries to Assam and arranged exchanges with Japan, Thailand, and other Buddhist countries. They did not join in Ceylon's vaunted Mission to Europe: "We did not think it was quite what it should be."

The Minister's time was precious, and I did not stay to dig with him in Buddhist theology. A day or so later I was privileged to have a leisured talk with the most famous man in Burma, and one of the most devout, former and future Prime Minister U Nu.

I was to meet him at the headquarters of the Anti-Fascist People's Freedom League (Clean), some way out from the center of Rangoon. I telephoned for a taxi. Telephoning was pain and grief in Burma. You twirled a little handle in the instrument, and if you were lucky a voice said, "Number, please," in English. You gave the name of the exchange and waited. More often than not that exchange was engaged. If it was free you asked for the number (hoping it was correct; the latest telephone book was two years old) and if the lines were not crossed and the exchange did not cut you off before your call was answered, a distant furry voice replied.

In New Delhi or Singapore a taxi comes to the door within a few moments of your dialing. In Bangkok you seldom walk ten yards without a gray taxi positively hooting to be hired. In Kuala Lumpur, a friendly place, any European will offer you a lift. The only taxi company in Rangoon, whose small fleet was a recent addition to the amenities, declined to book in advance, and when I telephoned they had, as I feared, none available. It was possible to obtain a jeep, but they were too oily for a best suit. I went out hoping to find a tri-shaw, which is Rangoon's version of the bicycle rickshaw and has narrow back-to-back seats in what looks suspiciously like a soapbox attached, combination fashion, to the rear wheel with a third to balance it. Tri-shaw coolies are shaky in their geography, so it would be a risk. I saw no tri-shaw in the quarter of a mile down to the main road. Hot, sticky, and already nearly late, I stood at the junction where old-fashioned buses rattled by, and with the help of a young Burmese succeeded at last in hailing a passing taxi driver who shouted that he would come back when he had dropped his fare. By now I was not entirely unflustered.

The taxi returned. Soon it was wedged in a huge traffic jam. At my insistence the driver tried another route and drove fast toward the outskirts. I knew the map sufficiently to become uneasy and then quite certain he was taking me wrong. When I discovered he was aiming at U Nu's residence, not his office, as I had ordered, I am sorry to say that I flared up like a Guy Fawkes rocket. It was most un-Christian, and the heat no excuse.

U Nu received me in a comfortable room where we sat side by side on a sofa. His head was wrapped in a yellow *gaung baung*;

a gray silk blouse, the gold stud on his white shirt, and a smart yellow and black check *longyi* made him extremely handsome. American magazines have called him moonfaced, for the Burmese face is round and smooth. His expression was meek, like an elderly high church bishop's. With us sat his secretary, a man older and more distinguished than he looked, U Ohn, formerly a minister, and ambassador to the United States, who joined in the discussion and took copious notes.

The first part of our talk, covering formal topics such as the relationship between missionaries and government, was interesting because of U Nu's years as Prime Minister and the personal affection and respect in which he is held, but not significant. Before long we were at the root of the matter, and U Nu was explaining Buddhism with the fervor of an evangelist.

"The supreme merit of Buddhism," he said, "is that Christianity tells you how to overcome the mind, Hinduism how to overcome the body, but Buddhism is the only religion which tells you how to overcome all matter." I let pass his misinterpretation of Christianity, for I was not there to argue. He enlarged on the transmigration of souls and how your status in this life depended on what you had done in the last (Buddhism is derived from Hinduism), and at length I was able to put the question I most wished: Did he ascribe divinity to Buddha? I mentioned the alabaster "gods" of Shan Buddhists, and said that a friend of mine claimed to have heard him, U Nu, in a speech ascribe godhead to Buddha. U Nu denied vehemently: "The Buddha never ascribed to himself godhead. Buddha cannot save—he cannot save. He is a teacher who shows us the way."

I asked about the animism that underlies Buddhism in Burma. I suggested that whereas the simplest peasant may be as true to the intrinsic spirit of New Testament Christianity as may the cleverest theologian, sometimes truer, Buddhism seems so esoteric that ordinary people require a leaven of former beliefs to make their Buddhism palatable. U Nu showed surprise. Then he admitted that when centuries ago Burma was converted to Buddhism (he told the story quite fully), much was left of the old religion. He went on: "It is not forbidden to Buddhists to worship the gods. Such worship is not essential, but they may give it if they also pay respect to the

Buddha." I asked if he believed the gods to be real. He shook his head vigorously.

U Nu, I had been told, had an interest in all religions, especially since coming in touch with Dr. Buchman's Moral Rearmament movement. He corrected me. He had not mastered the Bible. I had misunderstood. "I find Buddhism sufficient, but as a leader I am interested in the harmony of all religions—all faiths living together in peace. M.R.A. accept all religions. It was as a Buddhist that I went. They ask Islamics as well. Buddhism has nothing to learn from other religions. Life is all a matter of behavior. Indeed, Science has come round now, after 2,500 years, to what Buddha taught: there is no material, only behavior."

Here certainly we come to the crossroads. To the Buddhist: "Life is all a matter of behavior. . . . Your status in this life depends on what you did in the last." To the Christian: "By grace are ye saved through faith, and that not of yourselves: it is the gift of God. Not of works, lest any man should boast. For we are his workmanship, created in Christ Jesus unto good works. . . ."

I sought the former Prime Minister's views on Christ: "Do you think of him merely as a great Teacher, or as more?" U Nu, with U Ohn in support, asked me to make my meaning clearer. They were both very quiet but then hedged the question, I think in respect for my feelings.

Toward the end of our talk, when we had reverted to the current situation and U Nu had been assuring me that the coming proclamation of Burma as a Buddhist state "is a sop to popular clamor, it will mean nothing," I asked whether Christianity might have made more progress in British days if, among British administrators, business, and military men there had been more Christian living, more genuine faith. It was, perhaps, a question somewhat prim. He said, "Burma has been very blessed, very blessed." And he went on to eulogize the spirit of the men who had come out to administer.

Nor do I feel he was just praising to my face with his courtly Burmese grace. Remembered of British rule in a country such as Burma are not the political mistakes, nor the plentiful instances of arrogance or imperial bad manners of planter, merchant, soldier, or official; not the brandy and the whoring, such as it was, but peace and just government, respect for minorities in a multiracial land, high standards of administration, justice for which a long purse was not required. These are recalled, nostalgically, and these are Christian virtues. If this fact be doubted, English public life in the eighteenth century, its nepotism and bribery, provides a reminder as to how much present standards owe to the Christian revivals of the late eighteenth and the nineteenth centuries.

The day before we left Rangoon, Anne and I wanted a color photograph of typical dress. In Commissioner Road we asked an elderly gentleman whether we might take him. Afterward he asked where we came from. When we said "England," he drew himself up. "British good," he proclaimed, "their rule best."

SEVENTEEN ❧ *Bangkok to the Back of Beyond*

The B.O.A.C. Britannia from Rangoon to Bangkok, one and a half hours during the night of February 1st and 2nd was a contrast to Union of Burma Dakotas, but a crush, with a sleeping Sikh beside us. I enjoyed the London papers. When we took off they were still yesterday's, a reminder that the jumping-off place for earth's remotest end is round the corner. For after a few days we were really going to the back of beyond—little known tribal Laos.

Bangkok, the most extensive city of Southeast Asia with its fine buildings, well stocked shops, and clanging street cars made Rangoon in retrospect a sleepy country town and us, gingerly negotiating the dangerously roaring traffic, country cousins. From Bangkok forward much of our tour had the very considerable benefit of chaperonage and hospitality from the Overseas Missionary Fellowship.

In the mid-nineteenth century when China beyond the Treaty Ports was officially and dangerously closed to Europeans, a Yorkshire doctor, James Hudson Taylor, had penetrated inland with such faith, courage, and persistence that the China Inland Mission which he founded became the largest Protestant missionary group in the land until after the Communist "liberation" of 1949, when with all other foreign missions it had to withdraw. Becoming the Overseas

Missionary Fellowship, it then opened up untouched areas or spheres of activity in nine countries of East Asia. The Overseas Missionary Fellowship is interdenominational and international, with British, Commonwealth, and Americans more or less equally represented among the 650 or so members, and some thirty Continentals.

The wide geographical distribution of the O.M.F., the knowledge and experience of its directors and superintendents, the regard in which they are held by governments and other missions, and their generous understanding that my task involved far more than a look at their own work, gave me in each of their countries the benefit of, as it were, a courier and consultant service where otherwise I should have had to negotiate directly with a long list of organizations or persons.

Without the generosity of this and other missions and dioceses the tour would have been impossible, financially or otherwise.

As I lay in the sleeper of the Royal Siamese Railway carrying us eastward from Bangkok, I checked over in my mind what I knew of Laos where we were to visit the early stages of an entirely new evangelistic advance.

The Kingdom of Laos (pronounced "Louse"), one of the four countries once French Indochina and now free, is an inland state, with river plains on the west and highlands in north and east. Its economy had been so upset that until recently Laotian businessmen had accumulated easy fortunes by importing American wirelesses, motorcars, and refrigerators at one rate of exchange and reexporting them at another. Politics were equally haphazard. Before we left England the insurance people declined to cover our baggage in Laos because it was reckoned Communist. By now a different Prince had control, and the country considered itself aligned to the West. Six months later it was clamoring for United Nations intervention to suppress the rebellion aided from Communist North Vietnam.

In the plains live the dominant Lao, a race which is closely related to the Thai and spills across the border into Thailand: Buddhist almost to a man. The Roman Catholics, who had support from the French colonial government, made little headway except among Vietnamese immigrants. A small Swiss Brethren Mission had also worked valiantly for fifty years.

The highlands (I find after the Himalayas that the word "mountains" rather sticks in the throat) are peopled by primitive animist tribes, and round them the French drew a cordon which effectually excluded Roman and Protestant. In southern, or lower, Laos, the province where we went, Attopeu, was banned to foreigners except officials until Independence, and some of its more remote parts had still not seen a Westerner.

When the Viet-Minh war which followed Independence ended, the farthest corner of the land was opened to missionaries if any would come. The Swiss Brethren made occasional tours in the tribal areas and had a work among the Ngahaun tribe on the Bolovens Plateau; but, unable to expand through lack of personnel, they invited the Overseas Missionary Fellowship to make a survey. "We are expected," ran the subsequent O.M.F. report of March, 1957, "to accept responsibility for the evangelization of a third of a million people, some of them insular, rebellious, savage and even cannibal, scattered over an area equal to that of Scotland, but without Scotland's communication system."

On October 21, 1957, a small group of men and women assembled in Savannakhet, a lowland center on the border river which had been selected as base: a young international team led by an older American, John Kuhn, whose work in Southwest China and Northern Thailand makes him one of the most experienced of leaders in tribal evangelism.

At Ubon, the Thai railhead, next morning, no Mr. Kuhn. Afterward we learned that a telegram asking somebody to meet and hold us until he came took four days to cover eighty miles, arriving a day behind us. In Bangkok I had been given alternative instructions, unfortunately wrong, and told that the stationmaster spoke English, probably because he had once said "Good morning" before being answered in his own tongue.

I was passed like a rugger ball from Thai to Thai until gathered up by a doctor who tried a flood of French, switched to English, and dispatched us to our supposed destination, Savannakhet, by bus. The bus had a Chevrolet chassis and a Thai wooden body: smart blue-and-white lines, tail fins, a flat overhanging roof to hold luggage

and to shade the unglazed windows, which admitted plenty of cool
air but were too low to give a view unless you ducked your head.
The hard seats for three aside, with a three-inch aisle down the
center, were so narrow and each so close to the back of the next that
a European, even a skinny one like me, needed a dose of the bottle
which Alice found labeled "Drink Me." Fortunately the Thais are a
clean race—in India such conditions would have been insufferable—
and the young man in American cotton and kepi did not, as a Lao
in a later bus, start eating dried fish.

The countryside was out of season, arid and dull. The road was
wide but not tarmac, so that the vibration unscrewed a jar in our
basket and mixed sugar with ubiquitous dust. At intervals the bus
took flying leaps over wooden bridges or stopped for twenty minutes
while fried chickens on spits, rice wrapped in leaves, and meat
steamed with rice in bamboo were sold through the windows.

Four hours and 125 miles from Ubon we reached the frontier and
crossed by motorboat the wide Mekong River, lovely in the evening
light. I brushed up my schoolboy French. The Laos were impreg-
nated with the traditions of their former masters: a slouching customs officer up the riverbank yawned and waved us through; the
immigration official with slovenly uniform but excellent French
sleepily wrote our outlandish names, with my assistance, in his
book. We climbed into samlors, yet another kind of bicycle rickshaw,
and with some difficulty found Le Mission Evangélique, the house
belonging to the Swiss Mission placed at the disposal of the O.M.F.

"Oh dear," said a girl with beautiful hands and a gay little laugh,
"what can have happened? Uncle John was certainly going to meet
you." "Uncle John?" "Oh, we all call Mr. Kuhn that." The two
girls at the base, one English, the other American, cosseted us during
our brief stay, and not even the night-long firecrackers and blaring
gramophones of the Chinese New Year could keep us awake. The
next day was Ash Wednesday. I should have liked to have given
up Oriental buses for Lent. We discovered that Uncle John expected
us at Paksé, nearly five hours southeast of Savannakhet though only
four from the railhead at Ubon, and into another bus at midday
the girls bundled us, with instructions in case of a holdup by bandits.

Paksé, where that evening we found Uncle John in what he described as a "hot little place," is also on the Mekong River but deeper

into Laos. John Kuhn has a square-built figure and a square face, close-cropped graying hair and rimless glasses. He comes from the Eastern states, is Pennsylvania Dutch, and his speech has a strong whiff of the Pilgrim Fathers. His young team would follow him to the ends of the earth, and they say that in the hills he outwalks them yet. His first wife, Isobel Kuhn, author of notable books such as *Ascent to the Tribes,* died of cancer. He had recently married again, and we were still drinking Mrs. Kuhn's iced lime juice and unentangling our misadventures when in walked John Davis who had come down from Attopeu in an army lorry sitting on a pile of rifles.

That night we held a council of war, poring over such maps as existed. I was shown the strategy of their campaign, which had been worked out almost like a military operation. I was impressed most with their determination not to make hit-and-run evangelistic raids but to look to the founding of a church able to stand on its own feet.

First, at the Savannakhet base the team had accustomed themselves to Laos and had improved their Lao. Two further supply bases were then set up at towns on the Mekong River to north and south. From these lowland centers, as the next phase, a three-pronged drive took them to advanced positions on the edge of tribal territory, Nomarat, Tchepone, and Attopeu. John Davis had gone to Attopeu in April, 1958, working alone until joined by another young American, David Henriksen, a few weeks before we came. During one month of the rains he had been cut off from all communication with the outside world.

"Attopeu Province is shaped like a frying pan." said John Davis, drawing me a sketch. "Here is the flat circular valley with the capital Moung Mai, where I live, roughly in the center. The people there are Lao—they are educated, civilized, and Buddhist. Here is the rim of hills where the tribes live. The Oi, who have more contact with the Lao than most; the Soo, the Laveh, the Salang, and four others, all speaking different languages. And the Kasseng, farther away, right up in the mountains. A tricky people. We discovered the other day that in the fourth month of the year they occasionally make human sacrifices. Coolies who disappeared off the trail weren't taken by tigers after all. . . ."

Throughout the next day we were on the road, Anne, John Davis, and I. And this time we really traveled. From Paksé to Attopeu as the crow flies is not much, but as the lie of the land allows, nearly 150 miles, and required eleven hours. The first section was a swift hard-top road up to Paksong on the Plateau of Bolovens. From then onward the Chevrolet truck driven by a Lao in French *ouvrier* blue overalls and cap churned along a loose dusty track which at times reduced speed to a lurching crawl.

We made languid halts. At a Chinese cookshop; at a long rickety unfenced bridge which the truck crossed unloaded; and at a ferry where, after the driver and several of the passengers had had a swim, we were pulled across escorted by a duck that dived for scraps.

Acquaintanceship with John soon ripened into friendship. John Davis comes from Washington State in the Far West where his father is an electrician and his parents had also kept a farm. This might account for the practical aptitude with which he could turn his hand from mending a refrigerator or wiring a house to butchering and cooking, and for his fine physique. As I remember him in Laos when he was not yet twenty-five, he was touching six feet, with broad shoulders and strong chest. His wavy dark hair was thinning at the top and growing back. His eyes were brown and large, his chin firm, good for thrusting forward in the Lao manner of emphasis, while his lips were a trifle thick and prominent so that he could push them out, when talking with tribesmen, as they do to make a point. John has a great sense of fun and when relaxed would chatter happily about America, his early life, his parents, work, and the girl he was to marry. She was stationed at one of the other advanced bases with a Swiss couple and an English woman doctor. They had postponed their marriage three years in order to widen their experiences as missionaries.

As the interminable journey wore on, John made no bones about where we were going. "It's real frontier," he warned us, using the word in the American sense. "The Swiss missionaries have been a wonderful help but they think I live at the end of the world. One said I couldn't do it. And if I tried to reach the tribes there, conditions were so bad I would be dead in a year."

As night fell, the truck was making better speed through the forest below the escarpment of the Bolovens Plateau southward toward Attopeu. Once the driver saw a rabbit in the beam of his headlights, stopped, got out and ran back to try and catch it. At length the road suddenly improved for half a mile, having become, in fact, the military airstrip. A few minutes more and we had entered Moung Mai, the newer of the three so-called cities known collectively as Attopeu to the world, and were unloading at John's home.

A most extraordinary sound came over the partition from the house next door. A series of groans descending and ascending as if a performing dog practiced scales: the schoolboy son at his homework, reciting Lao vocabulary in the correct tones.

EIGHTEEN 🎋 *Forest Trail in Laos*

I awoke about seven next morning to see from the upstairs window no less than fifteen yellow-robed shaven-headed monks filing across the green, bowls in hand, to collect rice from the faithful. The small covered market was just closing down. John and Dave had already done their shopping.

I went downstairs and had a bath. Beside a tar barrel filled with water John had scooped a drain in the brick floor. You stood on a board over the drain and used a small tin (or can, as he would say) perforated at the base. This "shower" impressed me then; later I preferred the large Indonesian or Borneo scoop with which you can really douche yourself, but at Moung Mai water had to be carried some distance from the river at so much a bucket, and the perforated tin was more economical.

The house had six rooms, two up and four down, a barn-like ladder leading to the upper floor. The roof was aluminum, walls timber, partitions bamboo weave, and the street-side lower wall folded back as a garage door does. On the walls of the living room were posters of the parable of the Good Shepherd in a Lao-Thai setting, colored photographs of Swiss lakes, and snapshots of the lady who three months later became Mrs. John Davis. The back room was kitchen and scullery. The recipe in Lao for pancakes, pinned beside the shelf containing American cookery books, was a reminder that John had had a tribal servant for a month, who had been paid off yesterday to return to his village for the paddy planting. When without a servant John and David Henriksen, who was slim, of medium height, with fair hair and glasses, took the cooking in turns. It was John's day. For breakfast he gave us scrambled eggs, fried glutinous rice biscuits from a shop (pink; with jam to taste), pineapple, coffee, and a vitamin pill.

The bathroom, with lines for towels and clothes, and a general dump and bicycle store made up the rest of the ground floor; when the personnel of the Attopeu Mission increased, these rooms could be used more fully. The latrine was in a hut in the garden—merely a deep hole without box or seat; much the most convenient of that sort. Garbage went into a pit in the next garden, by kind permission, anything edible being disposed of by the neighbor's dog and its friends, the rest burnt.

After breakfast John set about getting porter-guides for the trek into the hills. Porters are not easy to find because local tribesmen have no tradition of professional carrying as have the Nepalese, and although by government order each village is obliged to produce two men for an official or for an accredited traveler the scheme is empty until you reach the first village. The only way is to find tribesmen going in the required direction, and our first intention was thwarted because none was. It was therefore agreed we should go with the former servant and his party to an area John had previously visited, where six men had "called on the name of the Lord," and we would be able to see how they had stood as Christians with no Bible, pastor, or further teaching. A starting time was set, and Anne and I wandered about exploring the tiny provincial capital, a half-horse town if ever there was one. We met John on his bicycle. "The outlook's grim," he said. "Those fellows cried off when they saw the loads. I am going to dig up some other tribesmen; I think I know where they hide out."

In due course two little men in G strings came to the door of the house. They saw the loads and wished to cry off, so we settled that the three of us men would carry also, heat notwithstanding. We cut down as far as we could, redistributed the loads, and after an expertly cooked lunch made our way to the river.

The trip would be to an unvisited area. Maps were so vague none of us knew quite what we should find except that we went to the Laveh tribe who can speak Lao as well as their own tongue, thus making communication easier. With at least half a dozen languages in the province, the trade language has to be used until sufficient response indicates in which tribe a settlement may be made. Even then the missionaries will face a conundrum: the Lao Government forbids tribal languages to be reduced to writing, being determined, rather optimistically, to replace them by Lao.

On the bank of the substantial Sekong River, a tributary of the Mekong, the tribal party gathered, short men and slender women, skins a darker brown that those of the Lao. One of our porters was naked except for his G string; the other had a little coat or portion of a shirt to keep the load from his back. He had teeth filed short (it is done when they are drunk); the lobes of his ears were stretched round heavy ivory ear-bobs, and he carried a beautiful knife with a tiger-tooth handle and smoked a stubby brass pipe. The two tribesmen had our heaviest things, in narrow baskets on the back. John had a big pack with aluminum frame, Dave and I each two sleeping bags, Anne two shoulder bags, two cameras, and a pineapple.

We crossed the river at about ten past three in a dugout. Eight people were in it. We had to sit very tight. Other canoes were crossing back and forth higher up; the plateau to our right was shadowy in the afternoon light, emphasizing our remoteness and the uncertainty of where we should be or what we should find next day.

Across the river, in a suburb of Moung Mai, the tribespeople said they must cook their rice at once rather than in the forest; we had to hang around again. They stuffed the rice into a bamboo, topped it with river water, and placed it on a fire. Lao gathered around, amused that we should be bothering to go to these "sinners," "sinners" because they kill animals and must have gained little merit in the last life to be born so lowly in this. They will be reborn as sand or mud, anyway. The Lao fear the tribes. "Going out there," one shouted. "Don't you know there's no water out that way?"

With two hours of daylight we set off at last through paddy stubble into the forest, a party of about fifteen tribespeople, men, women, and children. The men were in G strings, some with tattooing on their brown bodies; my favorite was a young man in a floppy blue sun hat on top of very long hair, ivory ear-bobs, a blue bead necklace which clashed with his hat, and a brass pipe; they were all great smokers, even small boys. One woman with a four-month-old baby in a shawl on her back carried a blue sunshade. Another young woman had a fetching blouse above her Lao skirt, which is longer than the tribal: the best dressed as well as the most dressed. Some tribes eat dogs. On the way up from Paksé, John had noticed two men strangling a dog, trussing and carrying it off for the pot. The Laveh are dog lovers. In this party were a full-grown terrier, smooth-haired, fawn, long in the head, and three puppies—Major, Minor and Minimus. Major walked all the way, Minor some of the way, Minimus none of the way.

We heard the distant chant of monks working in the woods. After an hour we stopped briefly in a clearing where the Lao use little huts during paddy times, and three trees in scarlet flower relieved the brown stubble. We went on. John gave a cry: "I've left the pork chops behind. There goes our dinner!" The sun dropped and darkness fell swiftly. We walked in single file through the forest by moonlight and by the glare of a far-off blaze, probably one of the frequent controlled fires of that season. At about 7:00 P.M. we came to a pool, and beyond the pool a *sala,* or enclosure, for travelers which was protected by bamboo stakes and brush fence from wild animals. We lit a fire. The tribespeople went straight inside, but we stayed out for a meal that was little more than soup. John very properly decided that we should go hungry rather than eat into tinned supplies, not knowing how long we might be away. After a wash in the pool, we unrolled sleeping bags. Anne and I had a mosquito net over our heads, but the boys did not bother. Our spot was quite soft. As I drifted into sleep I heard a trumpeting from the forest; next morning one of the porters said that it had been a wild elephant, and we passed fresh droppings on the trail.

A cup of coffee—a special concession—before we walked on at break of dawn gave the tribesmen the start on us, but we caught up at the first halt when the forest in the early morning as the sun rose through the trees was unforgettable. Our carriers by now were friendly. At first they had been afraid. One had asked for wages in advance, and when John declined, the man said, with bitter memories of the Lao, "We shall carry all day and then you will not pay us." "You'll see," said John. The trek proceeded; they saw that we did not shout at them, recognized when they got tired, did not mind sleeping in the *sala* or eating their poor sort of rice, and they realized that we were different. A special brand of Far Western smile did the rest.

At the second halt John disappeared, then emerged from a bush wearing, as I had been doing all along, a pair of shorts. "In deference to you," he said as he packed away his trousers. "They may not be beautiful but they are very useful." "Not beautiful? Haven't you seen immaculate British in white shorts and stockings and white shirt?" David, who comes from near Chicago, doggedly Yankee, wore "pants" throughout.

After four stages at an easy pace for the women and children, we made the main halt to cook and eat rice near a rather unsatisfactory piece of water. Another crowd of tribesmen were there. They dropped their work and thronged round, attracted partly by seeing a white woman in Western clothes: men's clothes excite no comment, since the Lao wear the same. John produced what looked like a large red camera, a foot long, four inches wide, one and a half deep. He opened it, extracted a handle with which he wound it up, set in place the arm and head, brought out from his pack a small record labeled "Buenos Nuevas: Words about Heaven (Laveh)," and in a few moments the tribespeople were gaping. With close attention they heard a message in their own tongue from one of their own race.

Gospel Recordings: I had come across them again and again, but Laos was the first place where I could watch their full effect. Gospel Recordings, one of the most significant and revolutionary developments in the modern mission field, grew from the idea of an American woman, Miss Joy Ridderhof, formerly a missionary in Honduras. Miss Ridderhof recognized not only that many hundreds of tribal languages were still unknown and unwritten but that a message heard in a mother tongue is worth a dozen in a trade language, especially if spoken by one for whom it is mother tongue. Without any powerful organzation behind her she began in the

1940's to penetrate tribal areas, first in Mexico, Central America, and Alaska, then in the Philippines, Southeast Asia, and Africa. She and her helpers, American and national, often with great difficulty and not without danger, found people who could be persuaded to record in their own words simple talks previously prepared.

From small beginnings Gospel Recordings has grown to include most of the major languages of the world, and its greatest impact is felt among illiterate tribes. By 1959 Gospel Recordings were nearing their 2,000th language, and over 2,000,000 records had been distributed free in more than 150 countries. "My motive for starting this work," Miss Ridderhof wrote to me, "was simply that I desired to give the Gospel to the unreached souls of Honduras where I had ministered personally for six years. While a missionary in Honduras I was constantly burdened with the realization that even with all my efforts and those of my national helpers I could not begin to reach all the isolated people of the outlying villages. I prayed for a way to multiply the Gospel message. Then, when detained at home in Los Angeles by a serious illness, I looked for a way to supplement the efforts of the all too few Christian workers I had left. When the thought of records came to my mind as a means of publishing the Gospel, I saw in it a means for attracting people to the Gospel through singing, and clear teaching through much repetition so that those who heard could not only believe but transmit the message to others."

In 1955 Vaughn Collins of Gospel Recordings working through Laos came to Moung Mai. The Laveh messages were done by an educated tribesman in government service, and today, deep in the forest, were sounding out clear from the little Swiss gramophone, to the intense amazement of forty or fifty people hearing for the first time "in our own tongue, wherein we were born, the wonderful works of God."

John had noticed a man's eyes badly swollen, and said: "We are not paid by the government, so we cannot give free medicine. If you would like to give me a little rice I have some ointment which would ease that swelling." He explained to me that they establish immediately the indigenous principle of not giving medicine, to discourage "rice Christians" or "medicine Christians" who in the old days, before such a principle was recognized on the mission field as widely as now, swelled statistics and grievously damaged quality. On the other hand, as John Kuhn once wrote, "Remembering the command and compassion of the Lord Jesus towards the sick, we should extend as much medical aid as is consistent with our primary objective of preaching the Gospel."

A woman smoking a short bamboo pipe brought a girl of eight or nine with a large splinter embedded in her foot. After sterilizing tweezers while we ate the rice, to which we had added a tin of corned beef, John approached the girl, who screamed. Held down by her parents, who alternately coaxed and slapped her, the girl, screaming to the end, was relieved of the splinter. The march resumed, I now carrying the heavy pack. At twelve-thirty we reached a fine pool. The tribesmen removed G strings and plunged in naked; with the modesty of their kind they were careful to cover themselves with their hands when out of the water. John gave me a length of wide cloth, called a *pha,* which I had difficulty in tying so that it should not fall off in the water, a weakness which persisted in Laos and Thailand.

During the afternoon march the tribesmen heard and saw a wild elephant over to the left through the undergrowth; they shouted to scare it, and quickened their pace. Dave caught a sight of the elephant. Whether I really did I shall never know. The trail was leading slightly upward through a narrow valley into hills which in this sector were not, as we had been told in Moung Mai, steep or high. Had we gone the route originally expected we should have had a long walk in the open sun, a stiff climb, and scarcely any water.

The next halt was in less than an hour because some of the men had caught frogs and decided to fry and eat them, shoving them in by great mouthfuls and sucking the grease off their fingers. We relieved Anne of her pineapple and decided on cocoa. Before the kettle boiled, John took a lick of the mix of condensed milk and cocoa in the bottom of his mug. "Um, this is good. Just like fudge," and took another. We followed suit. John announced that we might eat all that and mix another to drink. The Kuhn tribe are brought up on Winnie the Pooh; already, therefore, this was the "Expotition to the North Pole." As I scooped up the fudge I called out that here surely was Pooh and the Heffalump trap honey.

At a waterhole only a mile and a half from the village a tribesman chased a large tree lizard, killed it and tied it to his load: one more for the evening pot. A river came in from the right, about forty yards wide. We passed a small army post, recently built, crossed a pontoon bridge, and at ten to six entered the village of Ban Kong Mi.

Quite a surprise. It was larger and more substantial than any of us had expected. The wide "street" was lined with kapoks, sure sign of civilization, short trees with policemen-like arms, the product of which provides padding for the chairs of London clubs. Two timber houses had been built for Lao officials, and a timber school. The other houses, bamboo and somewhat similar to those of the Jinghpaw, were scattered about with no sense of overcrowding, the whole scene being backed by a circle of hills. The tribal areas had been lately reorganized into counties, one for each tribe. This place had been chosen as capital of the Laveh and a young Lao stationed as tribal chief; John had known the man without realizing where he lived and had already mentioned him. "A twirp of twenty-two," he had said with the superiority of twenty-four. The Twirp was amused that we should refuse quarters in the *sala* (the word is used for any sort of building set aside for travelers) and prefer the hospitality of a tribesman. He thought it more comic that we should accept our hosts' glutinous rice, cooked and eaten in the tribal way, instead of bringing the higher quality Lao rice and demanding that it be served the refined Lao way. His whole attitude was of contempt for his subjects: colonialism at its most arrogant.

"This is much the most civilized place I've seen," John said as we went for a wonderfully refreshing bathe from the pontoon, where as the light faded we soaped away the journey and splashed and swam in waters cool but not too cold. There would have been more romance in a huddle of huts, but the reality stressed the urgency of the evangelistic task. These tribes are coming into civilization, forced out of their isolation by the insistence of the Lao that they must be assimilated. Part of the process is to turn them into the Lao version of Buddhists, and apart from theological convictions I had seen enough of Lao Buddhism to know whether the tribespeople would be losers.

Back at the house a chicken nestling in the hand of its donor was presented for inspection—good-sized as they go in these parts, just plump enough for four. Anne screwed up her eyes, having heard they slaughter their gifts in front of their guests, but they took it away and we saw it next plucked, drawn, and spitted over the slow, open wood fire. When, after the meeting, we ate it with our fingers, dropping the bones between the bamboos in the approved manner, no chef at the Ritz could have produced a more succulently grilled, tender bird. If you want chicken barbecue as it should be, go to tribal Laos.

John had set up gramophone and posters. The schoolmaster brought a pressure lamp to give unexpected light, and the village father shouted to the people to come and hear what we had to say. They clambered up the bamboo ladder to the raised floor of the house, some seventy increasing before the end to a hundred, men, women, and children, including our friends of the trek. Several women had fresh colored blouses, but old Grandma had nothing over her shriveled breasts but rows of beads. The Laveh schoolmaster, neat in Western shirt and trousers, secure in his Lao education, smoked a cigarette with the expression of a Fellow of the Royal Society attending a lecture by another scientist. The Twirp had a towel round his neck. His white shirt, fine set of teeth, and generally well-fed appearance contrasting with the drabness of most of his subjects, he displayed amused tolerance. The tribesmen listened, some with interest, others with amazement, all with attention, to the records in Laveh, followed by an explanation, from John speaking in Lao, of the cleverly drawn posters, a series illustrating an allegory of the Gospel in terms they could understand. Occasionally a puppy squealed. I sat in the shadows, a bed bag and a blanket wrapped round my knees. As I watched this first meeting ever to be held, as far as we knew, in Ban Kong Mi, I wondered whether around were some future believers, fine standing Christians on fire for the Christ Who had liberated them from fear of evil spirits and fear of man, from the spiritual squalor of their present existence. One impression was strong: that once you get right in amongst these so-called primitive peoples they lose their primitiveness; those who seemed curious, even laughable, in the context of their more advanced lowland neighbors, in their own homes are ordinary people with the naturalness and self-respect of ordinary people. The impression was a little blunted here because of the Twirp, but it struck me forcibly whenever I got away to similar societies, the next day deeper into the hills; in Borneo, in the Phillipines. Dave said, "They seem 'simple' only because we don't understand them."

When John gave out tracts the response was gratifying. "Best I've ever had. I've carried this bundle two trips." He had no illusion that the demand sprang from the higher level of literacy in this village which had had forty-five students the last year, and a school for eight or nine years past. Direct interest in the subject was shallow; there were some questions and answers but no desire for further explanation, no sense of direct impact. The Twirp saw to that.

That night, after they had all gone, and the chicken and rice had been eaten and sticky fingers washed under a bamboo pitcher, we read together the tenth chapter of the Epistle to the Romans. ("I'm glad it mentions feet!" said John ruefully). St. Paul's words took on a new appositeness far away in the forest surrounded by men and women who had never before had the opportunity to hear "the gospel of peace . . . glad tidings of good things."

We marveled at the simple assurance, "If thou shalt confess with thy mouth the Lord Jesus, and shalt believe in thine heart that God hath raised him from the dead, thou shalt be saved." We knew that the word "saved" implied not only spiritual birth into the life of Christ but growth into the whole inheritance of the love of God. We read that "the same Lord is rich unto all that call upon him," and we took heart from the obvious fact that the promise, "whosoever shall call upon the name of the Lord shall be saved," included these men and women in their unlovely ways and their fears— fears to be brought forcibly before me the next day.

We looked again at the forthright questions, "How then shall they call on him in whom they have not believed? and how shall they believe in him of whom they have not heard? and how shall they hear without a preacher?" Because of the few national Christians, because of the scattered grouping of tribes in a rough, roadless country there was need undoubtedly for Western men and women, young, with as much physical stamina and endurance as any of the pioneers of the church in Africa in the nineteenth century: only a fortnight before, seven days out from Moung Mai, John had gone down with malaria. They had reached a place where there was no short way back. "Without Dave, I should never have made home," John said.

Such missionaries need to be spiritually mature if a thriving church is to rise here, in the heart of Buddhist lands threatened by communists, among a people not yet committed to Buddhism or submerged by communism. The Nagas in Assam, the Karen in Burma, the Lisu in China show how the spirit of God has moved among pagan tribes. If we doubted lest these people, some snoring peacefully, others merrymaking outside, could stand firm for Christ once brought into His fold, we had the promise before us: "the scripture saith, whosoever believeth on him shall not be ashamed."

The party which had returned were celebrating on the grass round a fire a few feet from the steps, over rice wine sucked up by thin bamboos from a large earthenware pot. As we crawled into our sleeping bags laid in a row on a platform of bamboos above the floor, their shrill laughter and the flickering of the fire on their bodies was Dantesque.

NINETEEN   *Fear Beside the River*

The trek and subsequent days gave ample opportunity to learn John Davis' story.

To see John into Attopeu, Mr. Kuhn had sent up his Lao Christian servant for a month. As the month drew to an end John felt an increasing isolation, centering partly on homesickness, partly on the fact that for the first time in his life he had no one with whom to speak English; the Filipino doctor was away and the governor's only European language was French. Forlorn in an alien land he found himself unable to tolerate the thought of losing the one Christian in the place, the Lao servant. So intense became the nervous strain that in the house he could not trust himself out of the servant's sight; he would break down and cry. At length he went upstairs to have the matter out. He prayed but his oppression did not shift. Suddenly the thought came:

You haven't sung a hymn in English for a long time. (He has a fine baritone, professionally trained.)

I don't want to sing.

Whether you want to or not, go on, sing!

He opened his hymnbook at Bishop Bickersteth's "Peace, Perfect Peace." He reached the third and fourth verses, "Peace, perfect peace, with sorrows surging round? . . . with loved ones far away? In Jesus' keeping we are safe, and they." He told me: "That broke the ice. Then I sang Montgomery's 'Prayer Is the Soul's Sincere Desire.' Once started, I couldn't stop. I sang hymn after hymn. Victory was won, I came downstairs perfectly all right. When the Lao boy went home, leaving me all alone, I could see him off with an unforced smile."

When he had settled in and had begun to make friends with tribesmen who came to town, playing them the records, he was ready to trek into their territory. The governor said he must take a police escort. This did not suit John's book. The governor refused him leave to go without. To a subsequent request he replied, "If you want to die, you may go," but still withheld permission.

Some Laveh tribesmen had heard the records on several occasions. Their headman said: "We do wish our women and children could hear these good words." "I would like to come home with you." John went, saying nothing to the governor. It was at their village, away to the east of Laveh territory, that six people said they would believe on the Lord, and turned to Him; among them was the headman, who publicly burned his demon altar. That night the village had a drinking bout. Drinking is bound up with the heathen worship; they will drink, eating nothing, for three days and three nights, and then sacrifice. The headman who had recently professed faith joined the drinking, and John was so distressed that in his praying, strong man that he was, he gave way to tears. Several times in the night he rose and prayed.

The next morning the whole village was drunk, a place of the dead. Suddenly John saw the headman, perfectly sober, the only man who had slept in his own home that night. Said the headman: "I came away quite soon. Funny thing, but the wine didn't taste as good last night, so I left!"

Back at Moung Mai, John confessed to the governor, who was amazed that he should be still alive, and thenceforth allowed him to go where he wished, provided he gave notice and took an official letter as passport; soon the letter was not required, only word of his route.

Subsequent exploratory and evangelistic treks, generally carrying his pack and sometimes alone, did not yield such easy fruit until, a few weeks before we came, at a village of the Jehe tribe near Moung Mai twenty knelt in the paddy one morning after John had taken them once and again through the essential meaning of repentance and faith lest they choose unwittingly. They called on the name of the Lord.

I once asked John what were his strongest temptations. He said that one was to fritter time in the mere business of living; his marriage stopped that. Another, to lack Christian love for the Lao, as distinct from the tribes. "You may be surprised, but I think the chief temptation is to be ashamed of the Gospel. When I have been worsted in argument with these Lao Buddhists with their nicely ordered scheme of making merit, I have been ashamed to go out of my house for days on end. To them the 'preaching of the cross is *foolishness.*' But when I saw those men kneel down in the paddy field and pray, that wonderful verse in the same chapter of Corinthians just came over me: 'It pleased God by the foolishness of preaching to save them that believe.' "

Cockcrow, a yelping dog, the steady blow of wood upon wood as the women of the house pounded rice below at dawn; there were four of them pounding in swift rotation, and the tops of their long, slender poles were cut from my sight by the lintel. They gave me the illusion, half awake on that first Sunday in Lent, of the change ringers in my old church at home.

The schoolmaster had told us of a village which he said was three hours deeper into the hills. Normally John and Dave would stay in one place for a night and a day, or possibly two, traveling to reach the next by evening, the whole trek extending about ten days. To fit our schedule they were foreshortening, and we planned to visit this next village in the course of the day. As we finished a rather dreary rice breakfast the Twirp turned up, asking to see the governor's letter.

"I'm afraid I haven't got one," said John.

The Twirp bridled. "You do not respect my position. I am here to see people's letters and you have not got one?"

John explained that he did not now carry one for himself, and the rush of getting away had prevented him taking us to call. The Twirp looked cross. Without his permission we could not go farther into his territory. John talked away in Lao, and even I could see the sun coming out again as the Twirp realized there had been no intentional belittling of his brittle majesty. He told John that he ought to have a letter, and could get one valid for a year. He would overlook the lapse and provide his secretary (who could neither read nor write) as porter-guide to the next village.

The governor when at length we called was graciousness itself, and brushed away the Twirp's objections. "You can have a letter if you like," he said, as if it were quite immaterial.

Dave stayed at Ban Kong Mi, where he was able to copy a detailed map against later expeditions. Freed from load carrying, we had a delightful walk in the morning sun, not more than two hours over into the next valley and along a river, probably about seven miles. Once we saw a strange pattern of twigs. A bird had called on the wrong side of the trail. Frightened tribesmen had hastily erected a charm to propitiate such a sign of ill luck. Our destination proved to be called Ekcampoohkaniang, promptly and inevitably dubbed Pooh Village.

Outside the gate we paused while John offered prayer. We were welcomed by the headman or village father who wore a G string, a set of light blue beads, and a worried expression; the lobes of his ears were stretched yet empty, probably because he had sold his ivory. He took us to his house where we rested, and drank from our water bottles in the porch which smelled of rancid meat and was decorated by a poster of the aged King of Laos, now deceased.

The village beside the little river was a miniature version of the tribal capital, bamboo houses clustering together with thatched or bamboo roofs. The site had recently been changed. Not all the houses were complete, nor had they held their opening sacrifice. We were right in the heart of the Laveh. No Lao lived here, though they passed through: the customary carving in the *sala* was not to be an elephant but a Lao soldier. "They come and play loose with our women," chuckled the village father; "we thought that would be appropriate." White officials had passed through in old days, but never, at this site or its predecessor, had the village ever before entertained a "Frenchwoman." Anne was their first.

The men were for the most part small with long forehead, deeply bridged nose and rather splayed nostrils. One or two wore rough shirts or sack waistcoats over their *café au lait* bodies, more *café* than *lait;* for most, G strings, tattooing, and blue beads were enough. Some of the women had wide elaborate necklaces, red, yellow, and blue, and nothing else but a vertically striped skirt except that girls between puberty and first baby wore a bodice. One mature, handsome woman had a great number of gay beads reaching down to her waist, three brass neck rings, fifteen brass rings on her left wrist, five or six on her right and, like several of her neighbors, large brass anklets carrying little bells. She carried off first prize. Close second was a naked little boy in a long bead chain of startlingly beautiful blue.

The place was alive with dogs and puppies. John saw a woman suckle her baby and then give suck to a puppy.

Tribal hospitality will always produce rice and a chicken for the first day of your stay, generally as a gift. During cooking several sick were brought. One had a septic vaccination wound, a girl had fever, a rash, and repulsive sores on her arms. Several complained of their eyes, and showed a rash. John thought it either smallpox or measles, but when on our return we described the symptoms the Filipino doctor diagnosed chicken pox. John did what he could, explaining his position but offering medical help free since they were entertaining us to chicken and rice.

The gramophone was set up after lunch outside the house opposite the father's. Low cane stools with skin tops were placed for us. The whole village, some fifty, squeezed round to listen. On my left squatted a man, his head slightly to one side, with a pleasant smile, too absorbed to notice that he was blowing smoke into my eyes from his short pipe; beyond him were a mother holding a four-year-old, a young man of typical Laveh good looks listening with a slight grin, an old man concentrating hard. A tiny puppy was asleep behind John and, as always, proceedings were occasionally disturbed by canine tiffs. Flies, midges, pecking chickens completed the setting.

Two or three Laveh records were played: "Words About Heaven," "Love," "Fear Not": "Do you fear sickness? Do you fear death? Do you fear the spirits? I will tell you of One who can remove these fears. . . ." The sun moving round, the father suggested going into the house where men and women, half listening, drank from a big rice-wine pot. They steam rice and husks until soft, put it in the jar, and seal it with clay or ashes until it ferments. When wanted it is un-sealed, filled to the brim with water, and sucked through long bamboo "straws," more water added as required until the brew is too weak. John said that records could not play during a drinking. Good hu-moredly, a last pull was taken and the "straws" stacked.

John next brought out the Wordless Book. This old friend of evangelists to illiterates teaches by a series of colored pages: black stands for man's sin and for judgment; red shows the sacrifice of Christ; white, the heart purified by faith in the blood of Christ; the last page is gold, for heaven. He took them through and asked them to explain it back. They were dumb. Expecting this, he ex-plained again, and they could remember the lesson of each page. Those who had not left when the gramophone stopped displayed close interest which the Wordless Book had clinched.

After a pause John turned to the headman. "How about the vil-lage father?" he asked. "Do you want to go to hell or to heaven?"

"I want to go to heaven," the father replied; "I want to escape from sin."

"There's only one way you can get to heaven, and that's by having Jesus wash away your sins. Would you like Him to do that?"

"Yes!"

"How many would?"

The headman said: "I don't know; I can't speak for the village but only for myself."

John glanced at the spirit altar just to my right, an affair similar to those in Burma. "Do you realize what this means?" he said slowly to the father. "You cannot walk two trails at once."

The father saw the point, and spoke to his neighbors in Laveh and then, in Lao, to John: "I want to go the Jesus trail, only one trail."

"That means you'll have to *leave* the old trail."

"I don't understand," said the headman, backing a bit and bring-ing up a little Buddhism. "What kind of work do you have to do?"

"You don't have to *do* anything," replied John, "to have Jesus. You do not need to avert His wrath all the time. Jesus loves you and died to free you. When you want to know where to make your rice fields, you don't kill a chicken and ask the spirits; you ask Jesus to lead you. Jesus doesn't eat chickens and pigs and buffalo. When you're sick, don't kill sacrifices, just pray. When you go into the forest or into the Lao country, you needn't propitiate the spirits with a pig so that you should be safe; just ask Jesus to keep you safe."

The headman said, "Why, if this is true it is the best thing in all the world!" He paused, and in his turn looked at the spirit altar. "But we don't quite understand." Another long pause.

John prompted: "What do you think?"

"I think we'll go on as before, but when we sacrifice, instead of calling on the spirits we will call on Jesus."

"That will never do," said John. "They are enemies. Jesus would not be pleased. If you want to believe in Jesus you will have to throw over the spirits and burn all this junk," waving his hand at the altar.

A long silence. There were beads of sweat on the village father's forehead as he thought of the awful risk. Even I who was unable to follow the conversation until John translated it afterward realized what was happening, could sense the conflict. There was the very smell of primitive fear in the room. If ever I had dismissed as allegorical St. Paul's reference to "principalities . . . powers . . . the rulers of the darkness of this world," such easy belief could not survive this incident. The spirits. All his life the man had dreaded them. Today he had heard "the best thing in all the world," yet dare he break loose from his masters, the dominant factor in his life as in the lives of numberless forebears back into the mists of time?

The handsome young man of the pleasant grin stretched out toward the wine jar, clutched a "straw" and took a long pull. "We don't know these words yet," he temporized.

"You don't need to study first," urged John. He asked for one of their pipes. "If I give you this pipe, my giving is no use unless you grab it" (In Lao: "reach out and take hold of it"). "God offers you a home in heaven, but His offering is no use unless you reach out and take hold of it." They began to chatter in Laveh. John sensed that they had gone off at a tangent. They turned to him. "We hear you saw a wild elephant on the trail yesterday. . . ."

Back at Ban Kong Mi after a bathe, we sat in the dark in the house. I asked John to sing.

As that rich, perfectly modulated voice echoed out across this pagan village, singing his favorites and mine, such as "Crimond," "And Can It Be," "O for a Thousand Tongues," "To God Be the Glory," and one I shall always recall in that setting, "Praise the Saviour, Ye Know Him," I looked to the day when Laveh should be singing their own Christian hymns in this place, when the exploratory period be over and response in the villages, together with increased manpower, had enabled missionaries to come out to their own little houses in the hills to spend periods teaching between spells at the Moung Mai base; when the tribesmen themselves became their own foremost evangelists and pastors, as I was to see in Borneo.

Next morning only two porters offered. We were entitled to eight and required four, having no wish to carry loads ourselves, as we aimed to cover the whole distance back to Moung Mai in one day. John went to the Twirp. "Look here," he said. "These two have come all the way from England to write about Laos. What sort of report will they put in their book? People say the Lao are lazy. Here is your chance to prove them wrong."

"These people are not Lao."

"Well, they are not American!"

"Oh, they haven't been assimilated yet. They don't count." John's remarks shamed the Twirp into producing a third porter, leaving John's pack and one bedroll to be carried by ourselves. We crossed the pontoon at 7:15 A.M., with twenty-eight miles to go.

A brisk pace covered the first stage in twenty minutes; we stopped at the Heffalump trap at the first hour, and by 9:45, already hot and covered with sweat, plunged into the big pool. The carriers when they caught up announced they would cook here. We added tinned meat to the rice, and I would have eaten much more had I known what lay ahead.

We had salt tablets to offset the loss by sweat. Take Awful Warning—never use hot coffee to wash down salt tablets; there were terrible moments of suspense in the bushes.

We divided forces. Keeping the carriers' pace would have prevented us reaching the river until well after dark, with no certainty of a canoe. John was anxious to call on the governor before he should hear of our expedition. Dave therefore would bring up the carriers, if necessary spending the night the wrong side of the river, and Anne, John, and I would press on by forced marches, he and I sharing his pack in strict hourly rotation. No danger of getting lost because all roads led to Rome.

The next stage in the heat and at the speed we marched made us thirsty, only to realize too late that we had left Dave not only the kettle but the chlorinating tablets, and since the occasional water on the trail was not safe to drink we had to ration the two polythene water bottles, which tasted of India rubber anyway. The forest shade was blessed, and a stretch in the open showed what we would have endured on the more easterly trails. In three hours we came to a *sala* damaged by a wild elephant, and having sat on a log for most of the ten-minute halt went to look, and remembering that a *sala* means water, sought it and rinsed faces. The day resolved into hourly stretches with that pack getting steadily heavier as the carrying hour seemed to lengthen. At first the chat went back and forth merrily as we spanked along. Gradually conversation slackened, and all energies were concentrated on getting there.

At 3:30 P.M. we reached where we had slept the first night. The tribespeople to whom we had played records on the trail were grouped around the pool. Leaving Anne dipping her legs in the water, John and I went out of sight and had a veritable buffalo wallow, lying in the water and going right under as long as breath lasted. John went further: his face took on the unmistakable expression of contented water buffalo.

Had we now had a meal and unlimited liquid we should have romped home. We had only five sweets between the three of us, having voluntarily outwalked our supplies, and a mouthful of water each. On the trail again just after four we scarcely slackened pace, but when the evening sun slanted through a part of the forest where a fire had burned most of the leaves off the trees, the pack, which I then had, took on alarming weight and proportions.

Our feet in gym shoes were exquisitely tender, our tongues cleaved to the roof of our mouths as we struck through the paddy stubble and could see the plateau beyond the town and river, sharp in the setting sun. We were racing the night; whacked, moving like auto-matons.

At 6:10 we staggered into the suburb beside the river. Clambering painfully up into a pop shop, we each downed two bottles of orange fizz (un-iced). Mercifully a man agreed to paddle us over, and I was so desiccated that just the touch of water refreshed as I held my hands over the side. The canoe landed at the governor's beach. Summoning the shreds of our courtesy we called on him. He was delighted to know we had been "à la Laveh," and his servant brought us iced tea. Tactfully and of necessity tying a woolly round the seat of my old shorts, I followed John and Anne down the stairs.

We went to another pop shop and had another two bottles each of orange (iced)—one was quite fizzy. We entered the local eating place, and ordered a Chinese meal from the shopkeeper. His wife, holding her baby, murmured: "Look, little one, Frenchmen! Take care, little one, take care; they'll get you, they'll get you!" A white man is to mothers in Laos what Boney used to be to nannies of the Napoleonic Wars.

There was a pot of Chinese tea on the table, unfortunately luke-warm. I drank a glass and a half, too fast. On top of iced tea and four bottles of pop in an exhausted, empty stomach, the effect was devastating. When the meal came, one spoonful and I had to rush for the gutter.

"Ugh," said the disgusted shopkeeper in Lao to John, "He's drunk!"

TWENTY   *The Land of Never Mind*

The Prince lit another cigarette. "If you prefer Kolynos and I pre-fer Colgate," he said, "why should I get upset? It's just preference. It is all the same, really, all toothpaste. In the same way I am Bud-dhist, you are Christian. What is the difference? It's all religion. Why, I won the divinity prizes at Aldro school!"

I was back in Bangkok. We had come down to Paksé in an overloaded bus-truck. Anne was squeezed into the cabin; John Davis and I sat on the roof, legs dangling over the side, a tribesman clinging round my middle, whether for his protection or mine I never discovered.* From Paksé next day Uncle John Kuhn had escorted us across the Mekong River and over those awful roads to Ubon in a jeep driven by Leslie Chophard, one of the two independent American Brethren who with the Swiss and the O.M.F. and six Japanese complete the tally of missionaries to the tribes of Lower Laos. Leslie had been a fighter pilot in the war, and drove his jeep accordingly.

Back in Bangkok: big buildings and air-conditioned offices; two-carriage yellow streetcars with striped sun curtains, crowded noisy main streets, Chinese food vendors hawking hot noodles at the curbside, hurrying coolies with loads swinging from bamboo poles over the shoulder, garbage in the back streets; stinking open ditches in the new city and, beyond the river, wide canals where floating shops ply in canoes with high prows curving inward: butcher, fruitseller, hairdresser, dressmaker, lottery-ticket seller, and the coffin shop; palaces and ill-kept parks, equestrian statues, officials all in similar American-style uniform so that only by capband may a soldier be distinguished from a streetcar conductor, a policeman from a railwayman. And always that violent traffic and the heart-rending squeals of the bicycle brakes of the samlors.

"Why should I get upset?" repeated the Prince. "Toleration is the hallmark of Thai life." A secretary of the embassy had kindly driven me out to my appointment with Prince Prem Purachatra at his small modern house beyond the Royal Palace, and now we sat on blue leather sofas beneath pictures and ornaments, a glass case of orders and decorations, and a bust of the Prince's father, one of the elder sons of King Chulalongkorn. Prince Prem, who after Aldro preparatory school had gone to Harrow and New College, Oxford, is a widely traveled man of literary attainments, a poet and novelist, editor of the leading English-language weekly in Thailand. About forty, he is small and chubby and quite fair of skin; he wore glasses and talked volubly in a frank way that I liked.

---

* Over a year later I heard that the impromptu sacred concert with which John and I passed the time had been a factor in the subsequent conversion of this very tribesman.

"Toleration is the hallmark of Thai life. Our history and our nature dispose us to be friendly to foreigners. The character of Buddhism is to show the way but not to compel anyone to follow it. I myself accept Buddhism as a philosophy rather than a religion; I don't believe all of it. It does not make much difference what you actually believe. Buddhism must not force. So it is against our faith to persecute or to object to people changing religion. The King is not only Head of the Buddhist faith but Protector of all religions. Therefore an offense against Christians for their religion, a persecution, is an offense against the person of the King, and it is so written in the Constitution. The King will subscribe to Christian or other religious institutions. Do not forget that earlier Kings gave land and money for churches and Christian institutions. Toleration is the hallmark of Thai life," said Prince Prem again.

Thailand or Siam (Prince Prem and many others still prefer Siam as the English name for the Land of the Thais), the real Thailand, away from the route of the globe-trot, is less familiar than it should be. "Siamese cats, Siamese twins, and *The King and I*— that's all that anybody in the West seems to know about Thailand," said one missionary.

Thailand is underpopulated for the extent of arable land, a fortunate fact marking it from the rest of Southeast Asia. No one need be hungry; most are as prosperous as they wish. It has known no modern war, and I used to wonder what that enormous Victory Monument commemorated. Thailand never had a colonial master, thanks to the astuteness and good government of its Kings, a wise American adviser, and the desire of Britain and France to keep a buffer between their colonies, and it is free of the self-conscious sensitive nationalism that complicates most Asian countries.

"We have not had foreign domination. Therefore we are friendly to foreigners and feel no antipathy to missionaries or others." This was the first point made by the aged Prince Dhani Nivat (Prince Bidyalabh Prutiyakorn), former Prince Regent and now President of the Privy Council and of great influence with the young King. Prince Dhani, grandson of the great King Mongkut, is an old Rugbeian and an Oxford man. He was wearing the formal Thai dress little seen today; his courtesy and charm were positively restful, his comments shrewd and wide-ranging, as would be expected.

Old Siam had certain foreign benefits without foreign rule. On the other hand the average road, a torment of stones, earth, and clinker, shows what it missed. Modern Thailand is proud to be the headquarters of SEATO, and America is the young Thai's idea of heaven. Bangkok likes foreigners. In the countryside, as we found for ourselves, they are as rare animals strayed from a zoo, to be stared at with avid but friendly and smiling curiosity.

The Thai is fairly small but well built. His face is round with somewhat puffy eyes, and he has a small mouth inclined to sag at the corners, a broad forehead, black hair, and a skin surprisingly light when not sunbrowned. He is cheerful, lovable, easygoing, and rather childish. You get the impression that his motorcar or his radio or the implements of his trade are toys, his fields a child's garden to be played with when he feels inclined.

Thais are very polite, except when in control of a car. The head is considered highest, the foot basest. It is impolite to point the foot, and if you want to be thoroughly rude, waggle it. When you pass someone sitting, bend the head to indicate no discourtesy, especially if he is your superior. The object is always to get lower than the other; a European accustomed to standing until requested to take a seat finds it strange that the Thai makes at once for the nearest chair to stop his head dominating his host's. Another courtesy is to place the left hand under the right arm when handing an object or serving a dish. Politeness crops up unexpectedly. We were walking along a river in Central Thailand when a row of schoolgirls in their blue skirts and white blouses coming toward us stopped, lined up and, though bursting with curiosity, bowed their heads as we passed, folding their hands in the *Wai*, the same greeting as the Indian's *Namastay*.

Thais are lazy. No one works harder than he must and no one need work hard. Strong houses are not required, firewood is unnecessary, and so are thick clothes. The farmer harvests his rice and then takes a long rest. We were there when the dried-up paddy fields were brown with stubble or blackened where good straw had been burned as an indolent way of clearing, and most of the country people sat about in enormous sun hats or knotted around the radio shops watching television. That the shopkeeper does not mind seldom selling sets to regular viewers is an example of the Thais' easy-going ways. They are mentally lazy, too, preferring magazines to books, seldom engaging in serious talk.

Mai pen rai—"Never mind"—is always on Thai lips. Two bicycles collide: "Never mind," they laugh. A man loses his watch. "Never mind," he says cheerfully. A military coup took place shortly before we arrived, and two others in recent years. No one noticed and no blood was shed. This easygoing tolerance has its limits; life is not always a song: cases of gunshot and knife wounds after armed robbery or drunken fights were regularly entering a Christian hospital where we stayed. Yet compared with most parts of Southeast Asia, the Thai lives one long beautiful morning.

An aspect of this merry country was a big surprise: the discovery of what Buddhism really involves.

Thailand and Cambodia are held up to the world as the centers of purest Buddhism. The temples of Bangkok, as every tourist knows, are serene and beautiful. The Marble Temple, the Temple of the Emerald Buddha, but not, I felt, Wat Arun, the Temple of Dawn, rising like a cone from the riverside, encourage stillness of mind as does no Chinese, Burmese, or Indian temple except possibly the Golden Temple of the Sikhs at Amritsar.

The patient and scholarly may drink deep of Buddhist philosophy, of the Four Noble Truths and the Eightfold Noble Path, at the feet of grave and reverend abbots. To the ordinary Thai, Buddhism denotes *sanug,* or fun. The temple is the center of social life where at community merit-makings or at family festivals neighbors and relatives have a good time, despite primitive Buddhism's outlawing of the pursuit of happiness. There is no regular congregational worship. The individual goes to the temple to offer flowers and incense, or to listen with others to the Buddhist scriptures being read in the ancient Pali language and expounded in Thai, but not for a "church service."

Apart from fun, religion is primarily the means of making sufficient merit to ensure salvation which, to the Thai, signifies a better life next time and eternal bliss some time; true Buddhism knows neither a heaven of conscious bliss nor a soul to enjoy it. For a male the immemorial custom of submitting, if only for a short period in boyhood, to shaving of the head and donning of the yellow robe and the discipline of the monastery goes a long way to meet the demand of the cardinal tenet, "By one's own good deeds salvation must be won." For a woman, feed the priest. There is much merit in the spoonful of rice ladled into the bowl of the yellow robes as they walk the streets or paddle the canals in the early morning. "Monk" would be a better translation of *Phra* than "priest," for as Prince Prem said, "They are there primarily for their own salvation rather than to help people, though they have a social value in bringing up boys, teaching and so on, as well as officiating at weddings and funerals."

Merit-making becomes more important in old age. The British ambassador, from his long experience in the Consular Service in Siam, put it rather nicely: "You get cracking when old, doing enough to make enough merit to be sure not to be reborn as a carp or a snake. But not too much in case you go straight to Nirvana and have no more fun on earth!"

The gap between primitive Buddhism and the Thai version is further evidenced by the spirit houses. These little constructions like dovecotes are everywhere, outside peasant cottages, outside the homes of businessmen and diplomats, and even in temple courts. The householder will never go away without telling his particular spirit, and will thank him on return for guarding the place. And the less-educated Thai has firmly deified Buddha and prays to him. "As they get education they know better," Prince Dhani said. "Buddha is not God. Buddhism directs you in the right way but does not take you there. That is left to you." For the common man, that is not enough.

Few get agitated. *Mai pen rai.* Never mind.

In this tolerant country it is a surprise that only a fraction are Christian: of a population of 23,000,000 some 30,000 are Protestants.

The Roman Catholic Church, as often in Asia, began centuries before the Protestants, but work is largely among Chinese and other non-Thais. Two Protestant missionaries, Europeans, entered in 1828. In 1831 the American Board of Commissioners for Foreign Missions sent their first representatives, and it is the American Presbyterian Church which is the greatest name.

The effect of the early Americans was soon felt; they introduced printing, surgery, vaccination, schools, winning the confidence of the Crown. F. B. Sayer, whose wisdom helped Thai foreign policy, was an American missionary. A few Chinese were baptized. The missionaries were men of that courage, sterling character, and deep faith which has characterized their mission ever since. It was not until 1859, thirty-one years after the Protestants had come, that the first person of full Thai blood was baptized. Only when they shifted their main effort to the north, where animism is stronger than Buddhism, did the Presbyterians see the birth of a church of appreciable size.

Today the Church of Christ in Thailand, the indigenous body which grew from the Presbyterians, has high prestige, and controls renowned institutions such as the Leprosy Colony at Chiengmai and the Christian Hospital at Bangkok. Relations seem excellent between Thai Christian leaders and those foreigners that the American Presbyterians prefer to call "fraternal workers" rather than missionaries. When after the Second World War a number of other missions at last approached Thailand, the C.C.T., far from being jealous of possible poaching on their preserves, sponsored them and did their utmost to smooth the way, knowing that geographically as well as numerically they themselves had been able to cultivate merely a few small corners.

Entry of missionaries is unrestricted. A Christian may preach on the streets, build churches, hold conferences, do anything reasonable he wishes. I found it refreshing to be in a country where no one need look over his shoulder, where names may be freely quoted, where the suave assurances of official spokesmen did not provoke long low whistles from those who knew the facts. The only intolerant time in modern Thai history was during the war when under Japanese influence Field Marshal Pibul Songgram, now safely out at grass in California, ordered all men to be Buddhists. "He did not like to do things by halves," said Prince Dhani. "He thought all in a Buddhist country ought to be Buddhists, and he tried to get Christians to change back." Christian government officials were forced to study Buddhism. Open pressure was slight.

Thailand is not quite so tolerant as Thais would like you to believe. By an unwritten rule an army officer must be Buddhist. "To be a Thai is to be a Buddhist and to be a Buddhist is to be a

Thai" is much quoted; family pressure can be strong even if no father would beat or disinherit his son for turning Christian, as in India. Compared with most other parts of Asia, Thailand stands for tolerance.

Why then so few Christians?

"Tolerance is like a wet blanket over the country," said an English missionary. "Tolerance" is probably the wrong word: indifference would be better. When talking with educated Thais I met the feeling that the contrast between Buddhism and Christianity was so slight that why should anyone change? "I'm a good Buddhist but I am Christian too," was their refrain, and always a little discreet questioning revealed that the speaker had no knowledge of the distinctive message of Christianity—perhaps because his ideas were based on misty memories of chapel and divinity at English public school. As for the ordinary people, *Mai pen rai*. It is the land of the Big Yawn—a cheerful yawn, comfortable, under the trees, out of the sun.

Nevertheless I began to share the feelings of those working there that Thailand may be the Cinderella of the Asian Church.

TWENTY-ONE   *Bread upon the Waters*

It was Roy Ferguson, an Australian, who told me of Mr. Samyorng. Samyorng Saelim's father was Thai and his mother Chinese, mixed marriage being frequent in Thailand. He was about twenty-six.

"When he was just leaving school," Roy Ferguson said, "Samyorng saw an acting troupe, and was fascinated. The old Thai dramas are very immoral, actors generally drug addicts, and looked down on. When his father, who was a respectable carpenter, refused to let him be an actor, Samyorng ran away. During the next nine years he gradually rose to be leading man.

"In September, 1956, the troupe was in the market town where we were stationed. Apparently he was very attracted by my little girl, who was then nearly three. Samyorng hadn't the courage to make contact with us, being very conscious of his low class as an actor, and because foreigners were unusual. His younger brother had joined him and was coming to our house every day, attracted by the Thai children who came to sing. He urged his brother to come and sing too.

"One night the electricity failed and they were unable to act. Samyorng and the joker of the troupe then came across to our house. I sang them a simple song dealing with the elements of the faith. Because of the Thai tune both of them were impressed. For three hours they listened and I played Gospel records, read Scripture portions, and explained them. Samyorng had never heard anything like it. It went like an arrow to his heart. He had no consciousness of sin, but in the course of this night and the next it was aroused.

"The next night—the electricity was still off and we were using a little oil lamp—during the playing of a record he suddenly jumped up and cried out: 'I can see it! I can see it! The light is shining into my heart.' His friend also jumped up. 'Where is it? I can't see the light!' I said, 'Sit down again and we will talk more until you see the light too.' After about half an hour they both said almost at once, 'How can we accept this Lord Jesus?' They were obviously sincere. I warned them that they might get persecuted by the troupe. They said: 'It doesn't matter what it may cost us. We must become Christians. This is the truth.' "

At this point in the narrative Samyorng himself came into the room where Ferguson and I were sitting in the Christian Hospital at Manoram, 125 miles north of Bangkok. He came by chance to give Ferguson a note on the way to church but stayed to talk to me, Roy Ferguson interpreting. Samyorng was slight, with a face well formed and a nose less squat than that of a full-blooded Thai, and hair well back from his forehead.

I asked him what difference Christ had made. After thinking a few moments, rubbing his hands up and down the bottle of water on the table, he said very quietly: "Joy and peace and light. This is obvious to all Christians. There is no need to speak about those things. . . . I had always had a fear of judgment and hell and a desire for heaven. By heaven I meant a place of blessedness. I knew nothing about the Buddhist Nirvana. Before I was a Christian there was one sin I was absolutely bound to, and that was hemp. I used to take it many times a day. The night when I confessed my sins and truly trusted Christ, I returned to my companions and the hemp, but behold! I was tired of it and did not want it any more. And I haven't smoked it since. The pipe belonged to the troupe or I would have broken it.

"There are many other sins which actors fall into easily, and I was no exception. We were afraid of the truth and told lies very easily but from the time when I became a Christian I have striven only to tell the truth. Women—these fellows were at it every night, including myself. When I became a Christian I made a clean break. I wanted to give up the acting profession, but it was eleven months before a way opened up." He said that the troupe did not persecute him. "In the acting profession we are very close friends and depend on one another for our livelihood. There was never any attempt to get me back into Buddhism. There were arguments, of course. Because of the big change in me some of them were interested, and said it is good. While nobody believed, nobody hindered."

Samyorng speaks beautifully, every word enunciated clearly, a smile lighting his face as he lifts his eyebrows and his hands to make a point.

He had, he continued, no other means of support, and would be obliged to leave his possessions with the troupe. The break came when he entered the Christian Hospital for the kidney trouble which, as he knows, will shorten his life. A Thai connected with the hospital supported him for a month and thereafter offered him a post as night cleaner. The manual labor and the humiliation of going down on the floor—foot level—nearly broke his heart. He itched to return to acting. At his most discouraged he had an overwhelmingly vivid sense of the presence of God: "You had no time to talk to Me when you were acting. Now you have. Is it not worth it?" Out of that experience he wrote a fine hymn which he set to one of the old tunes of the classic Thai drama. Since then he has written hymn after hymn. He sang two for me in his full tenor: a paraphrase of the Twenty-third Psalm and a song on the Wounds of the Cross. "The tune is the one sung by the King in the old dramas as he is being deposed. The verse is plaintive and the chorus stronger, to encourage himself. In my hymn the verses meditate on Christ's sufferings; the chorus is of thanksgiving and dedication."

Mr. Samyorng is now hospital evangelist and secretary of the

Thai governing body of the Central Thailand Church. His hymns are widely used. I asked him before he left, "What is the cause of the lack of response to Christ in Thailand?" He thought carefully and smiled, and thought more and looked solemn, and said: "I think it is because the Thai people are free and easy in their own national religion. They are most concerned about things of the world: to become a Christian there is the possibility of having to give up the things of the world and become devoted in their religion. When they have a merit-making they all flock to it, but their religion is entirely outward. When they become Christians it touches their lives—it is difficult to be a sincere Christian."

Mr. Arphorn had been a monk at Bangkok, six years in the novitiate and nine years a fully fledged priest. He was in his mid-thirties.

The temple had a library and he was thirsty for knowledge. In the course of his browsing he became interested in descriptions of various institutions connected with Christianity, such as hospitals and leprosy colonies. "The Buddhists have nothing like that of their own," he said, "though the influence of the Presbyterian Mission has made them start one or two hospitals." He could have stayed in the priesthood but, unusually for a monk, he felt a hypocrite. "I was sincere but conscious that I could not keep up to standard. I knew that as the rules increased in stiffness I would break them. Rather than do that I decided to come out." Furthermore, a thinker, he was worrying about problems to which he could find no answer, and saw that the theory and the practice of Buddhism are "poles apart," as he expressed it. He has now some pungent comments on temple leadership. "The leaders of the monks are greatly respected and worshiped. The more they are, the more proud they become. Instead of making them humble. In Christianity pride is a sin, and a big one at that. Christ was humble, so His followers should be. The more Christ comes in, the more humble you become. And instead of all your service being done for yourself, as the Buddhist monk's is, it is done for Him."

Coming out of the priesthood, Arphorn lived in Bangkok, then at Paknampho, about a hundred miles north, where he worked as storekeeper in an electricity works. At Paknampho, still interested in accumulating knowledge, he bought a set of Scripture portions from a missionary. "I wanted to go and study about the Christian religion but was embarrassed and backward about going there. It was a year before I had courage to go. A friend in Shell Oil introduced me."

He attended regularly at the missionary's Bible studies. Slowly he came to full belief. "What really made me believe was the realization that in Christ you actually meet the object of your faith. In Buddhism you have to acquire knowledge in order to obtain faith; your faith can never outrun your intellectual grasp. Faith in Christ actually brings you His life, and with His life comes the truth. In Him you have the fountainhead of wisdom which to the Buddhist is something remote, to be striven toward by long years of hard learning and good works."

When I put my question to Mr. Arphorn, why there was such small response to Christ in Thailand, part of his answer was most illuminating. "The Thai people follow what they hear about. The more they hear, the more they will believe. The more they hear about Christianity, the less they will regard with suspicion. They are suspicious of anything new. When this hospital opened two and a half years ago, they used to tear up the little tracts they were given, not out of hostility but because they knew nothing about the teaching inside them. Now they respect them because they know something of what it all stands for. Until the past few years this part of Thailand had no Christian work at all except for an occasional colporteur or a missionary passing through, or a Thai Christian moving in from elsewhere. They have hardly begun to hear. Custom is stronger than religion. Once we get them accustomed to the facts of Christianity, we shall get people. Once we get a lot of people following Christianity, we shall get others following."

"You are, then, expressing strong hopefulness?" I asked. "Granted that only the grace of God can win, you are saying that if we pump in *knowledge* of Christianity there should be one day a strong turning?"

"Yes. Definitely."

The river Suphan wound muddily but was beautiful within its verges of trees masking the dried-up acres. Birds were calling in the early sun. A kingfisher, deep red and blue, darted from a branch and curved close to the water. Now and again a timber house on stilts could be seen through the trees.

We were on *Santisuk*, the Gospel launch. Central Thailand is a maze of waterways, thousands of miles of connecting rivers and canals. Some are big, like the Chao Phya River we had left the previous afternoon, in dry weather flowing clear and full because of the new Chainat dam. The small serpentine Suphan would be unnavigable in February were it not for another dam built with American aid.

Water is both road and village street. In 1955 a British missionary, a former naval man, had the idea of using a launch as a means of itinerant evangelism. A somewhat unsatisfactory boat was bought secondhand and fitted out, to be replaced a year later by *Santisuk*. (The name means "Peace," literally: "Quietness of heart and happiness of mind.") Designed by the naval man and built at Paknampho at the cost of about £1,400, the gross weight of the *Santisuk* is 3 tons; it is 32 feet long, 10 feet wide, has a draught of 2 foot 6 inches, and is powered by an 18 h.p. Enfield Diesel engine made in England. In the dry season *Santisuk* is confined to conventional channels, but in the wet can career across the countryside almost at will.

The Gospel launch often carries as crew a married couple and a single man: the resultant squash and lack of privacy, admirably designed as the boat is, may be imagined. The present complement was two, an American, John Casto, doing a temporary spell before getting married, and a black-haired Swiss called Armin Staub, who holds Thai engineer's and navigator's licenses. For Armin Staub *Santisuk* is the dearest thing on earth.

We had been chugging downstream some minutes from the dam, John Casto at the wheel, when we saw a temple and beyond the temple a hamlet. "There is a family of believers there," said Armin. "I'll put on a record to let them know that we are about and will call on our way back. They will be in the fields behind the trees." Sousa's *Washington Post* march blared over the loudspeaker. Armin next put on a Gospel Record and continued to play Gospel Records interspersed with stirring music. We were making for a market some miles away but could play as we passed: merely a scattering of seed, for those in houses or fields or washing themselves or their clothes or their buffaloes would not hear more than a little. In a fortnight the launch was to return and spend several days.

I was surprised to hear that no missionary had been stationed in this part of Central Thailand until the 1950's. No one would quarrel with the decision of the American Presbyterians to settle in the North, in view of their limited manpower and the opportunity. Where, until so recently, were others, especially from Britain? The Churches of the West still do not take Thailand seriously.

At a turn of the river we came on temple school at the midmorning break. About a hundred children excitedly flocked to the landing stage. The little launch tied up. Armin plugged in the microphone and spoke to them, after which John Casto stepped ashore with bundles of brightly colored tracts. When there is a crowd of children tracts are not given away but sold, else they would not be valued, and one costs about the sum a schoolchild carries for sweets at midday; to buy means no sweets; fourteen packets were snapped up. "A Christian used to live just opposite, so these children would have heard before," said Armin as we backed into midstream, the P.A. system carrying a spirited record about the lame man let down through the roof to the feet of Jesus.

We overtook a rice convoy that had passed through the water gate with us, a slow, close-packed proceeding. The heavy barges have a long hold covered by a tin roof, and at the back the family quarters, some smart with polished wood, others a jumble of kerosene tins, hencoops, branches of bananas, cooking pots, perhaps a baby swinging in a shawl. Most have the typical dun-colored waterbutt decorated with yellow dragons; rudders and the high curving tillers would be painted blue or red. The barge people had asked for literature. "They probably have not traveled with us before," Armin had said, "but word has got round of a foreign boat on the waterways, a good boat which has not caused an accident, and what it's doing." The name is often remarked on, and the texts printed on boards port and starboard. As we went by, several waved and others were reading.

At a second, smaller temple school on the left bank we again tied up. Village men clad only in cotton trousers joined the children to listen. At the invitation to take a gift tract adults are sometimes bashful, but here a young man made the move. Everybody followed. Toward the end a gaffer with gray mustache and a fringe of beard and swept-back graying hair, and on his bare chest and arms elaborate tattoos, came running through the trees to get one. Finally a youthful monk bought a pile of the larger booklets.

We cruised on, then tied up to a tree stump in the mud. While Armin and John prepared a meal on the kerosene stove, I had a bathe. After stew on rice and bamboo shoots, followed by papaya, we took a snooze on the roof during the hour when not even a buffalo will stir in Central Thailand.

When *Santisuk* was under way again, the afternoon resolved into a zigzag from landing stage to little landing stage to satisfy the demand for literature from people attracted by broadcasting. Out of sight behind the trees were an astonishing number of homes. Even when we could see no one we were heard. I was equally astonished by the appetite for Christian books. At a stage on the left bank waited men in straw hats and blue cotton, their women with gray hair done in the typical "urchin cut," and their dog exceedingly puzzled. On the right bank was a granny whose teeth were rotted with betel chewing. She had amulets round her neck, and one shoulder bare, a triangle of white cotton loosely over her breasts, and a blue skirt. She was joined by a podgy youth with a hairlip so wide you could see his misshapen upper teeth.

A man in red-checked *pha*, his torso a mass of tattooing, beckoned us back to the left bank. A woman at the next landing stage ran away when she heard the price of the better booklets and returned with money, spitting out a sluice of betel juice. A woman just home from market set down two large baskets to receive a tract. Her small child had had her head newly shaved except for a long lock at the back, and silver ear-bobs, after a Buddhist ceremony.

Sometimes we stopped only long enough to give literature; sometimes Armin talked over the P.A. system or played a complete record, generally of an incident in the life of our Lord. "There!" he said, brushing sweat from his eyes as the launch reversed from yet another stage: "Only one incident of the life of Christ, but they know it now. Know *something* about Him. And they will read those tracts at night by the light of their little primitive oil lamps—just a wick in a tin with a little kerosene. Did you see those old Christmas cards from England which have had Thai texts written in? They love those."

We had to disappoint people waiting on the bank or be late for the meeting we had planned. Thao Keo (Glass Harbor), the market, was nothing but a bamboo jetty, a heap of garbage, a rice mill with tall chimney, a street with shops and timber houses, and a gate at the end leading straight into the fields—no road; the river is the road. The street had a cinema screen across it, for a white medical boat was in; they were going to give a film show; having got everybody to town, they would inject them against cholera. A man up-river had already told us. "They will always tell us where to find a crowd," said Armin.

Our program of records and talk did not, I thought, excite much interest, certainly not so much as that of another night at a different market, where Anne and I sat behind a substantial crowd on the bank watching colored slides thrown on a screen Armin had erected on *Santisuk*'s roof. The pictures of the life of Christ were accompanied by a taped commentary by a Thai, and the most impressive electrical storm I have seen. Here at Glass Harbor the crowd was thin (it included a rarity, a Thai albino) and not attentive. A record which cleverly compared Christianity with Buddhism rather as a political pamphlet will quote points from the opposing party to prove its own provoked animated discussion in a teashop between a man in a pink shirt, rather amused, another bare to the waist with a teapot in front of him, and a man of more educated appearance.

A passenger launch disgorged its passengers. A big barge tied up next to us. It had a treadle sewing machine and shining cooking pots. The man went ashore; the woman in skirt and bodice ate her evening rice, swilled the bowl in the turbid river, and drank.

TWENTY-TWO   *"And Put Forth His Hand"*

The meeting over, John cooked supper. We cast off and crossed back in the darkness to a point a half-mile upstream and ate pork chops in the living space over the engine, throwing the bones to the water.

A Thai hailed us from the shore: "Why do you tie up in the wilds like this? Why don't you go to the market?"

"We're all right, thank you."

"I'd go to the headman's. It's safer."

The plan was to find a Christian's house, call on him, and spend the night tied up to his jetty. Anne and I washed up in the tiny galley, Armin took the wheel, and John handled the searchlight. We failed to find the place before Armin said: "It is getting too late, and they will have gone to sleep. Life closes down early because they get up at dawn. We'll stop here." Two heavy poles were worried into the mud, and the launch was lashed fore and aft.

You could wash in the smart little lavatory or on the narrow stern deck with pails of river water, jumping down for a swim in the warm night; clambering back was more difficult. Because the two screened two-berth cabins were stuffy and cramped, the men nobly rigged us a mosquito net on the roof. A strong wind made it unnecessary at first. Bites awoke me at 1:00 A.M. The wind had dropped, so I dropped the net too.

As the river emerged into clear daylight, every scent and sound sharp, the freshness of morning made a memorable background to one's devotions. By the time we had taken down the net, dismantled the poles, stowed mattresses and bedding in the cabin, the others had prepared a breakfast of porridge, scrambled eggs, toast, coffee or postum, banana and pomalo, that outsize citrus fruit which is one of the best in the tropics. This very area produced the most famous variety in Thailand, exceptionally juicy, and with a taste more of grapefruit than of orange. We bought more from a floating market which paddled by, tooting the appropriate sound. The coffee man honks an old-fashioned car horn. The ice-cream man rings a bell. The butcher blows a ram's horn.

Inevitably, considerable time was spent on interior economy. We washed up again, Armin cleaned the engine, and John, donning a *pha*, washed down the deck and went overboard to scrub the sides, diving under to clean the propeller.

"What real exercise do you get?" I said.

"Getting the poles out. You try."

I did. I took off my shirt, and sweated at those poles. It is partly a knack but mainly strength. Once each pole is out and floating, it can be pulled in easily. On a later occasion I loosed them, without orders, when no one was at the wheel, and I am not clear why, being a landlubber, but the second pole promptly made off downstream and had to be retrieved by Armin. We were in a sluggish stretch or my zeal might have lost it.

On the last day of our trip, when *Santisuk* was anchored among the reeds in a back water of the big river, Armin and I discussed the aims of this enterprise. "We are definitely working on a long-term strategy," he said. "The scheme has been to spread a basic knowledge of the Gospel, mainly by literature—there's a high standard of literacy—all along the waterways; in other words, throughout Central Thailand. For the first two or three years we did the markets and big settlements. More recently, we have been working from house to house. The main aim is to do the areas still to be done, but we have in some places gone over a second time."

"Why do you cover so wide an area?" I asked. "Wouldn't it be better to concentrate?"

"You have to choose one method, and we chose the other. As a matter of fact, the earlier boat did spend a long time in one neighborhood, without any result so far as is known. Actually, I would say that when we see interest we do try to concentrate and give basic teaching. In January, 1957, we moved through another water gate off this river where we are now. The village beyond had been visited by some of our missionaries from Chainat giving out tracts. When the launch was there a small boy came up and showed a certificate from a Bible School and said half the temple school, about 120, were doing the correspondence course. The postmaster was always sold out of stamps. So we went to the temple teacher and got permission to have a Gospel meeting in the school grounds, and he let us have one on the Sunday when the school was closed. After that meeting two or three boys professed to have believed already. We invited them to the boat for further teaching. We decided to stay one week, and every evening eight or ten boys paddled across the river to the launch for teaching. Some definitely decided for Christ. But next Sunday no one turned up, probably owing to pressure from priests. Since then, missionaries have opened a station in the place, in a rented house. They did not find those students again, either because of pressure or because they had moved away."

At first I had been skeptical of promiscuous itinerating, the broadcasting of seed over so vast a field. Mr. Arphorn's words and my own observations convinced me that the Gospel launch, as well as a Land-Rover working on a similar pattern in the less watered area to the east, holds one of the keys to the evangelization of this strangely neglected countryside. It would be meaningless except as part of an over-all strategy which includes the Christian Hospital and missionaries living in the district centers, but it is going far to meet the special need, to "pump in knowledge."

Direct result may be small. Armin Staub says: "We are inclined to think of 'fruit' only as baptism or church membership. I believe that there must be many along the rivers who believe in their own hearts without anyone knowing it. Besides, I believe that our own contribution is to spread the basic knowledge of the history and teaching of Christ. There is absolutely no background. Why, when you speak of God—*pra*—the same word is used for Buddha, the King, and for a priest."

If Armin Staub had his way, and funds permitted, a second Gospel launch would specialize in reaping where the first had sown. Indeed, Central Thailand offers scope for a fleet.

I was interested to learn, considering the circumstances, that on that one stretch of river we should pass several Christian homes. "How did that happen?" I asked.

"Leprosy!"

Some mornings later I went out to a particularly lovely reach of the Chao Phya on its majestic way down to Bangkok and the sea, to a little *sala*. Waiting patients sat on bamboo benches. An English leprosy specialist on the staff of Manoram Christian Hospital, Dr. June Morgan, was examining a man with a beautifully tattooed chest. She took him into the bright sunshine, thereby practically eliminating risk of infection. Two American nurses put pills into envelopes.

The next patient, a man in a blue-and-white shirt, had sores. He told the doctor that he had not used his ointment because it fell off his bicycle and he lost it. He took off shirt and vest and they went into the sunshine. There was a roughness of skin round the waist and on one arm. "Some of those sores on his legs are certainly not leprosy," Dr. Morgan said to me. "In the tropics you get such a mixture of skin diseases it is difficult to sort them out. I shall treat him for a month and hope to clean the other things up, and then we can see if there is any leprosy."

Another Englishwoman, Miss Harris, began the midmorning preach. Gospel posters had been hung on the supports of the *sala*. Using an enormous hymnbook held up by one of the Americans, the Englishwoman took the waiting patients through a Thai hymn; the doctor and the other American continued examining and making up prescriptions. The clinic opened once a week, the patients attending once a month, and was one of a widely dispersed dozen superintended by Dr. Morgan, through which three thousand men, women, and children were receiving treatment or preventive treatment. When the informal service was finished, Miss Harris took two of the listeners away under a tree, and soon they were deep in talk, a Bible open.

A man in khaki and a small bush hat paid his fee, making a most respectful *wai*, pocketed his medicine, and went to the riverbank where he hailed and boarded a passing passenger launch. Medicine used by the clinics is given by the Mission to Lepers, but the work is not self-supporting, even apart from missionary salaries.

An infected mother, who had a bunch of keys on a brass belt peeping from under her blouse, brought her son because she was worried that he might have leprosy. He looked ten or twelve, and was actually seventeen. The doctor examined him but was not certain. She sat him down, blindfolded him, and touched him lightly with a piece of paper. He was to point to wherever he had feeling. Leprosy, being a disease of nerves and skin, may numb a hand or foot or other extremity. It appeared that the boy was numb in the left foot.

The next patient had lost his card and had to be traced through the register. When he was examined Dr. Morgan pronounced, "An active case, in the early stages. Look at that long red sore called a macule." The sore stretched round from his right breast down to the waist. It was worse when Kay Griffin, one of the American nurses, first saw him three months earlier. "He has been having a small dosage, as it is an early case. These sulphone drugs are very strong and effective," said the doctor.

I was introduced to a woman in a blue skirt and raspberry-colored blouse. She had lost her eyebrows and the bridge of her nose, and was numb from the elbow down, so that she constantly burned her fingers when cooking. A sore spot on her upper right arm showed that the leprosy was still active. This woman, a believer, was shortly going to the Leprosy Believers' Conference where some ninety people would be meeting at a market town up the river.

This use of leprosy clinics to spearhead evangelism was modeled on the scheme pioneered by Dr. Buker, working with the American Presbyterians at Chiengmai. Through the clinics flows a steady trickle of believers into the Christian Church. Leprosy is the soft underbelly of the yellow robe. Lepers in Thailand, not normally cast out by their families but considered by public opinion sinners, since Buddhists teach leprosy to be the result of sin, not only feel that they are unwanted by their own religion but are among the few Buddhists with a sense of sin, perverted though it may be. Therefore they show interest in the theme of redemption. Secondly, the continuous monthly treatment at the clinics brings them regular Christian teaching. They become familiar with the facts. Knowledge is "pumped in." And the practical love of Christian nurses and doctors directs their own sense of need to the place where acceptance of Christ is no longer a remote possibility.

By the leper his family and his friends may be reached. With Dr. Morgan and one of the clinic staff we went by road to a patient too serious to travel to treatment. He was a thirty-three-year-old schoolmaster and lived near a temple. We climbed the steep steps of his house, took off our shoes, and entered the clean main room, opening on to a veranda and a pleasant view of palms, kapoks, bananas, and bamboo. He was sitting in a *pha*, cheerful. His body was covered with bits of plaster and open sores oozing pus. Dr. Morgan sat in the manner of a well-bred Thai woman, feet tucked back to one side, and prepared penicillin. Virginia Mullin administered it in his upper backside and began to lance and clean his sores. He took the pain well and smiled at the jumble of inquisitive children.

As soon as we came, the neighbors and their children came too. One man importantly showed Dr. Morgan a torso covered with a skin disease he believed must be leprosy: it was shingles. The neighbors showed no revulsion from the leper. They watched sympathetically, received the tracts offered, and settled down expectantly for the preachment which is always given during a home visit. In one more way is the Christian Gospel made known.

"The general public at home still thinks a leprosy worker is heading for a martyr's crown.

"In actual fact there is little risk of contagion if you are sensible. To touch a leper is not the brave or the dangerous thing it used to be thought. The past fifteen years have revolutionized leprosy treatment. Those sulphone drugs [D.D.S. and Sulphatrone] are widely used, and for most cases are very effective, and D.D.S. can be given to children and to contacts in prophylactic doses. In the realm of surgery much can now be done for injured hands and feet, in some cases for eyes, and even noses can be remodeled and lost eyebrows replaced. Education is an important factor in the control of leprosy. The patients can be taught that they can live normal lives, and many of them are not infective and therefore of no danger to the community."

Dr. Morgan told me these facts and of her hopes of a treatment center attached to the Christian Hospital at Manoram, one Sunday as we went by motorboat to a service at a little hamlet where a leper lived. She also gave more details of the spiritual fruit of this work of compassion, the important factor being that the leper generally was only the beginning of a church. I had already visited, from the Gospel launch, the headman of a village who was not a leper but was a Christian—a new, shaky, but undoubtedly sincere Christian of definite spiritual experience; and it had all sprung from the life and words of a leper who had moved to his village.

This process was being repeated at the church near Wat Sing where we went that Sunday morning. "Church," in an architectural sense, is a misnomer: it was simply the ground underneath Tong Chai's house. His large-wheeled narrow country cart stood at the back. The space was well swept and benches and a table arranged; the Thai countryman normally sits on the floor, but Tong Chai wanted his church to look like a church. A middle-aged man, he was a leprosy patient without outward marks of the disease. He was wearing an old thick khaki shirt with black cotton working-class trousers round which was a thick leather belt with a brass buckle suggestive of an English gardener. His face was browned with the sun; he had a squat nose, protruding lips, and little horn-rimmed glasses. He looked solemn as he began the service, but when we talked afterward he sparkled merrily. He had been a believer two years.

The congregation apart from our party were his wife and three young men of the village, two of whom we saw baptized by Tong Chai in the river after the morning service.

"How did your first convert come?" I asked.

He laughed. "Ask my wife. She was my first convert."

A little apart was another, rather better dressed man, an interested listener but not yet a believer; two or three others dropped in and out during service, and local children wandered around inspecting us or playing with puppies or being ticked off by the preacher for making a noise.

Tong Chai alone was a leprosy patient. The others were won by him; in this way the church is growing. I asked him, Dr. Morgan interpreting, how he had become a Christian. "I had been attending leprosy clinic," he said. "I was given tracts, then I bought a New Testament. First I came to realize that the Bible was different, was God's book. As I read, I realized that men really are sinners, and that Christ had died for sinners. I was afraid I would go to hell, and wanted to go to heaven." Very gradually he came into the light. "My great day was when I realized that I would not have to go to hell because Christ had died for me."

Yes, he said in answer to a further question, he had had many temptations at first. "The neighbors taunted me that I was not a true Thai; I replied that it was better to believe God than the neighbors. Also, it was difficult that I was the only Christian in the district." As he said this he began to laugh, and chuckled away happily, perhaps because there were now at least four believers in the area, and all under God, through him. I asked him what difference Christ had made in his life. "I was so afraid of hell before. And I couldn't do good. Now I am no longer afraid, and I *can* do good because of the Holy Spirit. Also, I used to get so worried about things. Now I don't."

A Thai Prince once said to a friend of mine, "Do you really think that with this little Christian church you are going to pull down this great mountain of Buddhism?"

I think I know the answer, though I may not live to see it.

three

Isles of the Southern Sea

TWENTY-THREE

After the Shooting

In the early hours of Friday, March 13th, the International Express was slowing down to Tapah Road Station in Perak, North Malaya.

It was the second night from Bangkok. Opposite Penang that evening we had changed carriages from Thai to Malay. There had been a sumptuous Malayan coach right through; the windows were sealed for air conditioning which the Thais will not switch on. We preferred cool air to comfort and cleanliness. Since Penang the express had cut through the night at a pace that would have left an Indian mail panting.

Not long since all trains had been restricted to fifteen miles an hour and given armed escort. They were still made up with first class at the rear, second class next, and third in front, as if to take the brunt of being blown up and derailment.

Sleepily putting together our things, checking that no handkerchief lay forgotten under the pillows of the most comfortable sleepers in Asia, we were resigned to waiting on the station until curfew lifted at dawn and our hosts could drive in. There they were, at 3:30 A.M. Curfew had recently been abolished. We could drive with safety down the excellent road, headlights blazing, no telegraph lines sagging, no rifle fire to be feared round a corner. When we went for a pre-Easter holiday up at Cameron Highlands, declared White only a few days earlier, we could carry on walks what food we liked. Formerly, not even a cracker had been permitted, the idea being that if five men each carried one cracker, a terrorist robbing them could stave off hunger another day.

175

Except for a small area in the North, the shooting was over. Political danger remained, for the Communists had turned to subversion.

Malaya repelled me. It was not so hot as Bangkok, but it was more humid, so that you sweated when sitting still. The way to keep cool is to take proper exercise once a day. I never suffered from Malayan Foot (symptoms: inability to move more than a few yards except by car). I confess to attacks of Malayan Head (disinclination to work, inability to concentrate).

Roads fast and smooth made possible in a day an itinerary that in Thailand would have taken half a week. It was nice to find English widely spoken in shops and offices, to see English cars, and buses that ran to English and not Oriental schedules: they made connections. It was good to eat New Zealand lamb and drink water from the tap. That took some getting used to.

Nevertheless Malaya repelled. The four-fifths of jungle is drearily uniform green. The other fifth looks exactly what it is—artificial, cleared from virgin jungle for the purposes of gain by a population of immigrants, European, Chinese, Indian.

I am not so stupid as to deny the importance to world economy of those unending rubber trees, the tea bushes in the highlands, the messy tin mines; or not to admire the courage of those who faced death through the Emergency to keep them going. But the Federation of Malaya, of all the countries we visited, attracted the least.

The Emergency developed an outstanding example of cooperation between government and missionaries. The large population of Chinese, from which almost all the terrorists were drawn, had lived scattered in the jungle, market-gardening each in his own little clearing. At the height of the Emergency the government decided to uproot the jungle Chinese and resettle them in new communities near the roads so that the law-abiding would no longer be compelled to feed terrorists, and terrorists, who until then could combine market-gardening with murder, would be weeded out. Thus began the New Villages.

Field Marshal Sir Gerald Templer, who when High Commissioner and Commander in Chief of Malaya brought the churches into the

New Village scheme, very kindly wrote to me, in a letter of April 23, 1959, an account of what happened:

"When my wife and I arrived in Malaya in February, 1952," wrote Sir Gerald, "the resettlement scheme worked out by General Sir Harold Briggs was to some considerable extent completed in so far as the physical move of a very large number of people was concerned. Later on it was found necessary to deal with very appreciable additional numbers. But what had not been done, mainly because there had been no time to do it, or insufficient money, was to take all the many steps necessary to make the people feel that they had joined a community in which they could expect a higher standard of living and of amenities than in the isolated life from which they had been compulsorily ejected by Government. And naturally because of the compulsion, many of them had a chip on their shoulders for that reason alone, whatever their views might or might not be on Communism.

"It was a very great experiment indeed, for which General Briggs deserved the greatest credit. Like so many men and women who initiate an entirely new conception, he never got it. It was in fact one of the biggest mass moves of families that had ever been planned and carried out by any Government,—certainly in the Colonial Empire or dependent territories.

"When we got out there, General Briggs had left the country. He was to die soon afterwards in Cyprus.

"The people in the New Villages—or the resettled labor lines— were apathetic in every case. Many of them were working against Government whether or not as a part of the organized Min Yuen. They were a safe bet for food supplies from the terrorist point of view. And so we attempted to harness to our side every activity of human life and endeavour that we could manage. And managing meant money. By and large the Malayan Government of the day poured money into the business. It worked—to a very satisfactory degree. The official appointment of Village Committees, much on the lines of Rural District Councils in this country; the improvement of their standard type new houses; the provision of piped water (something quite new to most of them); the installation wherever possible of electric light which many had never seen before; the making of gardens and playing fields; the finding and allotment of

enough agricultural land to enable them at least to keep themselves
in vegetables and to own their own pigs; the building and running of
Village Community Centres; the installation of communal loud
speaker radio sets; the building and staffing of clinics whether stationary or traveling, in which the British Red Cross played a most
noble part by sending out a large number of volunteers from the
United Kingdom; the building of village schools with its con-
sequential problem of finding suitable teachers; the formation of
village troops of Boy Scouts and Girl Guides; the start of Women's
Institutes (though this applied more to Malay and Indian communities of which there were many in the whole resettlement picture); the 'adoption' of New Villages by the nearest Army unit;
citizenship courses to try to teach the elements of understanding
in how Government, whether central or local, worked; and armed
village Home Guard detachments—"perish the thought" many people
said. This list by no means includes all the endeavors that were set
in motion to try to get these people on to the side of Government.

"And what more natural than that the churches should lend a
hand? Unfortunately the large supply of British China-trained missionaries who had been forced to leave that country had to a considerable extent been dispersed world-wide and in positions from
which it was difficult to extract them quickly. And speed was the
essence of my problem. However, in spite of that, very considerable
results were achieved, and it would not be proper if I did not pay
my tribute in particular to the Roman Catholic Church who produced truly miraculous results very quickly, particularly I think
on the nursing and maternity side. I say that as a Protestant.

"It was indeed an inspiring experience to meet Christian men and
women of all denominations living and working in these isolated
communities under relatively primitive conditions, and often in
situations which the ordinary person would have considered dangerous in the extreme. They thought nothing of those things.

"All this was not done without arousing very considerable criticism, and criticism of a kind whose validity one was forced to admit
to some extent. Why indeed people asked, and in particular the
Malays, should all this money be poured out to help people who
had to be compulsorily herded together because they were so much
under the thumb of the terrorists if they were left alone in their

isolation? And goodness knows the Malay kampongs wanted great things done for them. And they were mostly doing their very best to support Government.

"It was all so exciting, and so very worth while. It was certainly one of the most inspiring tasks which I have ever helped to tackle.

"It's hard to isolate the missionary effort in the whole of this endeavour and to assess exactly its value. If one believes that Communism is an evil thing, as I do, and if one believes that human freedom from oppression and from the fear of the gun is one of the basic beliefs for which we are prepared to fight, then I have no hesitation in saying that the presence of considerable numbers of missionaries—men and women—of all denominations, played a very considerable part in the settlement of the minds of these people, a people who were rootless. They required to feel some spiritual influence. This was given to them by many devoted persons. And that is quite apart from the direct evangelizing work which they most certainly achieved. The hearts and minds of men, women and children were what we were all striving for."

New Villages have come to stay. By the terms of the old Protectorate and the interpretation of the new Constitution of the Muslim Federation, evangelization among Malays is virtually impossible. Only a quarter of the New Villages are Malay. Three-quarters are Chinese, either completely or with a proportion of Indians. At Kuala Lumpur I received the impression that Malay officialdom could not care less about the religion of any but Malays. Christian work is therefore unrestricted.

I was taken on a whirlwind tour of New Villages in South Perak and around Kuala Lumpur, a dozen out of the Federation's four hundred or more. Most of those I saw were worked by Anglicans, whether parsons, doctors, or nurses of the Diocese of Singapore, those in South Perak being connected with the Overseas Missionary Fellowship, those around Kuala Lumpur with the Church Missionary Society. I visited non-Anglican members of the O.M.F. in Selangor, and also talked with the bishop of the American Methodists who were almost the only missionaries in Malaya before the war.

General Secretary of the Church Missionary Society Dr. Max Warren had made a remark in England which I now recalled:

"Don't forget that pioneering may be just as real and just as tough in a city as hiving off into the jungle." A New Village today has most of the amenities of a city; many of the people possess fans and refrigerators, and therefore the missionary may possess them too. Communications are quick, shops are near. Another compensation was charming to watch. Most of the senior workers were old China hands. Those in South Perak came from a remote part of West China where mission stations had been isolated by hundreds of miles of roadless and mountainous province. A married couple was lucky if a European colleague came along once in three months. Now, after years of loneliness, they could drop in on one another for quick cups of tea—an Ex-China Old Folks' Club.

But the work is unromantic, slow. "Discouragement is the great difficulty," they said. The population is so mobile that when converts emerge after years of dry endeavor they may be gone within months. The nervous strain and the physical risks of the Emergency have gone. The spiritual strain remains.

We stayed with an Australian clergyman and his wife, China veterans, in a New Village in the Kinta Valley, one of the worst terrorist areas. The wire fence still ran round the village but the gate never shut; the Home Guard post was deserted and the wide ditch filled in or used as gardens. The tin roofs of the shack-like houses were dreary, but trees had grown in the main street.

That evening from the doorway of the little house, merely the end one of a row of shops in the village center, the activity outside appeared to differ little from that of a large English village. The house opposite certainly belonged to a necromancer and another was a gambling hell, docile enough to look at, and most families had an idol shelf where red paper represented the temple idols and incense was lit each day. The smart Chinese girls walking up and down, who had come in that morning from rubber tapping as tramps, who had bathed, and who were now filmstars, might have been English factory girls on the spree. A crowd streamed from the cinema; a shopkeeper drove up in an Austin car; bicycles sped by, and the air was noisy with wireless music, gramophones and gossip. The walls of the house are thin and its position central; noise is inescapable from dawn to midnight. You get used to it, as to a railway line below a bedroom window.

The next morning, a Sunday, I attended Mattins in the village church, simply the tiny front room of the house. The service was timed for ten o'clock. By ten minutes past, enough of the congregation had wandered in to enable Mr. Robert to start. A few more came, and the total of Chinese was eleven. Three older men were all baptized. One young man, little more than a boy, had been "received" as a catechumen. Another, a visitor in the village, had been contacted the night before and listened carefully, but his sincerity became suspect when he proved to be an insurance agent. Four women were in old-fashioned Chinese cotton tunic and trousers, dark blue and rather close fitting, and two working girls had smart nylon blouses and tight flowered skirts.

This represented the Christian congregation of a settlement of several thousands. One or two others were absent, but after years of work a church of this size, all but one being converts, was typical of a New Village in South Perak.

Different approaches to the problem find favor. The Church Missionary Society depends on Chinese pastors and evangelists, and has advanced quicker. Near Kuala Lumpur, where on Easter Day I was invited to celebrate Holy Communion and later to preach at St. Mary's, which certainly had big congregations at both English and Chinese services, I visited Jin Jang New Village and met the Reverend Lee Ling-Kwong, a charming and handsome young man born and converted in Formosa, educated in Hong Kong, and trained for the ministry in Singapore.

His stipend was paid from diocesan funds; Christ Church had been built by money from England. The work had been founded by an Englishman, and Lee came there six months before I met him. Jin Jang had a clinic, with a resident English C.M.S. nurse, two Chinese nurse-evangelists from Hong Kong, and European part-time volunteers from Kuala Lumpur. Those baptized numbered over a hundred. Jin Jang for various reasons was a star place, not typical, a promise of things to come. Lee was convinced that a "Chinese worker gets nearer the people." The O.M.F. on the other hand, both in its Anglican field and elsewhere, is at present against the paid employment of Asians in a spiritual capacity. It depends on the Western missionary until converts are ready to start a church on their own. Service must be on a voluntary basis unless the congregation is willing and able to support a pastor. In Selangor I went to a New Village where a church building has been raised by the efforts of the people; two men had taken responsibility, and the missionaries were withdrawn. What the building lacked in decorum it made up by signs of the enthusiasm and determination of the people even if, in that odd Chinese way, a pin-up girl calendar appeared on the wall beside Gospel posters, Bible pictures, and a roller of choruses printed in large characters and turned by a cunning wheel made of a Kiwi boot polish tin.

Opinion is also divided between town and country. Some believe that with the ending of the Emergency a more excellent way is to work the villages through strong congregations built up in towns, such as Teluk Anson on the Perak River, where we lunched in a parsonage newly built and so cleverly decorated that it made you cool just to look around. The strong congregation at St. Luke's, Teluk Anson was composed almost entirely of comparatively recent converts, and was already influencing its surrounding rural neighborhood.

Whatever the best strategy may be, the New Village field is one of the hardest in Asia.

At Bidor on the main north-south trunk road I discussed this with another former China parson, Don Temple, a slight gray haired man in the customary white shorts, stockings, open-neck shirt. His small house was well fitted because he runs the government Red Cross clinic. He was not like the Parson of Hogglestock, a gloomy man. In fact he listed encouragements: "There is always something to encourage."

Yet he faced facts. In an area of twenty thousand people scattered over several New Villages and a town his church consists of: three who had been baptized in China and who when the work opened were discovered, derelict Christians; a first convert baptized, now backsliding; a mother and daughter baptized later; four people professing to believe but not yet baptized; and three church members who had moved into the district from another part of Malaya. Conversely, one further convert had moved and joined the church near his new home.

"One of the factors why so few have believed," said Temple, "is undoubtedly political. Just talking to a missionary means that the Communist cell will accuse you of being a Christian—and hence anti-Communist. During the height of the Emergency you really did risk getting your throat cut. It's not so bad now, no physical danger now, but the feeling dies hard and the Reds are still very strong in the villages. Then, again, Communist indoctrination is all over the place, especially in the schools."

A third factor, he said, was the hold of idolatry. My mind switched to the temples of a religion which is Buddhist yet different from the Thai or Burmese; to the idols—Buddha and the old gods—and the red Ancestor Tablets before which incense burns to show respect and to give aid to the departed; to the paper cars and houses and furnishings burned at funerals to provide transport and ease in the next world; and to the Hell Bank Notes. Almost the only time I have seen a missionary shocked was when I walked through Sunday school carrying a Hell Bank Note. "Put it away at once," she cried. "They know what it means. Most improper!"

"Ancestor worship by its very nature is a barrier to Christianity," said Temple. "You've got to help your ancestors and you have got to appease them; if you become a Christian you are both leaving them in the lurch and annoying them. Oddly enough, the people are more idolatrous here than in West China, despite higher standards of life. And idolatry works. People go to a medium to find out which number to back in the state lottery. The local medium predicted that three here would win, and they did! Think of the hold of that."

He told me that Europeans speaking Chinese and visiting poor Chinese homes seemed utterly strange in a country where they had been known only as the rulers and the rich; at first the villagers could not believe they were anything but secret government agents. "We were taken as spies. We had to beat down this suspicion."

Above all, the Christian missionary in a New Village of Malaya confronts a blatant materialism. "The immense indifference of the Chinese!" exclaimed Temple. "Their real god is money, money, money. All they ask is what *material* advantages Christianity would bring. And they look around and conclude that it would bring ostracism and suspicion and offend their ancestors and the evil spirits. So what's the point? On top of that there is the strong influence of amusements, radio, cinema, cars, buses; there is so much to do and buy, and they all work so hard to get money that they have no time to think."

TWENTY-FOUR 🏵 *Last Days of a Colony*

Government House, Singapore, stands on a slight hill in a wide demesne, palatial, not ostentatious. There was poignancy in the marks of royalty in the anteroom: the statue of Queen Victoria, the rather faded Edward VII and George V; the postwar portrait of George VI in naval uniform. Within a year they would be gone. The Elections were a few weeks ahead. The city was already splashed with slogans and symbols, the forked lightning of People's Action Party predominating, and Bullingdon Place echoed to speeches. After the elections the governor, Sir William Goode, for six months would become a sort of portmanteau or tandem—two persons in one: Yang di-Pertuan Negara, or Head of State, and United Kingdom Commissioner. Then, with the installation of a Malayan-born Head of State the royal portraits would go. Rajah Brooke dancing his hornpipe over the dining-room table might be permitted to stay.

Throughout the tour we received kindness from British representatives. Sir William Goode at Singapore, now Governor of North Borneo, especially went out of his way to welcome us and give me the benefit of his wisdom and experience.

And so the day after our arrival in Singapore we sat at lunch. A cat may look at a king, and even on His Excellency's table the little ants scurried; they are tasteless and harmless.

"This is a free-for-all," said the governor, referring to religion in Singapore. "Whatever you are, you find something here: Muslim, Hindu, Bahai, Methodist, Seventh-day Adventist, anything."

"Like London or any big city in the West?"

"Yes, with this one difference: The great menace here and in Southeast Asia is Communism. It has been more and more felt that the only answer is religion. So whereas any religious teaching of any kind in government schools used to be taboo, it has been gradually felt that you can't turn out youth in a vacuum. So now the schools give religious teaching. It is at parents' decision. Muslim children go off to the mosque. Christian children have Christian teaching, and so on. If they have no religion they are taught ethics. Two hundred teachers have just graduated in ethics, whatever that may mean."

There was some anxiety among Christians that P.A.P. when they came to power would attack religious education. The governor did not think they would with deliberate intent. "On the other hand, they will do things the Chinese way. If anyone falls by the wayside they will just be left. If the steam roller rolls over anyone in its progress, just too bad. It can't stop. This is quite different from the British way, which is that if a child falls out of the train we pull the communication cord however much hurry we are in."

Singapore grows on you. It has neither the beauty of Hong Kong nor the vistas of New Delhi, and the rain comes almost every day. By the time we left we ranked it higher than any city, a position retained throughout the tour. We had no regrets when at the end of our second visit following return from Java the ship for Sarawak was delayed a day, and we lay at anchor within the mole. Between us and the islands to seaward were the aircraft carrier *Albion,* the pathetic Dutch mothball fleet fled from Indonesia in 1957, and some fifty freighters. The liners were out of sight in Keppel Harbour behind the hill. To landward, a quarter of a mile or less, a panorama of commercial might: Crosby House, the Asian Insurance (a skyscraper which New York would look down on), the new Shell building, still in honeycomb stage; the red roof of the G.P.O., its Union Jack half-mast for the Sultan of Johore, a glimpse of the City Hall where Mountbatten took the surrender, the trees which hid St. Andrew's Cathedral.

In churches, chapels, mission halls, and Christian schools Asian pastors and teachers predominate—Chinese for the Chinese, Indians for the Indians. On a larger view the significance of Singapore depends on what is accomplished for all Southeast Asia. It is a center of training not only of Asians but of Western missionaries; when we were staying at the compound of the O.M.F. a shipload of forty-one recruits arrived at the language school, British, Commonwealth, and American, twenty-nine women and only twelve men, a proportion unfortunately now common to societies and church mission boards. The recruits came to the headquarters for designations to the different fields, and sat around on best behavior. They were to spend four to six months in language study at Singapore before sailing on to their countries where study must continue: a reminder of the time required on the production belt before the product can be put on the road for breaking in.

Much administration is done from Singapore. As to the O.M.F., the compound opposite the Botanical Gardens is actually world headquarters, on their principle that the leaders must be missionaries on the field, that the supreme direction is best not by remote control from a home country but the other way round. Singapore, a hub of air lines, is the obvious center. The offices were adequate, but I coveted for them the air conditioning without which no businessman in Singapore would function. Air conditioning has become as normal an aid to efficiency there as a typewriter, however much out of place in forward stations where missionaries seek to live close to the people, and even that good principle needs marking. "What, no washing machine like we have?" says a neighbor in Japan. And then there was the couple from Formosa who had sweltered without electric fans. Rather guiltily they bought one. The Chinese girl who did for them exclaimed: "Why did you get such a small one? We've got a fourteen-inch!"

Air conditioning means money. Money is the thorn of these modern St. Pauls. I was impressed by the O.M.F.'s method of allocation. Most societies give their members a personal allowance. (They shy off the word "stipend" or "salary" for the same reason, perhaps, that when I edited a religious journal I called the fee I paid an honorarium: the sum was so small.) The personal allowance, however, is generally some points behind the rising cost of living. As a result I have seen a man's job being done on a diet fit for an old maid. The O.M.F. works differently. Its members do not have a fixed salary, and according to the principle of their society they must "look to the Lord and not to the mission to supply their needs" —in other words they have no claim, as of right, on the mission. In practice their daily bread is assured. They submit cost-of-living accounts which are a first charge on the funds allocated for the support of missionaries, after rents and other such outside obligations have been met. Education and board of the children is also a mission liability. The residue is distributed equally to each member; in some quarters he receives the figure agreed as normal; usually he receives less, occasionally more, once nothing. He does not have to live day by day on that; he is free from the temptation to save on food to pay for clothes or holidays or his son's schooling. As the general director said, "He has no personal gain in starving himself." As a member said, "It is like being in a 100 per cent welfare state."

Missionaries do not come abroad for financial profit. But they have the right to expect the tools to finish the job and the wherewithal to live. Theologically and practically there is the positive factor of faith, of our Lord's words, "Your heavenly Father knoweth ye have need of these things." From an accountant's view missionaries are not adequately supported, certainly not from Britain.

America has learned to give. The giving of a tenth of an income is as frequent in the United States as it is rare in Britain. American missions therefore have bigger funds even if the most affluent are not always the wisest or the most orthodox: the Seventh-day Adventists possess some of the largest resources.

The American likes to see his money tick, bringing quick and tangible results, and to point to a project expanding, a person striding through the wilds because of his gifts. Do not ask him to drop dollars into the dull ditch of mission administration. Despite recent changes United States tax laws strongly encourage charity. Fund raising by churches rather than by appeal to individuals is widespread and produces higher yield. And, obviously, there are more Americans.

Yet all this is as nothing beside the lamentable fact that Britain does not know how to give. I shall always remember the incredulous laugh of a young American in the Philippines when I remarked, and felt foolish as I did so, that if an Englishman gives $5 a year to a mission he thinks he is generous.

Transplanted Wimbledon. The accumulation of Westerners in Singapore brought to a head thoughts which had gathered all the way round, on those who go abroad professionally or on business; their relationship with missionaries; the influence for good or for ill of their personal characters.

Wherever I came among a business or professional community I met kindness. Singapore was no exception: at Bangkok an air-conditioned office was at our disposal, and honorary membership of the British Club so that we could play tennis. And there were always a few whose Christianity was far more than nominal, though their interest might be limited to the chaplaincy church; the congregation of Christ Church, Bangkok, seemed quite surprised to learn about Laos, although it is their back yard. They resolved to do something about it.

Only in a few areas of Asia do the paths cross—in the big cities, in plantation districts, around engineering projects. Relations are not cordial. As a young professional man in Hong Kong said, "There is every sort of attitude from incomprehension, through indifference, to contempt." Missionaries on their part feel that businessmen and their wives, all "Christians" to their neighbors, let the side down by endless drinking and smoking, card playing, and gossip. Each side has a caricatured image of the other. A missionary certainly has less time for gossip, the primary relaxation of expatriates after a hard day's work. Where available, an occasional game of golf or tennis or a friendship outside his colleagues may do much. It is often edged off by absorption in the job, and owing to the contrast in incomes the businessman must make the approach. Sometimes he does, with mutual benefit.

It is doubtful if the character of a businessman has much effect negatively on non-Christians around. There may be Brahmans who continue to believe that the Bible, as the Christian's book, is a guide to choosing wine or cigars. Christmas may be called "the Big Day when even the best Christians get drunk," but no Muslim, Hindu, or Buddhist expects every adherent of a religion to be the perfect exemplar.

Positively, a Christian who is really a Christian can do much: for his national employees and associates by personal qualities and spoken convictions; for local mission work by financial support and giving service in his leisure should opportunity offer. At home, which he visits more frequently, he can inform circles untouched by mission literature of the needs social and spiritual of non-Christian countries. This applies also to the Armed Forces, with one qualification. At Kuala Lumpur and at Singapore we were royally entertained to dinner by members of the Officers' Christian Union, and it was clear that those present considered the primary mission field of an officer to be among his own men.

Civilians or servicemen, the heart of the matter lies in the home churches. Expatriates are the normal run of Englishmen.

The "colonial" attitude of Westerners in personal dealings with Easterners used to appear in the missionary as much as in the merchant, planter, or administrator. With few exceptions it is gone.

The change was discussed by the Governor of Singapore in a further talk at Government House. He pointed out that in the old days there was clearly a sense of being superior because, after all, these men were making Asia work. Without them railways would come to a standstill, ports silt up, political chaos break out. He compared their attitude with that of an English squire of the old days. "Most of the people out here were imbued with the public-school spirit. They may have been superior in their ways, but they had the squire's strong sense of responsibility for their dependents. If any one for whom they felt responsibility was in need, they saw him through."

At the end of our talk, when he was showing me to the door of his office, Sir William said: "This is the end of an era. You see the end of a chapter. All this"—waving his hand around at marks of British sovereignty—"is going out. We have done our bit, and now they are being left to carry on. It is rather as if school is over and they are all being let out into the playground."

TWENTY-FIVE   🪶   *South to Java*

"You tourists? Whatever do you want to come to *this* country for?" We had crossed the equator huddled in blankets at nine thousand feet, and now at Djakarta airport waited interminably for Immigration. The Englishwoman who spoke, and her husband, an oil executive, had been through it often. They warned us that this was a foretaste of Indonesian officialdom. They were right.

The customs man was surly and opened every piece. We had already been in the country over an hour and a quarter when we climbed into our host's car. His house was within walking distance, yet owing to the contortions of the one-way system it was quite a drive, for most of the main streets of Djakarta are, in Dutch fashion, beside canals, and the Indonesians like to send the traffic down one side and up the other. If your particular turn is just the wrong side of a junction, you may go an extra mile at least—half a mile down, over a bridge, half a mile back. To offset this and ensure that Djakarta traffic shall be the most constipated in Asia, the police in long narrow two-way streets order No Parking at one end but at the other parking on both sides; if a vehicle is parking, certainly if two are trying, one at each curb, every other driver might as well go to sleep.

Djakarta, like a decayed gentlewoman, by reason of past beauty and prosperity is dowdy without being squalid. A little imagination and the acres of untidy grass are again close-trimmed, flower-splashed, and very Dutch. The principal shops fretfully displaying a thin windowful of foreign goods at exorbitant prices have names eloquent of the days when Batavia was a queen in the East. A lick of paint could transform unkempt houses into those gay imitations of Delft or Amsterdam wherein the Dutch, preferring home-like atmosphere to a bodily discomfort which must have been appalling, squeezed themselves, their large wives, and large families. The original Batavia is so close a reproduction of Dutch cities built for comfort in cold as to be almost unbelievable in the tropics. The Dutch had moved out of that area in the past century. It was now typical Chinese slum. And gloom, if that were possible in a Chinese community, was settling in because of government economic policy. Foreign businessmen had coined a joke: "Indonesia is like an egg. They have eaten the white. Now they are attacking the yellow. Soon there will be only Shell."

We planned to go straight to East Java, about four hundred miles from Djakarta. I had been warned that the railway to Surabaya was slow, no less than seventeen hours, six hours longer than three years earlier because rolling stock and track had deteriorated; and crowded, because a railway ticket was one of the few cheap things left. The government had chosen the month of the Muslim fast to assault a practice whereby tickets bought in bulk at the agencies were sold outside at black-market prices. No agency might sell, every traveler must go the day previous to the station whence he intended to travel, and should he, after queueing five hours, find every ticket sold—too bad.

The holidays for the end of the fast and the Muslim New Year increased demand. Two days before we wanted to travel it was ordered that a ticket could be bought only immediately prior to boarding the train. The chaos may be imagined. A child was killed and three hundred extra police were out. Anne and I would need to start queueing at 6:00 P.M., wait all night, buy the tickets, board the train which was due to start at 6:00 A.M., and travel all day. About midnight, if the train was not too unpunctual, we should reach Surabaya and there wait for the connection next morning.

Fortunately, in our ignorance, I had written from Malaya that we preferred to go by air.

I had not realized what that request would mean to our host. George Steed, a Canadian, is a most patient man, and in his task of mission organization in Indonesia he needed to be as patient as Job. And to walk as delicately as Agag; I might add that in some of my Java account I have had to use pseudonyms. One man, a Chinese, whom I expected to meet studiously ignored me for fear of indiscretions in print. An episode specially enjoyed receives no mention because its leading figure, a Javanese, subsequently suffered an acute attack of cold feet. That George Steed—his real name—is not in a madhouse shows him to be the sanest of men. That his sympathy is still foursquare with the Indonesians shows that under irritating absurdities of officialdom there beats a national heart which is fundamentally sound and a national character which, the more you explore it, is attractive.

George Steed got air tickets for us. A common mortal cannot walk into the office of Garuda Indonesian Airways and order a ticket, except for the tourist flight to Bali. He must have a priority. For some weeks Steed had been inquiring, only to be told that the Surabaya runway was under repair and no Convair could land. He knew that a Dakota got in on certain days, but the clerk denied it. The day before we arrived, Steed addressed an application direct to the head of the Department of Travel in which he shot a line in outrageously flattering terms. After four separate trips (you never can tell what documents they will require) he emerged for the first time in his career with a Priority One, went at once to the air office, and received tickets. It had taken him four hours. "That was nothing," he said. "Quite common. Often I have been kept waiting in outer offices for ages, only to find that the man inside was reading the newspaper."

Before dawn next morning we were at the airport. Domestic flights throughout this far-flung pattern of islands begin at first light from Djakarta, so that every plane may be back by nightfall, safe from rebels or other calamities. The flight was scheduled for 6:20 A.M.; we had to be there at 5:15 or risk our seats.

The Dakota was bare of interior decoration, the seats mere canvas chairs, the service good. As the plane began to lose height nearing Surabaya, the principal naval base of Indonesia, passengers read or dozed. The stewardess woke them up by pasting brown paper over the windows. "Military installations," she said. The brown papers were not quite large enough. As we swept in over the harbor, every window had a face glued to the cracks.

Java, I had been told, is one of the loveliest of countries.

It is, with loveliness all its own which the sun, the mountains, and man have conspired to form. Paddy fields of every stage, so kind is the climate, provide brown and yellow, shades of green, strips of blue water all in one glance. Beyond, a grove of coconut palms. The white of a house may peep here and there, but it is hard to realize from the camouflage dictated by desire for shade that parts of Java are among the most densely populated of the world and that the long lines of woodland are unending villages. As background, the smooth slopes of volcanoes, mostly inactive, not harsh and ashen as in Japan, but soft green to the summit. Occasionally, to bring you to reality, there is the shell of a Dutch mansion burned in the War of Independence.

I knew that East Java possessed a body of ex-Muslim Christians.

Muslim areas of the world flaunt the power of Islam, its apparently impregnable strength impervious to the Christian message. Pakistan—a fleeting glance on this tour but I possess earlier memories of majestic mosques, proud jealous tribesmen of the Northwest Frontier, the faithful saying prayers at sunset on a wayside platform in the Bolan Pass. True, there is a substantial church in Pakistan, almost all derived from the non-Muslim sweeper caste and the outcastes. Malaya—a few weeks back Tuan Hassan, the most brilliant Malay in the Civil Service until his retirement, a kindly, broad-minded man, was saying: "We have nothing to learn from Christianity. Indeed, we look on ourselves as the religion that reformed Christianity."

In Java this body of ex-Muslims would be small, struggling, of recent growth.

I am ashamed of my ignorance.

The story of the origin of the East Java Church was told me by Dr. Phillip Van Akkeren at the Theological School Balewyoto at Malang, fifty-five miles south of Surabaya. Dr. Van Akkeren is one of the comparatively few Dutch missionaries retained by Indonesian churches, a tribute to his personal qualities. A spare man of medium height whose thin silver hair testifies to three years in a Japanese concentration camp, and not to age, like most of the missionaries of the Dutch Reformed Church he is learned. He wears his learning lightly. Blue eyes twinkle behind glasses.

The Van Akkerens received us at short notice with utmost kindness. An expert on Javanese history and lore, he conducted us over ruins of thirteenth century Hindu temples in the Malang neighborhood and explained the important position of the ancient Hindu culture, coming after the Buddhism which finds expression in the wonders of Borobudur, and before Islam. Mingling with them all is age-old Javanese philosophy.

This, very briefly, is the story he told.

In the late eighteenth century a German sailor called Johannes Emde joined a ship for the East Indies to prove the absurdity of a tale he had heard that no winter came there. On retiring from the sea he took up watchmaking in Surabaya, and married a Javanese. He was a man of genuine if overpietistic faith, and drew around him a little group of Christians, mainly Eurasian. When Stamford Raffles ruled Java for Britain in the later Napoleonic Wars, a Dutchman of the London Missionary Society helped Emde to such effect that on the missionary sailing farther east Emde had a group of over a hundred, including some Javanese.

The Dutch returned and reimposed their ban on missionary work;

like the British East India Company, but for forty years longer, they regarded it as a menace to commercial profits.

To Dr. Van Akkeren this policy of exclusion was not merely un-Christian but tragic. Around 1830 Muslims in Java began to respond in numbers to Christianity for the first time. Historians wonder why. Van Akkeren believes the explanation to be that the fall of the old Javanese kingdom in 1825 after a bitter war produced widespread expectation of a new era, a Christian era under a Christian King. Traditionally Java took the religion of its monarch, and now the monarch was William of the Netherlands. A jihad, or holy war, had failed. Men recalled that Islam was only three hundred years old, and foreign; songs were sung of the prophecy of the last Hindu King that a true religion of the spirit would arise, ushering in a golden age. "In short," said Van Akkeren, "expectations made it easy for Christian preaching, although done in a very primitive way, to be heard and accepted as the new promised religion. But as the Netherlands Government stopped everything furthering the Gospel, this movement at last more or less died out."

An Eurasian of Emde's group, in his own odd way, became the leader of a group of ex-Muslims.

Coenrad Laurens Coolen had been born in 1774 of a Russian father and a Javanese princess. He grew up an eccentric, a dreamer of dreams. While serving in the artillery at Surabaya he joined Emde, until, being unhappily married, he deserted wife and children and went inland where he took a Javanese woman who bore him six children. In 1829 he turned to reclaiming jungle, making a rice farm at a place called Ngoro. As this remote settlement grew, country people joined him, including fugitives from justice.

Coolen taught them a mixture of Javanese lore and Christianity. No plowing or reaping or building of houses might begin until he had uttered a blessing. Some of his prayers were to God the Father or to Christ, some to "Highest Smeru, mount in Java's land." It was a religious life essentially Christian but too heavily veiled in Javanese terms and ways. Undoubtedly he evangelized and obtained converts from Islam. He refused to send them for baptism because the Dutch minister in Surabaya declined to baptize his bastards.

In the late 1830's one of his converts was a *modin*, a Muslim summoner to prayer called Paq Dasimah, who formed a little group of

Christians at his village of Wiung, for if Coolen taught odd doctrines he imbued his followers with evangelistic zeal. About 1840
Dasimah met Emde and discovered the deficiencies of Coolen's
Christianity. He learned of baptism and the Holy Communion and in
1843 he and thirty-five others were baptized by the Dutch chaplain
on terms that they crop their hair and abandon sarong for trousers;
small wonder they were dubbed by neighbors "Dutchmen without
hats."

Many of Coolen's settlement, against his wishes, went down to
Surabaya for baptism. By 1845 the baptized, over two hundred, split
away and after wanderings made a new clearing in the jungle. They
called it Modjowarno and it became the Jerusalem of East Java.

For in 1848 the Netherlands Missionary Society sent out a Dutch
missionary who became the third founder of the East Java Church,
the Reverend J. E. Jellesma. When the ban was lifted in 1851 and
he could begin work beyond Surabaya, Jellesma decided to throw in
his lot neither with Emde nor Coolen but with the new settlement of
Modjowarno. Emde identified Christianity too much with elements
European; Coolen overlaid it with ideas Javanese.

Jellesma was before his time. His thesis was: "Javanese are the
bridge through which to reach the Javanese." Emde died, over eighty,
in 1859, Coolen, just missing his century, in 1874. Jellesma and his
Dutch colleagues and successors absorbed and developed their movements and corrected their course into the channel of regular Christianity. In their hands, and springing from such sources, the East
Java Church became what it has remained: a farmers' church, not
in the least urban; basically indigenous, depending much on carefully trained lay readers; parochial in form, no wild stream but
linked with world Christianity through the Dutch Reformed Church.
There were quarrels and setbacks but the movement spread.

East Java Muslims, unlike those of Madura island nearby, are not
fanatics. Nevertheless, social pressure prevented Christians settling
among Muslims. By the turn of the century Modjowarno was overcrowded. Young men pushed out to the only land which remained
underdeveloped, on the hilly south coast. Christian villages sprung
up and thrived. They were Caves of Adullum—Muslims who were
in distress or in debt or discontented gathered themselves unto

them, and became Christians. The weight of the movement gradually shifted beyond the Southern Mountains.

The Geredja Kristen Djawa Wetan (Christian Church of East Java), one of the thirty-one churches who are members of the National Council of Churches in Indonesia, now numbers about 65,000, more than twice the Protestant strength of Thailand. Whatever its sources or its present position, to the Dutch belongs the honor of making the largest ex-Muslim church in the world. In 1931 it became independent in name if virtually controlled by the missionaries until they were interned by the Japanese, when the church did not suffer, nor did it suffer in spirit during a persecution in 1944.

To the eyes of the Muslim majority it was still tarred with a Dutch brush. In the War of Independence its members showed conclusively where their loyalty lay. Even the people of Modjowarno burned their Dutch-built institutions.

TWENTY-SIX   *The Edge of the Volcano*

The Southern Mountains: neither high nor extensive, dwarfed on the north by Smeru, which celebrates its twelve thousand feet by a supercilious spiral of smoke. The Southern Mountains guard the Indian Ocean, and now, the sun behind us, we looked on distant waves beating around offshore rocks. The next landfall would be Antarctica. If you turned southwest, Australia lay the distance we had come from Singapore, 850 miles.

We began the descent, an adequate road but rough for Peter's car. Peter, an Englishman, was driving us, his wife, his small son, his small son's Teddy bear, and a Javanese friend to one of the Christian villages. The mountains brought no sense of desolation. We continued to pass strings of small white houses, furnished with table and chairs, since the Javanese do not sit on the floor, and above each, in a cage attached by rope and pulleys to a tall pole, sat a parrot. The jungle thickened slightly; the road twisted down, and at the head of a valley we found ourselves under the palms in sight of a white rectangular church severe of line but imposing in size and position.

Peter interpreting, we chatted in the pastor's house and walked across to the church. The interior was austere in the Dutch tradition, relieved by a little colored glass in the upper windows. Behind the preaching desk in the center hung a cross and a face of Christ and the text John 15:3 in Javanese, "Now ye are clean through the Word that I have spoken unto you." On the desk the phrase "God so loved the world" was inscribed in the old Javanese script. I turned round and looked the length of the church. As the eye took in rows and rows of benches it was an effort to remember that we were in a village, and in the heart of a Muslim country. The pastor counted 600 adults as an average congregation, out of the 1,500 in the village. Peter said that on his first visit the place was packed for a baptism service: in front sat thirty mothers holding thirty babies with thirty fathers standing behind, and thirty grandmothers waiting to take the babies when the parents submitted to long exhortation.

The pastor conducted us out of the church, down steps, over a footbridge, and along a neat street. After a hundred yards we turned by the Independence monument on to a parade fronting placid waves of rice backed by a craggy sandstone ridge where are tigers. The mountains behind and the Indian Ocean two hours' trek beyond, the whole place suggested a tropical Shangri-La. The more substantial houses faced this open view, and we came to the pleasant home of the head of the village. Dutch missionaries had created this community. They had gone but their work remained.

The head was a remarkable young man, ruling the whole settlement. He had been a theological student at Malang. When the Government gave autonomy to the group of villages, the inhabitants asked him to sacrifice his plans of ordination to be their head. He was vigorous in manner, with a quick, genuine smile; his skin was fairly dark, lips typically prominent, his high forehead sloped to black hair *en brosse,* and spectacles covered a slight squint. We sat on comfortable chairs and sofas. The coat of arms of Indonesia over an inner door was flanked by indifferent portraits of his parents. The walls had garish Java landscapes.

The head said that he worked closely with the pastor. He approached the job as a Christian service. "When I came," he said, "few of the village leaders attended church. Now they all do, and after service they come back here with me and sit in that big meeting veranda over there and all the needs of the village are prayed for. Especially we remember those in trouble and difficulty. I do not say this to boast but that you should know. Spiritual and secular work is all one as far as my job is concerned. Sunday is kept as a day of rest. Even the few Muslims in the village keep it." In Java on a Sunday the fields are usually full of workers.

Thick sweet black coffee came, cakes of fried rice and coconut, and bananas. Good manners prevent anyone touching plate or cup until the coffee is even colder than when it is brought. Admittedly hot drinks are not the fashion, but I do like my coffee hot.

Pastor and head sketched in for me the background of Islam in Java, for the pastor had been born a Muslim, converted through a Dutch mission school. Except in certain areas Muslim teaching had never gone deep. Men were Javanese first and Muslims second. Peter's Javanese friend Muljono demonstrated this by seizing a banana and pulling at the skin. "This represents Islam," he said, "just a skin. This," jabbing at the flesh, "is the old Javanese lore."

"And what about the early Hinduism and Buddhism?"

"That's there too, deep down inside."

The Christian villages have been nurseries of pastors. They have also produced, for a wide area of Java, schoolmasters, male nurses who are usually the only medical men of a place, and midwives. In Madura almost the only Christians are the local "doctors." It has been said that such went to extend the faith. In fact they lie low, even when absolved by their neighbors from being pro-Dutch. They would show their Christianity by ordered, monogamous lives, upright characters, and good deeds but they kept their mouths shut.

Now they are coming alive. A new spirit is abroad. Many of them have met a man who has shaken them from their lethargy.

It was the same in the village. The pastor had met this man and his ministry had been revolutionized. Neither the pastor nor the head mentioned him when they spoke of the new spirit. "Since the past two years people have been wanting to evangelize," said the head.

"Why? How has it happened?" I asked.

"The Holy Spirit, the Lord moving them."

A good Calvinist reply. I could find no other answer adequate to explain the influence of Pastor Markus, round whom the movement centers, an insignificant little man neither eloquent nor clever.

We spent several days in Pastor Markus' district. If it had not been for Peter, I should not have got near him.

In no place in Asia has the white man lost his status as in Indonesia. All over Java we felt pent as never elsewhere except in the Shan States, where we could not be let off the lead for fear we should be picked off by bandits or picked up by police. A white stranger in the Java countryside is assumed to be Dutch. "Why is he here?" they mutter. "To spy!" Not as a military spy, but to examine land which since Independence has been occupied without title.

The West New Guinea (West Irian) question has kept alive detestation for the former rulers. The Dutch colonial empire was efficient, and Java owed it much: jungle almost entirely cleared, roads and railways built, medical services, peace and prosperity maintained. Indonesians felt that this was done for Holland, that their proper station in life was to work for the ruling race. Education throughout the Dutch East Indies was grievously restricted; efforts to promote a single language were frustrated. When finally Holland failed to defend its possessions against the Japanese, the Indonesians threw off the mask of docility. After the war a compromise might have been effected. In that the Indonesians consider the Dutch to have double-crossed and broken word, their great contribution to the welfare of the East Indies, Java especially, is forgotten. "The Dutch got what they deserved," is the attitude, "and not all they deserved."

Once a "Dutchman" proves to be an Englishman, once you have smiled at a man planting rice or trotting by in a *dogkar* or walking beside a heavy, decorated shaded oxcart, and have raised your hand and called *"Tabeh!"* in the customary greeting, he smiles back, courteous rather than friendly, a little surprised at a white man's attention. Follow *Tabeh* with *"Ingresi!"* smiles broaden, words of welcome flow. Once in West Java we were accosted by a man on a country road running through a rubber estate. Production of a British passport, of necessity carried everywhere in Java, did not soothe because he could not read and as robbers were in the district we beat a retreat, he and his gang at our heels, in the direction of the nearest military post. One of the men cut across country, and I expected to find the way barred by roughs. We walked them so fast that the gang leader stripped. At the village he spoke to a man of more important appearance who roughly waved us to the guard post. They believed they had caught spies. The soldiers, better informed, were courteous. On seeing the passport they were all smiles but nearly fell through the floor when they heard how far we had walked. I said, "But we are English, not Dutch." This naughty remark was a huge success.

Javanese have an instinct for hospitality. Peter's car broke down in a village. An elderly gentleman in the Sukarno black velvet cap, a red-brown sarong and an ordinary coat, his wife in blouse and striped brown sarong, came out and invited us to rest in their house and they did not know we were not Dutch. Bottles of orange fizz and coffee mocha and excellent chocolate biscuits were laid before us. Their son came in, a lawyer on holiday. He spoke English. The formal atmosphere evaporated. When the car was ready, the old man said, through his son, "We are so very pleased to be able to entertain strangers—respected strangers."

Christians in East Java are afraid of dealings with the Dutch. A Dutch missionary who visited the villages was asked by the synod to stay in the town. Several of our calls were made after dark lest a Christian should be embarrassed by the appearance of an unknown "Dutchman." And a European who asks questions makes them afraid that in some way they will be suspected of liaison with Holland. Only because they knew and trusted Peter were they prepared to talk—more than Peter expected. A happier legacy of Holland is their high regard for order and dignity in worship and church government; this begets an enormous regard for red tape. It was lucky that I could be introduced as (in their terms) "a pastor of the English state church" and that though a delegate of nobody I carried impeccable Episcopal credentials.

Through Peter I began to discover what had been happening in these villages in the foothills of Mount Smeru where until recently Christians were a tiny, dumb minority.

We called one night on a farmer called Sihardjo. His room and clothes were shabby. His numerous children ought to have been in bed. His wife, small and shapely as are East Javanese women, suckled a two-year-old.

"All the difference in the world," said Sihardjo smiling at my question, "all the difference. The heart is happy"—thumping it. "As a boy I greatly desired to meet the Lord, and therefore this room you are now in was filled with people studying Arabic to try and understand the Koran better." This did not satisfy. He turned to the old Javanese lore with no better result. Years passed. In 1952 a Batak Christian from Sumatra stayed a week and taught him much. In 1956 Muljono, the Javanese who went with us to the Christian village, helped him.

"It was Pastor Markus who helped most," remarked Peter in an aside. "That's the extraordinary part. He never obtrudes, and people forget how much he has done for them."

Muljono and Sihardjo lost small boys at the same period, and in their grief discovered Christ as never before, and threw off hesitations. "There are many difficulties," he concluded, "but the heart is happy. The heart is happy. I'm like Daniel in the lions' den." Roars of laughter all round.

Muljono entered. He has a trace of Arab blood which gives him height and a strong-boned angular face and a restless energy lacking in a Javanese. He dominated the room, extinguishing his friend Sihardjo, and talked excitably, screwing up his eyes, never looking straight at you, never keeping still.

He is in government service. His father had been a teacher of Javanese lore, his father-in-law a strong Muslim with a mosque in his own grounds. Muljono had been set searching for knowledge through the influence of a Dutch schoolmaster in his boyhood and at one time attended mosque on Friday and church on Sunday. With his father-in-law he had "great argument about it and about."

Once again it was Pastor Markus who brought him a clear grasp of Christian truth, and once again he received no mention. Muljono is now a fiery apostle whose zeal inclines to outrun his discretion.

They sang a paraphrase and Muljono prayed. We rose to leave. Muljono lit a cigarette, for in the tradition of the Dutch missionaries nearly every Christian is a heavy smoker. Grandpop toddled in, grinning from ear to ear, dressed in the old Javanese style, sarong, white jacket and turban. "Oh," they said, "Grandpop believed when we all stood round his deathbed—as we thought—and prayed, nearly two years ago. His way of spreading the Gospel is to go into a neighbor's house with a Bible or New Testament under his arm, sit down, and ask one of the children to open and read it. He then expounds."

"Probably very unsoundly," said Peter afterward. "He can't read the Scriptures himself!"

I learned more about the shadowy Pastor Markus.

In his south-coast parish after the war he became involved in an unfortunate dispute and went to prison. Until then he had been a typical Dutch-derived pastor: product of long training, dependent for his effect on such learning as he could muster, long words, a strict orthodoxy, afraid of anything unseemly.

In prison he rethought his message. His sorrows, the unjust accusation under which he lay forced him to reconsider the Gospel he preached. When he came out of prison and was put into another parish, he proved so zealous and effective that the synod recognized in him a special gift for reaching beyond the church. Early in 1956 they freed him of pastoral responsibility, took him from a Christian village, and placed him in a Muslim area where there was no church. Such a step was highly unusual. Markus and two others appointed at the same time elsewhere are paid indirectly from Dutch sources.

At first Markus was a little bewildered and lonely. Within two months he had results.

As Peter said: "He is a child of the East Java Church. He did not do as a Western missionary might do—giving tracts, having meetings. He went about in a very soft-slippered way. He sought out the nominal Christians such as the schoolmaster, or those who had some contact, went to their houses and talked."

One by one scattered Christians took their candles from under bushels and let their light shine before men. One by one Muslims entered Markus' flock. By February, 1958, two years after he had arrived, there were so many converts that a new parish of the East Java Church was inaugurated, extensive, expanding, with a young pastor so that Markus might remain free to evangelize. Converts continued to enter, an important feature being that the typical one was a family man who brought in his wife and children. Often he would be prominent already in his village and thus, almost without effort, a new group had respect.

Several causes of the movement may be listed. National independence and the troubles that have followed—rebellion, economic upsets, roads going to ruin—have produced a widespread hunger for divine help and light. Many older converts were strong Muslims but not well taught or fanatical, and the chairman of the East Java Church said: "Most of the new generation of Muslims are not satisfied with their Holy Book. They do not understand Arabic. They are interested in finding a Saviour, which Islam does not offer. A church that holds a strong belief in Christ as world Saviour is bound to create a strong impression." They seek truth. In conversation converts referred to St. John's Gospel with its emphasis on light. "There is a lot of indifference," said one of them; "there is a lot of searching too."

Christianity is no longer closely identified with the Dutch. Yet I heard of a convert whose daughter announced, "Daddy has become a Dutchman."

Another factor: Markus is an ordinary son of the soil, a complete peasant, and the presentation of the Gospel is Javanese. An evangelistic meeting takes place in a home, not in a European-style church, and is carried on in a way that makes a man feel at ease: it does not begin on time; it goes on to any hour, 1:00 A.M. or 2:00 A.M. or dawn. At full moon the Javanese like to gossip the whole night through.

"Last Christmas at one village," said Peter, "they had a meeting with a very wonderful symbolism which just about sums it all up. The lamps in the room were all turned out. Markus lit a candle and came forward. The doctor, who had been only a nominal Christian not long since came forward with an unlighted candle and lit it from Markus'. The schoolmaster did the same from the doctor's. The village head, a former Muslim, lit his from the schoolmaster's. The four of them holding their candles circled a Christmas tree and lit forty candles on it to symbolize the forty converts in the village."

There is nothing to stop the movement. They all hope that more of the Christian villages will catch the spark, with effects throughout Java. "We are trying to light a trail," said one of them, "that leads back to barrels of gunpowder."

Whatever the factors, they would not have coalesced without Markus, a man, as they say, on whom the Spirit rests.

At last I met him. He was not much to look at. You did not feel a tingle of personality.

Scarcely were introductions over when he was telling Peter the latest news in a matter-of-fact voice. "The Muslim headman of a village thirty kilometers away came in yesterday," he said. "I remember he had called about two months ago when I was to take a wedding of one of his relatives. We had chatted and he took away a Gospel. Now he tells me he has been over since then to a church a little nearer his place but on the far side, but he hasn't found the teaching very clear. He's come back here. He wants to be baptized right away! I have put him off for a bit but have promised to have a meeting in his house when we are next over."

He jumped up to consult a wall calendar. "He'll get everybody in he can, you know. Now let me see, could we go over this Saturday fortnight?" He turned to me. "It's like the Acts of the Apostles," he said. "The Gospel is proclaimed, people believe, and then temporary leaders are chosen from among the people."

TWENTY-SEVEN 🌿 *Indonesian Look-Around*

"I hope you are prepared to be uncomfortable," a man who knew Indonesia had said in London. As we drove up to the imposing façade of a hotel in mid-Java, I wondered what he had meant.

Our sitting room—most hotels in the tropics give three rooms—was small and extremely public. The cheerless bedroom had two hospital beds end to end, covered by dirty mosquito nets. In the bathroom the water closet had no chain, the basin, its glaze mostly chipped away, no plug. The bath, as expected, was the usual cold refreshing scoop-and-splash. There was a shower: it did not work. The wall socket for my electric razor did not work. At least we were a married couple; a single man is expected to share, and in

Djakarta hotel booking is almost impossible owing to permanent residents, mostly diplomats or businessmen who can find no private accommodation. At dinner the meat of indefinite origin was tough, the potatoes cold. The waiter, a charming man, announced, "The sweet is always a banana but tonight we have no bananas."

The lights went out. That was not surprising, as they failed for a shorter or longer time every night throughout our visit to Java.

Next afternoon when we returned to the hotel our beds had not been made; this merely involved placing together two sheets, one pillow and one Dutch wife, a horrible bolster which always spent the night on the floor. The cheerful room boy was very willing to make them when called, and the same next day. He could not see the hurry; it was not bedtime. I tried to be stern but it was difficult. Dinner was precisely as before, a banana included; the third and last night it was garnished with fried potatoes and thunderstorm. The final joke came with the bill, made out to a nice long Indonesian name: *Mr. J. C. Pthereverend.*

Having toured mid-Java, including Borobudur, we took train from Semarang all day, partly beside the sea, partly through great sugar estates with factories and light railways, or rice fields where neighbors in groups of up to fifty or sixty worked together, the women in cartwheel straw hats having conical crowns As backdrop, always pleasing, the volcanoes shaped like the hats.

First and second class are air-conditioned. I had never thought of air conditioning as an instrument of torture. Indonesian railways have perfected it. Their air conditioning works only when the train is running, and at the long halts you descend slowly into inferno, rescued just in time by the train restarting. Later it was inferno throughout. A coachful in Java is given just enough conditioned air to keep alive. As the day grew hotter and the train more packed, the third class, loads and all, spilled down the aisle of the first-class coach, sucking up our miserable ration of refrigeration. Amused though I was to watch merry little boys with chocolate-drop eyes, I found it hard in that atmosphere to endure a brace of peasants blowing hot down my neck. It was necessary to keep an arm firmly on the armrest, or one of them sat down and blocked what little air was left; after all, I had paid for the seat.

Anne got out at one station to photograph the scrimmage, and there she would be now had not a young Dutchman kindly pushed her from behind.

In the suburbs of Djakarta after dark the air conditioning was summarily turned off. Officials forced their way through the aisles to remove the dust covers from the seats. I say nothing of the state of the lavatory. On the credit side: the train arrived on time.

On a four-week tourist visa it was impracticable to go beyond Java, for Indonesia extends across a distance almost that from Los Angeles to New York, and communications are poor. Nor is that all. I made plans to visit the famous Batak Church in Central Sumatra. The first missionaries, Americans, to the Bataks were eaten. Before the Dutch occupied the area toward the end of the nineteenth century, German Lutherans began a work so thorough that the Batak is numerically the largest missionary church in the world. I had heard strong criticisms, heard also that over one hundred Bataks were evangelists among other peoples. I made inquiries about the route. I could have reached the edge of Batakland. And there the military would have stopped me.

I had to be content with studying the general Indonesian situation from Java. This was not easy. Making appointments with official or public figures in Djakarta is like biting at toffee apples on a string with your hands tied. It was the one capital where the embassy was unable to secure a single interview. The embassy at least could telephone, but the wanted man was always out, away, or busy, every specious promise made came to naught. For private persons the telephone was a mocker. The only way to see anyone was to drive across the city and call, preferably before breakfast, make the appointment, and return at the agreed time. Taxis were rare as gold. The usual public transport was by *opolettes*, jeeps or station wagons plying for hire along fixed routes, which you had to know. There were a few creaky three-car trams and former Australian buses and 38,000 *betjas*, a fresh variety of gaudy pedicab or bicycle-rickshaw pedaled from behind, as in Malaya. If a *betja* boy annoys a policeman, the policeman removes his tire valves.

Fortunately I had George Steed. He was able to introduce me to those who mattered. And he nobly gave hours to drive me back and forth.

Christians in Indonesia number over 3¼ million out of 85 million. Of these about 2,237,000 are Protestants. The largest Christian groups are in Sumatra, where they total 7.1 per cent of the population, and in the thinly populated Celebes, 14.27 per cent. In Java, predominantly Muslim, they are only 0.7 per cent.

The weight of Christian influence on the central government and administration is considerable. I was unable to meet Dr. Leimena, one of the senior members of the government who had been in sixteen out of the eighteen cabinets up to that time, but another prominent Christian layman, Dr. Tambunan, a Batak, received me twice at his home in Djakarta. Dr. Tambunan had been Deputy Speaker but resigned to be Vice Chairman of Parkindo, the Christian Party. He is held in highest regard by the state and the churches and has a most engaging modesty and friendliness.

Indonesia is the only Asian state with a Christian Party. "In 1945," said Dr. Tambunan, "when it was decided there must be political parties, a number of Christians met together—I could not be there as I was a judge at Cheribon—to decide whether there should be a specifically Christian Party or whether we should work through others. There were arguments for and against, as at all meetings. The decision was to have one." It had been of considerable effect, he said. Every cabinet had had one or two Christians; it had kept the extreme Muslims from making Islam the state religion; and although in practice the President would always need to be a Muslim the Christian Party prevented the Constituent Assembly inserting a clause that it must be so by law: "This seemed to suggest that there were first- and second-class citizens."

As we were talking on the veranda of Dr. Tambunan's little house on April 22, 1959, President Sukarno was beginning his long speech at Bandung in which he appealed for a return to the "1945 Constitution," a speech which led to the abolition of the Constituent Assembly and to the establishment of direct presidential rule. In his analysis of the national troubles, Sukarno pointed to the continuation of corruption and dishonesty.

Christians owe most of their political influence to their unimpeachable integrity. "As to Christian influence on the government," said Dr. Tambunan, "it is not exactly the Christian churches but individuals, such as Dr. Leimena, who are greatly trusted. You cannot find corruption in Christian officials, Members of Parliament or teachers. We are a group that do not ask so much for favors but do our duty. We have no corruptness." The evidence is that he was not exaggerating.

All Asia is concerned in the future of Indonesia. "A strong Indonesia is good for her neighbors," I was told in Singapore. That she could be strong is plain from her present achievement in lifting literacy from 7 per cent to 60 per cent. The dangers of weakness are obvious to any man walking through the Java countryside where every village has a house with the bright red P.K.I. sign of the Communist Party of Indonesia.

"Practically speaking, there is no anti-Dutch feeling in church circles." These words of Dr. Tambunan were borne out by other men.

Christians of Indonesia owe too much to Holland to allow politics to obscure gratitude, however they may wish to disassociate themselves from the charge of having been tools of the colonial power. Conversely, government circles recall that churches and the missionaries did much for the independence movement by creating self-governing churches when political autonomy was a slender hope. Dr. Hendrik Kraemer is regarded as one of the forefathers of Independence.

Dutch ways have not been removed from the services of the major churches; in the circumstances it would be an unfortunate invasion of political animosities if they had. A service transports you to Holland—closed windows and all. Hymns are slow, prayer is long, the sermon read. An Indonesian way of worship will develop, but must develop naturally. Certain funds still come from Holland, although the former state churches in the Outer Islands, and the chaplaincies, have nothing more from government. The National Council of Churches is rather proud that Dutch missionaries are still among them. A secretary who was instructing me in his own church, the Batak, listed their twenty foreigners, Germans, Scandinavians, Americans and, very coyly, "we have three Dutch." Christian leaders say, "We are open enough and unbigoted enough to want them still."

Compared with old days they are few. Those who go home are

not always able to return. New Dutch missionaries can scarcely hope for a visa. Those who have remained are men who have adapted themselves to the new order. In personal relationships, oddly, many of them in Indonesia seem to have retained a starkly colonial attitude. An American, certainly not uncharitable, narrow-minded, or ill-informed, said: "Most American missionaries who come here very soon become anti-Dutch. . . . I never realized before what the term 'Dutch uncle' really means, or 'blockheaded Dutchman'!" Emotionally the Dutch regard Indonesian Christians as children, rather stupid children, and they maintain the attitude of a school-ma'am. It appears to be instinctive. This factor alone increases the pleasure of Indonesians in the friendship of non-Dutch Christians. One Australian girl completely won the hearts of her local church because she helped to wash up after a social. "We have never had a European do that before," said the people.

My experiences with Dutch missionaries were of the happiest, both in Java and elsewhere, and some I met evoked profound admiration. I recall a talk in Djakarta with Dr. J. Verkuyl of the Re-Reformed Church. His house is on a corner, and our conversation was punctuated by the loud clappers of intinerant vendors drawing attention of householders to the shops carried in heavy boxes on poles across their shoulders.

Dr. Verkuyl came to the East Indies in 1940. To a remarkable degree he holds the confidence of the Indonesian Government. "I am working very hard," he said, "to make peace between Indonesia and the Netherlands. If West Irian is settled, I am absolutely sure the door would open again." When on furlough he had addressed a meeting of the Netherlands Cabinet. His plan, to which he says the Indonesians are amenable, is for a condominium in which Indonesia should have the sovereignty while the management shall be vested in herself, Holland, and Australia.

It is most unlikely, as I soon realized on leaving Java, that Australia or the United States would permit sovereignty of any part of New Guinea to be in the hands of an unstable Indonesia which is inclined to lean toward Russia. It is unfortunate that Indonesia should allow this blunt fact to sour her.

To offset the difficulty of getting in Dutchmen, Verkuyl said they must concentrate on strengthening Indonesian Christian leaders and on obtaining missionaries from other countries: "We have got to be ecumenical." As far as the churches are concerned, Indonesia welcomes men and women, especially those bred in a Presbyterian tradition, who have gifts and are willing to work under nationals. Government, unfortunately, is not so welcoming.

To get a recruit into Indonesia may take years, certainly very many months. The Chief of the Protestant Section of the Ministry of Religion was good enough to say he would see me, and introduce me to the Minister, a Muslim. The appointment evaporated as official Djakarta appointments do, and thus I was unable to discuss the question. The Chief of the Protestant Section, a Sundanese pastor who has held the post since Dutch and Japanese days, very faithfully upholds the government's strict immigration laws, but there is a feeling that the Roman Catholics, whose priesthood is heavily weighted with foreigners, bring pressure to bear in this and other matters and get more than do Protestants.

A decisive voice in all matters is that of the National Council of Churches. Partly to strengthen opposition to the forces working toward making the state officially Muslim, partly because the existence of at least thirty separate churches of different languages over more than a million square miles cried aloud for unity, the Council was formed in 1950. It has not achieved unity such as in South India, but it is of outstanding importance.

The value of national Christian councils in non-Christian lands is obvious. They negotiate with governments, act as fact-finding bureaus, as organs for the distribution of relief from overseas; the list could be lengthened. They are linked to regional councils and to the World Council of Churches.

It would be folly to deny that the World Council is viewed with uneasiness in certain quarters. Apart from those who draw the margin of cooperation so narrow that they reckon the ecumenical movement a work of the Devil, many moderates and men highly regarded do not subscribe fully to the ideas behind it, especially since the decision to merge the International Missionary Council with the World Council.

There is fear that the World Council wishes to be boss, and this fear persists despite the oft-avowed disclaimer that the W.C.C. is or ever ought to be a superchurch. To a lesser extent is the fear that the ecumenical movement promotes hotch-potch theology. And there is the feeling that too many conferences at distant centers deflect desperately needed funds. "Such a waste of money," said an Anglican bishop, in other respects a supporter of the movement. "All that hot air too! Think of what we could do with the money they spend getting delegates to these conferences."

The World Council is as permanent as the United Nations. A strong evangelical in Malaya said, "These national councils and the World Council are a picture of things as they are. We have got to accept that and work through them. If we do not we cannot complain at unwelcome decisions made in our absence." The World Council organization at Geneva and its chief supporters have a slight tendency to treat themselves as sacrosanct, like the Vatican, and to dismiss as "sects" those who will not go along with them.

In Indonesia, discounting pentecostalists, Seventh-day Adventists and the like, several excellent groups are not members of the National Council of Churches. The Southern Baptists could not be expected to join. For them it is too broad a union. "Our emphasis is," said a pleasant young man from Texas, "that you should only co-operate where you can go the whole way spiritually." They do not keep mission comity, preferring to open Baptist churches in the big centers, spreading outward. Wherever there are no Baptists is considered free. The Southern Baptists are one of the wealthiest missions. "Our people at home are blessed with this world's goods. They ought to give. Tithing is the basis of our giving." The Christian and Missionary Alliance operates in isolated parts of Borneo (Kalimantan) and the Outer Islands. Mr. Rudes, the field chairman, whose guests we were at Bandung, pointed out that membership would bring little obvious gain to either side. It would, I suppose, be a piece of tidying, but that is not sufficient cause.

Those who do not support the World Council or its local unit may be in danger of making isolated pocket churches each in its small corner. Yet many who are wary of the ecumenical movement have as strong a sense of the universal church, the Body of Christ. One man on virgin soil of another country said: "From a very early stage the doctrine of the church should be taught, to show that a saving faith is not just for personal enjoyment but brings them into a Body. We must teach corporate worship. We must teach them their relationship to another; that because they are related to Christ they are related to the whole Body of Christ. The third stage is to teach the doctrine of the universal church. We don't want to confuse the ecumenical movement with the universal church, the Body of Christ."

Before flying back to Singapore we stopped for three days in the mountains. We had hoped to visit the most famous active volcano in Java, close to Bandung, from where a motor road leads up to the crater. But in the previous week bandits opened fire on the leading cars of an escorted convoy of sightseers and killed six people. A Chinese Christian couple, personal friends of George Steed, saw their two eldest children killed.

TWENTY-EIGHT ✻► *No Gaiters in a Canoe*

Borneo from a distance seems a steamy, unattractive place. I could never understand why those who worked there should rave about it. Now I know.

From the moment I awoke among the mangroves in S.S. *Auby* at anchor in the Sarawak River before she continued with the tide up to Kuching, Borneo cast its spell.

The Bishop of Borneo was leaving next day on an episcopal tour in the Second Division and invited us to join. Breakfast was served before sunrise, and sharp at 7:00 A.M. the government-survey launch *L'Aubaine* was away downriver. On the left bank stood the Astana, residence formerly of the white rajahs, the Brookes, now of the governor, a country house rather than a palace. To the right on a slight hill was the Bishop's 110-year-old house, and beyond it the tower of the fine new cathedral.

The launch was fourteen registered tons, screw-propelled, Diesel-engined. The foredeck, roomy under an awning, had a survey table, and below was a cabin with bunks, a table, a sink, a kerosene cooking stove and a refrigerator. Off the cabin was a small bathroom the state of which would have greatly distressed Armin Staub. The crew were Malay—a young captain and four others. The bishop normally used Chinese passenger boats, crowded, ugly, slow, airless, on which no European other than a missionary will travel, but as he had guests he wished them to have comparative comfort. There were four of us—Canon Oliver Brady, an elderly Australian who had been Archdeacon of New Guinea; ourselves, and John Crowe, the bishop's young secretary who was out for a year between school and university. The "Year Between" scheme was a brainchild of the bishop which had been taken up by British colonies in Asia and Africa to enable boys waiting for university places to do social or educational work in underdeveloped areas. There were eight or nine boys in Sarawak. "From our point of view an unqualified success," said the governor, "though they probably get more out of it than we do."

After we had settled our things, the bishop read Mattins on the foredeck. When the service was finished, *L'Aubaine*, at 7½ knots, was well down the twenty-eight miles to the sea. The bishop spread out a map and explained the origin and extent of his diocese.

In 1848 Rajah James Brooke, who had been invited to the throne by its then suzerain, the Sultan of Brunei, obtained for Sarawak a man who was both parson and doctor, Macdougall, the first missionary and later first bishop. The Society for the Propagation of the Gospel had built up the mission and diocese. The diocese was now independent and the S.P.G.'s part was limited to finding personnel—a sort of missionary broker—and contributing funds, as does also the Protestant Episcopal Church of America. The bishop thought in terms of *Ecclesia Borneo*, not of this or that mission. There was nothing he disliked more than to hear his clergy referred to as "S.P.G. priests," especially since the Australian Church Missionary Society had recently sent men. The diocese was conterminous with Borneo, the third largest island of the world, but no Anglican work existed in Indonesian territory. In Sarawak, under an allocation made by the rajahs, to practical intents its mission was limited to the First Division where the Land Dayaks live, and the Second Division home of the Sea Dayaks or Ibans, a different race with a different language. In North Borneo, apart from the big towns, operations were those of the Australian C.M.S. at Tawau, mostly among Chinese, and the new Dayak Mission of the Epiphany in the remote interior.

Nigel Cornwall, Bishop of Borneo, is an athletic man in his fifties. He has a square face with Churchillian curves, a strong but not prominent chin, a small mouth, wiry black hair going gray. A face you can trust. He was wearing white shirt and gold pectoral cross and chain, blue shorts, fawn stockings and sandals. His episcopal ring had belonged to the first bishop, given by a descendant.

The bishop was reputed impervious to heat, cold, wet, hunger, and fatigue, and throughout the days to come I scarcely saw a yawn. His unostentatious piety was infectious. He was a most thoughtful host and organizer, just the companion for an expedition such as this.

A few days after our return to Kuching he would be leaving to be married in Colombo. His bride was on her way from England.

The South China Sea was choppy, and John Crowe and the Land Dayak boy whom the bishop had brought as servant, felt it. The Land Dayak, Rabat, sat below with an expression of deepest woe.

The bishop put on a kettle, opened a tin of Macvita and, to my joy, Oxford marmalade, an extravagance explained by the excellent uses of those distinctive jars. The coffee had been left behind— shades of pork chops in Laos. We had tea instead, and watched the lovely deep green coast line and the hills behind. We were cutting across the wide curve where Sarawak turns north. The whole distance from Kuching to Saratok, our nightstop, being ninety-seven miles.

The bishop and I washed up, and as Rabat was now in piteous state the bishop peeled and put on the potatoes. He is a most practical man but he did burn those potatoes. The rest of us sat reading on the deck. The bishop put his head through the hatch. "What would you like for lunch? Cold ham, luncheon meat, a sort of meat roll, fried sausages?" "No," said Canon Brady firmly, "*not* fried sausages."

Canon Brady, Father, as we all called him, was one of those churchmen of stanchest views who yet hold the utter respect and affection of their opposites. Father was an Anglo-Catholic who had been chaplain and confidential friend to an evangelical Archbishop

of Melbourne. He had a profound sympathy with the late Archbishop of Sydney, Dr. Mowll. "An uncompromising evangelical," he
would say, "but—but—Christ came first!" I can imagine that the
saintly Dr. Mowll used a similar expression about Canon Brady.
Father had been twenty years in Melbourne churches when a visit
to New Guinea led to an unmistakable missionary call. "It was like
Francis Thompson's the Hound of Heaven." He responded in
1940, and for nineteen years had been principal of a teacher-
evangelist training college: "All our teachers had to be evangelists
too."

In early afternoon *L'Aubaine* entered a most beautiful estuary
and called at a contrastingly ugly confusion of gray huts of dried
nipa palm: Kabong. The crew said we must wait until the river
filled. The bishop said: "What they really want is to buy fish. A very
good place for fish." The native officer, a Dayak, led us over a
rickety landing stage across a mud flat where little sand crabs bur-
row, through one of the shops on to a red-brick narrow causeway in
the grass, up to the District Office. This green timber affair was
called, in echo of stern days of head hunting and piracy, Fort
Charles.

The native officer was a Christian. It was good to be in one of
the few territories where the word "native" has not lost its dignity;
the Malays and more recent immigrants, Indians and Chinese, are
known as Asiatics. The indigenous tribespeople, pagan or ex-pagan,
are still native in name as well as in origin.

Said Evensong marked the continuation of the journey up the
Krian. Under a sun still strong in a clear sky all faces were scarlet
after exposure to refraction at sea, even the brown torso of the
muscular Malay cross-legged at the wheel was patched in red. Compared with Thailand these waters are uncrowded. Sarawak is an
empty country, and the distances between settlements increased by
the twisting of the rivers, the only alternative to slippery trails. How
the Krian wound I realized when I flew over it. Tides were important factors in the bishop's life. The three books always with him
were the Bible, the Book of Common Prayer, and the *Sarawak
Gazette* Tide Table.

At dusk 6:00 P.M., we reached Saratok, tiny capital of a district
and center of a vast parish. The parish priest, Father Basil Temeng-

gong, accompanied by a crowd of his congregation, escorted us to the mission house close by St. Peter's School. Here we had splash baths and dinner. With his white cassock Father Basil shed a slight solemnity. He was a most intelligent man, a Sea Dayak who had been trained at Bishop's College, Calcutta and in England at Mirfield and an East End parish. He spoke excellent English with a Mirfield accent, that slight drawl combined with a clipped enunciation which seems characteristic of a certain sort of English clergyman.

The bishop thoughtfully had arranged that Anne and I should sleep on the launch, where we made ourselves comfortable on the deck. John Crowe slept at a teacher's house, Father and the bishop at Basil's.

The bishop had already traveled twelve hours and was not at his destination.

Water Rat in *The Wind in the Willows* would love Sarawak—it is all messing about in boats.

Two canoes with outboard motors roared away up the Krian, bows out of the water, a man standing at the prow to signal a rock or obstruction, another at the motor in the stern. We sat in the bottom, the bishop, Father, and we two in one, John Crowe and two Dayaks in the other driven by Basil, for clergy and missionaries in Sarawak require to be expert at outboard motors.

In twenty minutes, at 8:35 A.M., on a curve past a longhouse of impressive length, we disembarked at stairs up a steep bank. At a little house standing by itself the bishop confirmed a young blind woman. We knelt in a room lumbered with water jars, mattresses, bright red rugs, two gongs and a banjo, family snapshots, and magazine pictures royal and ancient. Basil prayed, and the bishop read the service in Sea Dayak; he cannot speak the language but has taught himself to read the services of the church. Irreverent geese and cocks cackled and crowed beyond the thin partition, and mosquitoes, which evidently do not bite bishops, for me made the service a trial. My neighbor obligingly squashed a few on my ankles.

At Kaki Wong (Foot of the Rapids) we spread into a third canoe and the crewmen changed from shorts to bathing trunks. The river narrowed, came flowing faster, tunneled under more forbidding trees. The jungle looked thick but was only secondary, and now and again a rubber plantation came to the water's edge. No estate is owned by a European: the rajahs would not allow it. They ruled the country for its people. Since a rubber boom the natives had made money—hence all the outboard motors. Obstructions increased; we turned a corner and took the first rapids.

Rapids are fun, especially these puny ones. High up on the bigger rivers they can drown the rash or the inexperienced. At the first proper rapid we were told to get out on a midstream rock, and the canoe shot the rapid at a roar and a bound. After that, rapids came frequently. Some were small enough to take in our stride with one tremendous splash, the man in the prow expertly using a pole and driver lifting the motor at the critical moment. At others the canoe had to be manhandled, and at shallows, where we walked in the water, the driver kept the engine turning and the prowman hauled. He would not permit me to help.

Hungry and thirsty we came to Kabo. A discreet pause at the landing stage for the reception committee's benefit, and with cymbals and gong, Chinese firecrackers, and the lay reader in white cassock leading the procession we were escorted through a short path in the undergrowth, past a nefarious open latrine which had been placed there at the instance of the Community Development officer and up the steps to the entrance of the longhouse.

Kabo was a barrack of a longhouse, the most substantial though not the longest I saw, and had been Christian for two or three generations. In Sarawak the native village is the longhouse. Each family has a private home, but instead of opening on to a street its door opens on to a covered communal space the length of the longhouse. Size is reckoned by the number of "doors." Built entirely of timber, Kabo had floor boards with measurements putting to shame the finest Elizabethan gallery. The more prosperous "doors" had excellent paneling, and one or two not only possessed portable wirelesses and pressure lamps but had built an upper story. Through most houses, but not Kabo, runs a strip which is the trail. A wayfarer must pass that way, and if he wants refreshment he sits down and will receive it.

Almost always everybody is related, and affairs of life are done together. Friendships and feuds ripen fast. Conspicuous by his absence from the festivities at Kabo was the Tuai Rumah, the headman. He had fallen out with the lay reader, who was not blameless in the dispute, had ceased to come to church, and would have nothing to do with the bishop's visit. The bishop spent a long hour attempting to mediate, suggesting that bygones be bygones, but the man was obdurate. He had been wronged by the "parson," and was through with the church. It might have been an English country parish.

We mounted the steps, took off our shoes, and entered. Eyes glistened at the array of bottles on the table, but we had to process right round, the lay reader and Basil, the bishop, ourselves, most of the villagers, singing an Iban hymn. At each door the bishop blessed the home, making the sign of the cross. When we reached the entrance again, all knelt for a final prayer.

Then we set to. Every family had bought or made something: bottles of still orange and lager beer, rice cakes, and a fried rice biscuit sticky as it was succulent. We washed and swam in the swift narrow river and next were treated to an enormous lunch. Most "doors" had one or two chairs and some had tables; these had been placed so that we could eat in Western style, forks and spoons complete. The lay reader had killed a pig in our honor. On to rice we ladled pork and venison and lightly boiled eggs, as much as we could eat. There is no hunger in Borneo, or poverty in the Indian sense, and these Sea Dayaks near the coast were among the most prosperous natives of Sarawak. They did not celebrate like this except on great occasions, and the late nights we had on this expedition were not normal, for they rise early and go early to bed. Those who work there are critical of books which imply that Sarawak life is one long feast. All the same, I enjoyed being in the tail of a V.I.P.

We were resting on the sleeping mats laid as beds on the floor upstairs when a storm began, so heavy and prolonged that Evensong and Confirmation did not take place in the church but in the longhouse. The one sheet in the party (brought for Father) made a fair linen cloth across a table for the cross and two candlesticks brought from the church. Candidates and congregation squatted on mats; we were given benches behind. Some children made a row down at the far end until told off by the lay reader. In England my late diocesan recently had stated that he had no authority to prevent a rector bringing his dogs to the parish church. No Bishop of Borneo could hope to keep dogs out of a service in a longhouse.

English hymns translated into Iban were sung loudly; it reminded me of a garrison parade service. The bishop in red cope and miter confirmed eleven candidates, mostly boys, and gave through Basil's interpretation a simple address.

I noticed men down in the semidarkness at the back. Were they backsliders or under discipline? I asked the bishop afterward. "They are from another longhouse," he said. "They are pagans. That is one way the Gospel spreads."

TWENTY-NINE   *Sarawak Storm and Sunshine*

It was astonishing how much time the bishop had to spend in travel. The next morning after early service in the church, a huge breakfast and a call at the school, we were on the way to Ensawa. It could be reached by a twenty-mile canoe trip back downriver and up a tributary, or a five-mile struggle overland. Sending Father and the luggage by canoe, the bishop decided to show us a trek such as he often made in the First Division.

Quite different from Nepal or Laos, a Sarawak trail was all ups and downs—little ups and little downs, but so slippery that even with sticks we were on our bottoms now and again. Two girls going to Ensawa, in sarongs, blouses, and men's brown trilby hats laughed at our antics and were so surefooted that they could give helping hands. I lost count of the brooks we forded, the bamboos we balanced on across mud or marsh; some treks include miles of marsh. The jungle, nearly all secondary, shaded us most of the time. Once we came at a rise on a fine view of blue hills far away.

We were not more than one and a half hours before the trail reached a small longhouse, pagan. A branch lay across the entrance. "It is taboo," said Basil. "We cannot go through." A woman came to the door. "Only a child's play," she said in Sea Dayak. We entered. On a pole in the center was a bunch of heads hanging by the hair, the skulls black with probably a hundred years. "In the first bishop's time they would have been dripping blood," said the bishop. The last recorded headhunting in peacetime had been in 1935, and rare for many years before. In war it was different. The governor has a story of the head of a Japanese education officer whose gold-rimmed spectacles are taken off each day and polished. At Ensawa I asked what happened to a collection when its owners turned Christian. A man replied, "When my grandfather and father became Christians, they had pity on the heads and buried them with prayer."

We came to the tributary, running full after the storm. Almost at once a canoe whined from round a bend, loaded us, and careered back, the gunwale so low that no one dared move a muscle. Ensawa was a smaller longhouse than Kabo, only four families. We were greeted in Sunday best: men in fresh-laundered shirts and shorts; the women in Dayak blouse and sarong, hunched and grinning little balls of grandmothers, gums blackened by betel, young mothers self-assured, all of them wearing what looked like sovereigns. They were engraved with the head of Queen Victoria and the words "Gold medal for jewelry."

Father and the luggage arrived. We were given refreshment and left for another house, scarcely a longhouse, some miles up the tributary where the bishop was to baptize and confirm an adult. The bishop, Anne, and I were in one canoe, the rest in another. It came on to rain. It rained hard. All the Chinese umbrellas were in the other canoe and, looking back, we saw a row of green or black paper circles moving on the water, a curious sight. We caught our cotter pin on a hidden rock and had to stop for repair—in the rain. The other canoe broke a propeller blade and arrived long after.

The rain soaked us through and was cold. Greetings at the house had therefore to include the provision of dry clothes, and after some difficulty owing to the un-European dimensions of Dayak women, Anne emerged in a long sleeved muslin blouse and sarong, an outfit which she reported hot. The bishop and I sat in sarongs, naked to the waist until the other canoe arrived and the bishop could put on his white cassock with purple cincture. For our strong thirst these people had only bottled beer. Neither Anne nor

I likes beer; odd to come all the way to Borneo to drink Scottish lager from Glasgow.

Before a lunch of rice, fried eggs, meat, and chicken the bishop was invited to bless the house in a short service. He said that several such services had been worked out by the diocese. "The pagans have so many ceremonies connected with the farming year that the Christians want something to replace them." The customary snooze took place in a line on mats on the floor, and then the bishop blessed a graveyard, and proceeded to the baptism and confirmation in the diminutive church high on its stilts, very simply furnished, not even a cross, merely a religious picture. I entered toward the close. The bishop was delivering his sermon, a dog was asleep behind the congregation, and beside the font full length lay a man. "He had a fit during the baptism," said the bishop afterward, "and then was violently sick, so they laid him there."

"I did wonder what he was up to." "I expect you thought it was another of those terrible high church practices," laughed the bishop.

The Sea Dayaks, who number over a third of the Sarawak population, and the other indigenous tribes have a surprisingly fair skin—where not exposed to sun it is little darker than a tanned European. They are small but well formed. Their bodies are not hairy like Indians, and their faces give a rather flat effect, possibly because their mouths, which are large, do not have prominent lips like the Malays and their noses are splayed. The forehead goes sharply back to thick black hair which is sometimes kinky. These we were visiting had advanced farther than those in the interior, and the men wore Western clothes. Even when working in the sun they had shorts or bathing trunks, not a loincloth. Nearly every man at Ensawa had a wrist watch. They are easygoing, lighthearted. "The real masters of the longhouses are the children. There is no discipline." To Europeans the adults, like the old English countryman to his squire, combined complete respect with unconscious personal dignity and friendliness.

Back at Ensawa that evening we were given a welcome such as the bishop from his ten years in the diocese could not recall.

Following a bath in the river we assembled for dinner. "What wouldn't you give now for a nice plate of roast beef?" murmured Father to Anne as they looked at piles of rice. The Tuai Rumah, complete with pencil, board, timetable, and lists, dashed about as if a military staff officer. In the communal part each of the four "doors" entertained one of us, Anne and I very properly counting as one, and an interpreter (in intention at least) was provided. We sat at tables loaded with food, rice, eggs, liver, bits of chicken, soup, more than we could possibly eat; no matter: our hosts, sitting with us, would eat afterward and on the floor were scores of friends from other longhouses. Our interpreter was a middle-aged man who had been to a catechists' school twenty years ago. During the war he had been taken by the Japanese to Kuching for forced, unpaid labor. Like all the men in these longhouses, he was a heavy smoker. Neither of us found the other's English easy.

He talked of the rajahs. "The rajahs were *very* popular. But we felt we had to be modern and keep abreast of the times. We are glad to be a Colony." I asked whether Christianity was spreading among the Sea Dayaks. He said, "They go to mission schools and hear the way of religion and want to be Christians." He told me that he would say to a pagan, "It is the will of God that you should have the way of religion."

We all withdrew to the new church built on their own initiative with their own hands. The bishop dedicated it next morning before Holy Communion, a service to which all came, and the singing was excellent, but the sandflies interfered with my concentration.

After Evensong the next item was listed as Chat. We sat at the same table, three solemn young men at the other side. "They are heathen," said the interpreter rather scathingly. They brightened when I made him draw them into the conversation. One said, "I am not a Christian—yet." I tried a little evangelism, but the interpretation was not adequate. The Tuai Rumah came up and said, "Father Pollock, the bishop wants everyone up at the other end." By the Tuai's scheme the six of us went together to each table in turn, the bishop blessed the household who knelt before him; they solemnly shook our hands and regaled us with orange, beer, rice beer, cakes, and biscuits. The art was to eat sufficient to please without getting indigestion.

Speeches, Basil interpreting. The Tuai made a speech of welcome, and the bishop's reply left no doubt how touched we were by the hospitality. He continued with gracious reference to his "distinguished guests," mentioning each of us until his minnows became whales. "And all of them," he said, "are here because of the Gospel of Jesus Christ." He concluded with words specially for the pagans: "On the river today I counted no less than seventeen outboard motors at one place. You would not have seen them ten years ago. I have heard of the thousands of dollars passing through the Community Development shop. . . . When you die, will you be able to take those outboard motors with you? All those dollars? Take care of your souls. . . ."

When all matters had been discussed, it was midnight. Coffee, biscuits, margarine, jam, marmalade, honey, *and* cornflakes were produced. No one could eat any more. Narrow mattresses had been laid at one end of the longhouse, and on one two pillows side by side. The bishop was highly amused. "Look what's prepared for the married!" Mercifully, another mattress came. While the bishop and his companions knelt at their prayers, the chatter at the other end continued, and far into the small hours, breaking into a sleep otherwise luxurious; indeed, I believe some of them never went to bed. Certainly we were all up before dawn, I for a bathe before service, though the river had risen too high to risk swimming. When the time came to leave, another canoe had to be brought into use to keep the loads light.

The farewells were affectionate. The old women hugged Anne. "Come again, come again," Basil translated; "we have loved having a white lady." The river back to Saratok was so full that rapids and shallows passed unnoticed. Dangers came from flotsam, from hidden rocks—and the Tuai Rumah's improvidence. We were in his boat, the extra one. He ran out of fuel and had to trust to the swift current for the last mile to Kaki Wong.

Late on the afternoon of Whit Saturday Anne and I looked in on the bishop at the Saratok mission house; in his kindly way he had given us *L'Aubaine* as home, and Rabat to look after us.

He had a pile of papers. "Adult Baptism applications," he said. "You know the Prayer Book says 'timely notice shall be given to the Bishop' before the baptism of those of riper years. I make the priests send applications to me. It is a way of preventing unwise baptisms." He looked at the next and scored it through. "No," he wrote across it. "It is very dangerous to baptize a girl of eleven in a house where there are no Christians."

In those days in the Second Division and afterward at Kuching there were opportunities to discuss the general work of the diocese. As the bishop said, "The Gospel is spreading faster than we can keep up with it."

The church people of Borneo have a strong sense of their part in historic Christianity. The stream which flowed from Galilee and Jerusalem through Rome and Canterbury flows strong in the tropical forests. The Anglican communion brings them awareness of their place in the universal church, although I detected in some of the clergy that tendency to assume that non-Anglicans receive gifts of the Spirit only accidentally, sent to the wrong address.

The family feeling the Church begets, a settled church order under a pastoral ministry, a consciousness of the Fatherhood of a God of Love, a way of life which may not be unimpeachable but has a foundation of purity and of compassion—these signs mark Christians from pagans. The contrast between darkness and light is far stronger than comparisons between different theologies within the broad stream of catholic Christianity, however deep a man's convictions lie. These signs also are a powerful draw to pagans.

One way the Gospel spreads, as the former catechist at Ensawa said, is through mission schools. In the last century S.P.G. began the only schools in the interior. Now the diocesan schools range from those in villages to the famous foundations of St. Thomas and St. Margaret at Kuching, Engish-speaking secondary schools.

Much depends on the Asian ministry, Dayak and Chinese. I asked the bishop about the strength of these men. "I can tell you where their weaknesses lie more easily," he replied. "Lacking in initiative and enterprise, with the notable exception of Basil." They will not plan ahead. They lean heavily on the bishop for anything, even routine matters often being passed to him. Some of the recently ordained have done well, and he hopes to be able to send more men abroad for advanced training in England or Australia. "Our greatest need is a better educated ministry. I go back to that again and again."

Urban Borneo is largely Chinese, Kuching bazaar almost entirely so. The diocese has five Chinese priests, and four of them are over sixty. The reasons so few volunteer for the Sacred Ministry from the large Chinese congregations are revealing: they are not of the background from which priests and teachers come, the bishop said. Their forefathers came to make money; every possible avenue of employment is wide open and they do not consider that the Church provides sufficiently favorable terms and conditions; the government offers overseas scholarships which have the effect of deflecting possible recruits; objection from parents, including Christian parents.

On the other hand the diocese is encouraged by the increase of funds from within Borneo, over 500 per cent in nine years, yet not enough. "Our aim is to become self-supporting, at least for our Asian ministry."

The bishop said: "Frankly, I am a bit worried about the laity, the laity out in the districts. I feel they are not being fed sufficiently. The same in the towns where they are overwhelmed by the materialistic atmosphere." One weakness inherited from former times is lack of a Bible in vernaculars other than Chinese. The mission has been in Sarawak 110 years, and apart from the passages in the Prayer Book has nothing but the New Testament in Sea Dayak, reprinted in 1952 and widely used, and a Land Dayak New Testament being polished preparatory to printing. In former days illiteracy in the interior was almost complete because (the Sarawak official record states) "it was the considered opinion of the rajahs and their principal advisers that the Sea Dayaks and kindred tribes would be happier and more contented without education as represented by reading, writing and arithmetic."

In the neighborhood of every Christian longhouse are others which are pagan. Father Basil mentioned two districts completely unevangelized. "The priest has to confine himself to the evangelized area."

"Could not teams of laymen go?"

"They could, but they don't."

There is a distinct fear of letting the laity loose. "If," said the bishop, "we had lay teams going out to evangelize, we would have to have the clergy coming in immediately after to give the continuing foundation."

The price of a strongly sacramental emphasis is often a laity which leaves the initiative to the clergy, and clergy are few in Borneo. The coming of the Australian C.M.S. is an encouragement to expansion, as is also the diocese's new North Borneo Interior Mission. The bishop is working toward schools of evangelism. Weekend schools dear to an English diocese would be impossible: the people might take a week to get there. He aims to appoint as canon missioner a missionary of experience and ability who knows three languages; he would travel to centers, gather the laity of the district when they can spare time from farming, and teach.

"But you see the Holy Spirit working, the Church growing," said the bishop. And we did.

After Whitsunday at the parish church at Saratok we went on the Monday to Robon, a place marked quite large on the map. Getting to Robon involved either an overland expedition with carriers, twelve miles, or by river down the Krian to Kabong almost on the coast and back up the smaller Seblak, a total distance of about fifty miles. The launch could just make Robon on the tide but would be grounded if it stayed. The bishop, uttering warnings that it was a most grueling route, consented that Anne and I should walk, the rest to come by launch, which would return at once to Kabong with Father and us. The bishop, Basil, and John, their duty done, would rejoin by canoe next morning.

The trail, almost level, had been made fit for jeeps, and the four-hour walk was hot but not hard. It was memorable because of the extreme friendliness of such people as we passed. Nearly everyone insisted on shaking hands. Coming more or less directly from Java, I found it a moving tribute to the popularity of the Brooke rajahs and their successors, the British Colonial Government.

Robon was a delightful small timber-covered bazaar on the farther bank of the little river and in a tropical way recalled a Constable landscape of the Upper Thames. The reception committee was a little dashed, as they expected the bishop; Basil's message had been garbled. The afternoon journey downriver surpassed in beauty any before enjoyed, and at Kabong we fortuitously coincided with the regatta and next morning watched races between the traditional Dayak war *prahus,* some twenty-four or twenty-eight paddles strong. The winners were generally so excited that they sank.

We were all tired and should have been glad of immediate return to Kuching. By next morning we were equally pleased not to have missed St. Michael's, Plassu.

Two and a half hours in the open sea brought *L'Aubaine* to the mouth of another estuary, still part of Basil's parish, and up it with the tide until we saw in the distance three canoes, and a waving, and heard a Dayak band. As we closed with them, a young man dressed, or undressed, rather, in traditional costume, red loincloth draped fore and aft, a silver belt and bracelet, headdress of humming-bird feathers, danced gingerly in one of the canoes. The bandsmen thumped a long drum similar to those of the Burma Jinghpaws, beat two gongs, and played on a sort of xylophone of circular brasses.

We transferred to the canoes, one with an awning of *puas,* those beautiful red weave mats which are a speciality of the older Dayak women, and turned up a narrow creek through forbidding mangrove forest, the blue sky saving the scene from gloom.

The chief bandsman, the effect of whose red waistcoat and head-dress was spoiled by spectacles and a toothbrush mustache, was the key to St. Michael's, Plassu.

He had gone to live at Plassu in 1956, a middle-aged solitary Christian. He persuaded his pagan neighbors to ask for a school, a mission school. Four longhouses contributed money, cleared jungle, built a school, houses for teachers and huts for children to sleep during the week nights if their parents desired. St. Peter's, Saratok, provided teachers. The government had no part except to congratulate and accept St. Michael's as an unaided school. One longhouse had already turned Christian, and now they had their own St. Michael's Church.

The creek narrowed so that you could almost touch the mangroves on either side. We drew into a sidestream to let the band pass, the "ancient" Dayak dancer busy with an outboard motor, his feathers pushed back on his head, and in due time we landed in the middle of a vociferous greeting of music, firecrackers, and the discharge of an ancient musket which knocked its firer back. From all four long-houses they had lined up, the old men, the young, the boys, in order of size: the old women, the younger and babies, the girls. We walked through an arch marked "Welcome" and shook 144 hands.

The compound had been marked with English notices: "Exhibition Room," "Way to Bathing Place," "Bathing Place," "Urinal." The blackboard in the schoolroom proclaimed "Welcome to His Lordship the Lord Bishop of Borneo and His Company."

That evening in the church, which had the narrowest benches I have ever had to perch upon, the bishop confirmed after Evensong. Because the people could have their vicar to preach only once in a while, to listen to the bishop on his first visit was epochal. And the bishop cut through the barrier of interpretation, making his points plain by actions. He spoke of the Heavenly Friend. "At the start of each day kneel on your sleeping mat" (the bishop knelt on the floor) "and place your hand on the shoulder of your Friend." (The bishop stretched out his hand as if he could feel the shoulder.)

After dinner and the bishop's speech, Basil summed up in English the three Dayak replies. To the urgent plea, "Send us a European to come and live here to teach us more," the bishop could only say that it was "a good dream but dreams sometimes come true."

They danced, shyly. A man did a shadow dance, another a sword dance, the effects rather spoiled by Western clothes. The young man with traditional costume had a fit of giggles when his feather head-dress fell off. And all the time the Dayak music, gongs and brass and drum, clanged in a rhythm rather than a tune, a constantly repeated theme like "Ole Man River."

Sleeping mats on a bamboo floor seemed no discomfort by now, but absence of pillows made the night fretful. Next morning after service we were given breakfast in the schoolmaster's house, the biggest bowl of porridge being laid before the bishop: the schoolmaster evidently knew the story of the Three Bears.

The 144 hands having been shaken all over again, we reembarked. The tide was low, and outboards could not be used. The day was dark, the mangrove roots muddy and gnarled, and the whole scene requires a heavy word like umbrageous.

Anne, Father, John, and I were in the canoe worked by Basil with, as prowman, the young man who had danced. We could not expect *L'Aubaine* at the junction with the river; she would be coming up as far as the tide allowed. Storm clouds gathered. We had umbrellas and believed that the bishop had his. Rain. Umbrellas served for a bit, but we were soon drenched by hard, unyielding rain which blacked out the scene, poured down our necks, and began to fill the boat so that one of us had to be bailing. The engine ran dry and we drifted inshore to refuel. By now, in this tropical country, teeth were chattering. And no sign of the launch. We sang to keep spirits up; it seemed to make us warmer. At last, nearing the fishing hamlet near the estuary mouth, we saw the outline of the launch at anchor. The crew, lazy Malays, stirred not a finger to help us clamber up. The captain was hiding under an umbrella in a bath at the stern.

With an ill grace they consented to turn about upstream for the bishop. We removed our soaking clothes, put towels round our middles, and started a kettle. Ten minutes later we picked up a frozen bishop. He had been reading theology when the rain came—and had no umbrella. He had paddled to keep warm. His fingers were stiff, and when we gave him scalding coffee his lips were numb. The Bishop of Borneo burned his throat.

THIRTY *In the Interior*

The red single-engined Piper Tri-Pacer on Sibu Airfield looked minute from the Dakota as we came in to land on June 2nd. In that frail craft we would be venturing into the interior.

After a fortnight writing at Bishop's House, Kuching, a capital with such village atmosphere that it might be called the Lichtenstein of the Far East, we were to join the Borneo Evangelical Mission. There are five missions operating in the areas allocated by the rajahs: the Anglicans, the American Methodists in the Third Division, whose warm invitation we had no time to accept; Roman Catholics, Seventh-day Adventists, and the Borneo Evangelical, originally and predominantly Australian but now with several British members.

The Malayan Airways plane from Singapore had been delayed at Kuching by radio trouble nearly three and a half hours, and the time was 3:40 P.M. The tiny Piper taxied onto the runway. Borneo afternoons in the interior are notoriously bad for flying, worsening with evening, and though the sun was strong at Sibu the B.E.M. pilot, Captain Harold Parsons, a beefy Australian over forty, had an eye on the clock.

Anne sat beside the pilot, I on the floor behind facing backwards, the rear seats having been removed to allow us more weight for luggage. Harold Parsons braked to a halt, engine ticking over. He went through the pre-takeoff routine—fuel gauges: checked. Fuel valve:

proper tank. Carburetor heat: off. Carburetor mixture: rich. Engine gauges: checked. Flaps: up. Stabilizer: set. "Shall we pray? We never fly without prayer. Lord, we commend ourselves into thine everlasting arms. . . ." Harold in simple, humble words asked for skill and safety. He pulled at the throttle, and we were climbing steeply, not at the maximum angle lest Anne be nervous; the plane can rise almost like a lift. We headed for the coast.

A Shell Oil man at Harold's "Shall we pray?" had said, "Is it as bad as that?" Prayer is as routine to the B.E.M. pilots as any other preflight check. I had heard a sneer that the B.E.M. took a slapdash line, "Trust the Lord and let routine go hang." Nothing could be further from fact. The pilots are skilled, very experienced, and their attention to safety factors as close as that of B.O.A.C. And because they do not maintain a schedule they need not and do not fly in risky weather. I was nervous at first because of unfamiliarity with light aircraft. My confidence increased rapidly. The dozen landings I made in the next three weeks, several in difficult conditions, were painted on with a brush, and if it were not insulting to the B.E.M. I would say that I felt safer in their aircraft than in Tokyo taxis.

We touched the coast at five thousand feet where the beach is used as a main motor road and came down to Bintulu, an airfield of the Borneo Airways Twin Pioneer. Anne and I changed places after refueling, and the Piper VR-WAY (Whisky Alpha Yankee) headed inland toward the hills. Our trip from Sibu to Belaga, two hours' flying, would otherwise have taken three days by outboard-motor canoe up the Rajang River. Whisky Alpha Yankee used fourteen gallons of fuel; the canoe would have taken forty. We were right off any commercial air route. When the B.E.M. began to fly in 1951, no official inland services then operating, the government thought them mad to use single-engined aircraft in the interior, but officers soon asked for lifts.

The evening was perfect, so unwontedly perfect that Harold's estimate of us shot high. It was certainly encouraging when time was important. Without wishing to seem pretentious, for "providences" surely are the birthright of a Christian, I recall on this tour of Asia scores of apparently casual circumstances—luck, if you will—which strengthened our sense that we were not planning or working unaided.

Primary jungle lay unbroken below. Ahead, nothing but jungle-covered mountain and, beyond, higher mountains away toward the Indonesian border. Somewhere in between lay the Belaga River. The world appeared desolate, forbidding as the evening light hardened the beauty. A little plane in such a world could easily lose its way, fail to strike the river, run out of fuel. Behind us was the coast line where you could easily identify position, reach an airfield. We approached a mountain, climbed to eight thousand feet, crossed it. Harold was looking at the map.

"Mount Lumid?" I asked loudly above the engine noise.

"Too high," he shouted back, pointing at the altimeter. "I don't know quite where we are."

"Do you want to turn back before it is dark?" I asked nervously.

Harold laughed, and pointed at the compass. "I'm traveling on course! I will never rely on sight rather than compass. We must be a mile or two too far north."

Almost as he spoke, the mountains disclosed the Belaga. We turned, followed its twists and lost height, crossing over the puny town at the junction of the rivers and on down the broad Rajang five miles toward the new airstrip just built by the government but used until then only by the B.E.M.

Harold made his prelanding check: Brakes. Undercarriage. Mixture: rich. Petrol: enough in tank in use to go round again. Radio aerial in. We circled the airstrip which had been smoothed out of bumpy ground in the one approximately flat place for miles. We flew in, engine purring, across the river and between the trees.

We touched down, flashed by, and taxied back. A gentleman stood there with hair cut straight round the front and done up in a bushy pigtail at the back, and the lobes of his ears stretched into a long ellipse with little brass earrings, holding a large straw hat edged with brilliant red and black patchwork, a broad smile on his face—a Kenyah Christian, Tama Do. Behind were sundry men and women from the longhouse where we would stay. And Ray Cunningham. You could tell he was Australian by the cut of his jaw. He had been mentioned warmly in government circles in Kuching, and I had met him a few moments when he passed through after damaging his leg. Harold switched off. "There's a pioneer missionary for you. And what a missionary!"

Ten minutes in an outboard canoe, and we were balancing ourselves across the mud on a treetrunk so long that I counted seventy-five notches, up to a rough longhouse which stood in the undergrowth on strong timbers twenty feet high and stretched for about three hundred yards. The people were Sekapans, a small tribe, and the place was called Puso's after the old opium-loving chief who lived there. Beside the great log stood the elaborate grave of his father, and archaic guns given by the Sultan of Brunei to encourage opposition to the Brookes.

We sat for the evening in the chief's room. They had recently had a bumper harvest of illipe nuts the oil of which is used in the best chocolate, and showed signs of wealth; a marble-topped table, chairs, a pressure lamp, Thermos bottles, despite the old man's opium. Over one door hung a hornbill's skull and yellow beak tipped with red, over another, antlers. Six months previously the human heads had been thrown into the river. The longhouse had turned Christian.

A Murut missionary pastor had been sent there when they turned. "At first they weren't interested in throwing out the sins of the heart," he said when I met him later, "but only in a more convenient life by no longer needing to propitiate the spirits. No one came to my first meeting. On the third night three came." When he left after two months a hundred or more listened nightly, and now we were there to pick up a man and his wife, who had tattooing all up her arms like an old lady's black lace mittens, to be flown to Bible School at Lawas. They would do a four-year course and come back to be pastor and wife.

The Christians sat around smoking, chatting, and watching us. Most were in singlet and shorts or just a sarong, with straggly hair cut pudding basin in front. They served us on the floor a good dinner of rice, fish, and pork, having already provided snacks. Owing to our late arrival Ray Cunningham could not hold a big meeting; just a few to sing and pray before bed. Our hostess led Anne and me to the unexpected luxury of a double bed behind a curtain and a mosquito net. Being wooden without a mattress it was by far the hardest night of our entire tour; a timber floor at least gives a bit. And they put the puppy outside the door so that it should not disturb us—with the result that it murdered sleep until removed half an hour later.

The next day as usual in a longhouse began noisily at dawn; we returned to the airstrip, waved goodbye to the trembling couple making their first flight, and after the palaver without which these natives can do nothing, took canoe for Belaga. Belaga consists of the local government office, Fort Vyner, a school, and a covered bazaar where the shops are stacked with tins, Australian fruit and cheese, Japanese fish, Dutch and British biscuits, and also Indian and Japanese cloth, Chinese Thermos bottles, Hong Kong umbrellas, and all manner of local produce. And if you want to know where Californian newspapers go when they die, get something wrapped up in Belaga. A man clambered up an orange tree, and the fruit Ray ordered dropped into pineapple plants like enormous thistles. There were coffee bushes and banana plants, and bright sarongs drying on the rails, and a man building a canoe fifty feet long.

We met some young men whose canoe had capsized in dangerous rapids which, had Ray's damaged leg not changed his plans, we should have ascended on our way to his place at Long Geng. The men had lost thousands of dollars of equipment belonging to a Chinese photographer who sat disconsolate in a pop shop, but no lives. Recently they had nearly turned from paganism until thwarted by a group of priests in an all-night discussion in the longhouse. "These people want to become Christian," said Ray, "but lack personal conviction. They are afraid of the others. It's the communal tie. They don't see that the Lord will undertake everything personally for them."

That evening I saw what the communal tie may mean.

The native officer had passed on a request from Uma Kahei, a Kayan longhouse upriver, for Ray to visit them. The whole area was one of new advance Ray had entered in 1957. Some unfortunately had adopted the comparatively new Bungan religion, a Kenyah cult spreading to other tribes which eliminates certain of the terrors and discomforts of paganism without admitting truth. Uma Kahei had retained the old custom but now wished to turn Christian.

We arrived there, a fairly small longhouse of bamboo, and noticed beside the log up from the river fetishes and sacrifices, including a row of bamboos like organ pipes with eggs stuck in the splayed tops, and bunches of dried grass hanging from the timber supports and, in front of the priest's room, a gong and whole array of fetishes.

We came back from a river bath to find Tama Do holding forth to a group of leading men. Neither the headman nor his son who kept a shop in Belaga was present but had promised to come for the decisive discussion. Tama Do spoke Kenyah but Kayans could understand. "By this way," he was saying, "you can go direct to God. Why should we have all these fetishes and things, and try to reach God by the spirits? It's much better to be able to go straight to God. The astonishing thing is we didn't think of it before. After all," he said, his face wrinkling in laughter, "God made us and gave us ears! Don't say it's no good because you can't *see* God. Could we see the spirits? Could we see . . ." and he ticked off the names of the spirits.

This was not a first contact, as in Laos, but the deliberation of a people. The growth of literacy, the steady opening of the interior had made them ashamed of the old custom. The Bungan pseudo-cult had unsettled them. A Christian from Indonesian Borneo who was a schoolmaster at Belaga had taught the children hymns. The conclusive factor was the undoubted change in the other longhouse, Puso's, formerly the most unsavory in the district.

"If we follow this way," said an old man in a loincloth with scraggly hair and incongruous steel-rimmed glasses, "shall we have any one to teach us till we understand?"

"Only yesterday," replied Ray in Kayan, "I had a letter from the head of a Kenyah village away across country saying he feels the Lord is calling him to preach to Kayans." He read out the letter: the man's village was many days off but only an hour by air.

Everything depended on the headman and his son. "We can't do anything without them," the people said. "What we decide on our own doesn't matter. We can't just decide on our own." The headman apparently was prevaricating.

"He wants to say farewell to the spirits slowly," complained a man in bathing pants and a circlet of leopard skin decorated with hornbill feathers. "He wants to be able to call on them again. What's the good of that?"

"If we are going to trust the new God, we must trust Him wholly," said another.

Tama Do said: "The truth is, once we trust the Lord Jesus the others can't come back and interfere. They are afraid to come near Jesus."

In the inner room over a poor dinner served by the head's women assisted by a typical Sarawak cat which, Manx-like, has a stump for a tail, Tama Do remarked: "This place seems all of one mind. There seems no opposition at all. They said to me, 'We all want to go ahead. If we can get the head's agreement tonight we will all become Christians tomorrow.' "

As at Puso's it would at first be more a turning away from the old custom, with its attendant inconveniences, than deep faith. The mission works on the belief that some will come to genuine personal experience of the new life in Christ. "Whenever we go to a new place, we are looking for the two or three to whom the gifts of the Spirit are being given—not the fruits of the Spirit; many should show these—but the gifts, so that they shall be 'able to teach others also.' "

The head's son, Nyipa, but not the head, came bustling in. Before the meeting, cups of Lipton's tea were brought us from the family's best china. The young head took off his shirt and made himself comfortable. Ray unfolded picture posters, and taught. Someone occasionally smacked a midge, or a puppy gave a yelp. Ants scurried along the windowledge. "If anyone has got a log stopping the river," he concluded, "do tell me now and we will talk until it is clear." The situation was straightforward. Everyone wished to turn, but no one might until the head gave the word. Before bed they decided to beard him next morning.

We visited him ourselves in Belaga before they came. The old man stood outside his shop in a thin white sarong over dark pants, his bare trunk plump, his hair falling over his shoulder. He would not look Ray in the face, and fingered his chin thoughtfully. Ray appeared to bring him near decision, and the head said, "You go to the airstrip to meet the plane, and when you are back we shall have discussed it and will let you know the verdict."

By the afternoon when we had to fly away, the village was still arguing with the old man, sitting and standing all over the shop.

"He was on the verge of getting angry," said Ray. "It was best for me to leave."

All ended well. Months later in Japan I heard that the longhouse had turned. "I believe the headman was persuaded only next day," wrote Ray. "His son and all the rest were so insistent that he agreed, and Nyipa sent a telegram to Lawas. Before the telegram got through, we had arranged for the two Kenyahs from the Baram, Tama Pudun and a young companion, to be flown over. They taught and prayed and went from room to room to clean out all the evil stuff. Tama Pudun was amazed at the quantity of fetishes and religious trappings. . . . Their testimony before government and others at Belaga seems to be good. It reflects the benefit of steady shepherding from the start."

Ray Cunningham, the same age as myself, had been serving in the Royal Australian Engineers in New Guinea during the war when the words and teaching of a Papuan Christian changed the course of his life.

Ray's slight figure, well-brushed black hair, and his neatness do not proclaim the pioneer, nor do his deep brown eyes and the wrinkle which generally puckers his brow reveal the tremendous determination in his character. He takes no unnecessary risks, nor does he refuse to carry comforts such as a stretcher to sleep in longhouses if circumstances allow, thus showing himself a true pioneer, not an adventurer. Ray and his wife, whose fair hair, blue eyes, and figure make her seem frail for such assignments, speak three Borneo languages each and both are able translators. Ray had been a wool grader, Evelyn before joining the B.E.M. a teacher with an economics degree. Their little girl was nearly one when we were there.

In 1957 the Cunninghams were at Lio Matu further north, the center of the Christian Kenyah area. They received a request from the longhouse at Long Geng, and from the Indonesian Christian who taught hymns to his pupils at Belaga, to come over and evangelize this area which was untouched by any mission. Ray trekked from Lio Matu across almost uncharted country. I did not learn from him, but this was an epic feat of endurance, partly by canoe, partly on foot, sixteen days. To arrive on schedule for an airdrop he and his party of Kenyahs did the last days at such speed that they reached Long Geng, on time, exhausted. They laid out the markers. They saw the plane pass over and fly away. The pilot had an unsuspected tailwind and thought he had ten miles farther, in a country of few landmarks such an error being all too easy. He returned, spotted the markers, and made the drop—food, tools, medical supplies.

Ray had worked on his first Borneo airstrip as an Australian sapper. At Long Geng he surveyed and with the Kenyahs cleared the jungle and built the strip. "It was a great time," he said, "a wonderful way to get to know them all." And so Long Geng was opened, duly approved by the Civil Aviation Department.

Twenty-four miles by air from Belaga, twenty minutes' flight. "Lean over, Harold, so that John can see the rapids." Harold banked, and there they were, far below, white water boiling through the jungle. Two days by canoe, or it can be done in one at a stretch. Away in the distance stood the jagged Hose Mountains. Harold circled twice over Long Geng to lose height. Little figures ran to the airstrip which lay by Ray's bamboo house like an extended lawn at right angles to the river. On the second turn I could identify Evelyn Cunningham carrying a colorful Kenyah hat, she and the baby on her back the only white people, as Kenyahs lit a fire to show the direction of wind. We lost sight of the house, entered a shallow valley, emerged over the approach where the trees had been felled, over the river—too low, give her a little throttle—cleared the bank, touched down on the narrow strip, drew up with a few yards to spare.

Long Geng. Certainly earth's remotest end. I cannot begin to convey the sense of remoteness that pervaded the place, not isolation but serenity. The clear blue river, shallow and not too swift and the jolliest to bathe in since Laos; the variegated jungle and low hills changing color with the sun; the two rough longhouses a few hundred yards upstream, the one on the near bank being Christian, turned out of the other which follows the Bungan cult. The people are more slit-eyed and round-faced than the Kayans or Sea Dayaks. The women wore fez-like hats of straw weave and the married walked bare-breasted. Richer girls and women carried in each elongated ear up to twenty-five or thirty brass rings. Some had bone bracelets or bead necklaces.

These cheerfully noisy but not very clean people (they bathe daily but chew betel, spit, eat messily, and in the pagan longhouse I counted no less than fifty dogs) were a most welcoming crowd even if they took seats as for a play when we fed. The plane in its coming and going brought them all to the airstrip, and naked boys danced in the slipstream.

At the back of the Cunningham's cabin stood their latrine, and beside the latrine a shed for the airstrip motor mower which when not in use was attached by a belt to a generator. The cable from the generator acted as Evelyn's washing line, and it powered the 10-watt 3 BZ transmitter.

Long Geng and all the B.E.M. stations are in radio touch with mission headquarters at Lawas, using Australian war equipment. Every morning at 6:30 A.M., before the daily prayer meeting, the stations tune in briefly to Lawas; requests are made, weather information given if the plane is coming, news passed. "The radio and the plane enable unmarried women, normally in pairs, as well as married women or single men to work in the interior," say the mission. "The loneliness is offset, and though they may see the plane seldom, if anyone is sick they can be got out."

The radio at Long Geng saved Ray's life.

In 1958 he was on a prolonged trek. Evelyn was at Lawas. In a distant longhouse he fell sick, vomiting, unable to keep down food: typhoid fever, though he was within the inoculation period. After three days' misery he faced the fact that unless he could be flown out he would die, and the nearest transmitter was his own at Long Geng—two days' journey. In the bottom of a canoe clumsily navigated by an inexperienced crew he lay racked with pain, constantly vomiting his remaining strength. In one rapid they lost a traveling tin, and for agonizing moments Ray believed the little receiver had gone, and with it his hope of hearing what medicine would save his life. At a worse rapid Ray had to force himself up, take charge, and get them through before collapsing. Toward the end of the second day he ceased vomiting, and when Tama Do's wife at Long Geng gave him a raw egg he kept it down. His watch had stopped. He would have to guess the time when Lawas would come on the air.

At Lawas the English medical officer and secretary of the mission, Dr. Bill Lees, went down to the radio room before time. "Generally I read, but that morning I happened to start twiddling. I heard a very faint voice saying with terrific effort, 'Long Geng, Long Geng testing'—the station had not yet been officially approved —'Long Geng testing. Aircraft please.' " The aircraft was unserviceable. The magneto had failed and the spare proved a dud. Replacement had not come from Singapore. "We nearly lost Ray because we then had only one aircraft. The first thing I had to do was to boost his morale before breaking about the plane. I had to give him a sense of 'we can control that, fix that,' to prepare him to wait. I could tell at once what it was, but if he lost hope he would die."

The mission sent launches to Labuan, but the magneto did not come until Shell flew it in by an air drop. Ray had now waited a week. The weather was poor, but Captain Bruce Morton, the senior pilot, a former R.A.A.F. fighter pilot who was on leave during our visit, knew that this was an occasion for risk, and with great skill got Ray to the Shell Hospital at Brunei where he had an immediate blood transfusion of two pints.

Earth's remotest end. Yet thanks to Harold and the Piper, Malayan Airways and B.O.A.C. Comet, I could have been calling on the Archbishop of Canterbury within three days. In fact, technically (though ideal flight schedules are generally spoiled by weather in Borneo) you could leave Long Geng by the Piper at 9 A.M., local time, pick up the commercial flight at Sibu at 12:45, change at Singapore and be at London Airport the following afternoon at 4:50 P.M., Greenwich Time.

The Air Department is essential to the Borneo Evangelical Mission. "God told us to evangelize the interior. We could do it only by air."

Their transport system operates on a six-hundred-mile front along the Indonesian border. No lengthwise surface communications exist —from one station to another the only land route is down to the coast and back. They gave me a few examples. From Lawas to Ba Kelalan carrying a payload of 540 pounds (that is, apart from the weight of pilot and fuel) is 45 minutes by the Piper. The alternative is to walk, seven days, with the weight distributed over at least six native carriers: 42 carrier days for the one aircraft load. Two missionaries would probably have to go with them. From Lawas to Lio

Matu before the airstrip was made a missionary walked for 29 days. His next trip took one hour and twenty minutes. From Marudi near the border of Brunei to Long Geng is one hour by air, or nineteen days' surface, five by river, and fourteen on foot.

The planes are gifts, the new Piper from an English businessman, the Auster, still in service, from Shell. Running costs are the chief item of the mission's expenditure, though they buy less gas than they would require for river transport. And it would not be feasible to maintain such extensive operations except by air. The Piper, manufactured by a leading American light-aircraft company, is powered by 160 h.p. Lycoming engine and has a ground speed of 103 m.p.h. under still conditions from point to point; the rate of climb fully loaded in the tropics is 500 feet per minute. Weight empty with 2-way 5-channel radio and battery is 1,118 pounds, and the maximum allowable weight is 2,000 pounds. The engine's life is 800 hours.

B.E.M. pilots—they have three—require to be extremely experienced. They are not accepted unless qualified commercial pilots with over 300 hours, if possible more. Captain Parsons came out with 700 hours, was restricted to coast work until he had logged 1,000 and now has over 1,200 hours. A B.O.A.C. pilot's log will be more imposing, but in a six- or eight-hour trip he may make one landing under standard conditions at an international airport; the B.E.M. pilot's single hour may involve two difficult landings on narrow airstrips. He does his own loading and unloading. On the other hand he flies less than does a commercial pilot. The B.E.M. argument is: "Aircraft do not make mistakes—only the pilot. Therefore keep your pilot on top of his form, never let him fly when slightly unwell or against his better judgment. Aircraft do not stop in the air except through faulty maintenance. Therefore let your pilot do his own, but not under pressure. We treat our pilots like artists!"

The result is an exceptional safety record, higher than other operators flying similar country backed by a more extensive organization. In over eight years B.E.M. aircraft have had one crash, without casualties; it occurred after rain on a soggy airstrip, and although the pilot must accept responsibility he allowed his judgment to be overruled by impatient oil operatives who were his passengers.

The interior of Borneo is a strain. The skill needed to fly the first time into a new airstrip in hilly jungle country is obvious. Routine flights are as taxing. Much of the country is featureless, maps are inaccurate, and regaining course after alteration dictated by local weather requires expert navigation. The only answer is perfect knowledge of the geography and meteorology. Flying blind, though instruments are carried, is avoided on principle, and no aircraft in Borneo, commercial or private, flies at night. In the interior, weather, especially in the afternoon, is so changeable that a pilot is continually faced with major decisions: a cloud bank is ahead; he sees a break. Is it a way out or a trap?

On treetops the survival margin of light aircraft is higher than that of a parachute, and the Piper can stall down to as slow as 49 m.p.h. A cutout is very remote, since both aircraft have two magnetos, the Piper being fitted also with a special feed safety device invented by Nate Saint, the young American missionary pilot who was killed with his companions by the Auca Indians. Each plane carries survival kit, but should he be ferrying ladies the pilot has the additional strain of knowing that in the event of forced landing he must get them out of the jungle, and on some routes they might be days from habitation.

Harold Parsons by vocation had been neither a missionary nor an airman. He ran a small upholstery business. In his thirties he felt life was becoming too prosperous and self-centered, and he and his wife decided that they should offer for the mission field. He was past the normal age; he knew he could never learn a language; his gifts lay in the technical, not the intellectual sphere. He took flying lessons, qualified, sold his business and found a job as pilot in an agricultural spraying firm. He secured commercial licenses for flying, for aircraft-engine and for airframe maintenance and, over forty, was accepted for Borneo.

The takeoff at Long Geng appears to head straight for a hillside. Climbing at maximum angle, banking to the right, we entered a hidden valley, rose above it, circled to gain height, and set off across an uninhabited carpet of jungle to the Baram River. The Dulit range to the left was attracting bad weather, and we sidestepped a rainstorm, crossed over longhouses at a bend in the wide Baram, and an hour after leaving Long Geng were eating rock cakes on the Long Atip airstrip, fourteen days away by surface.

Again we had uninhabited country on a northeasterly course with a fine view into gorges and caves as we passed beside Mount Mulu, second highest mountain in Sarawak. Over the Limbang, Brunei Bay was in sight, and the sun pinpointed the distant dome of the new mosque. Over the Trusan, we noted the new jeep road looking better than it is. And so to Lawas.

THIRTY-ONE ❦ *The Tribe That Nearly Died*

"Who is this white man who wants to see you, Panai Raub?"

"Perhaps it is one of the men I hid in the war."

From his home in British North Borneo, Panai Raub walked all one day, three hours the next, took a canoe down the Lawas River, and here he was, washed and refreshed in a white check shirt, khaki shorts, and bare feet. He did not know his age but probably was in the mid-fifties. He had a strong, squarish body and face, surprisingly brown skin, a broad forehead topped by thinning black hair well oiled. His ears each had a small hole. He had a slight growth of beard, possibly by mistake.

Panai Raub, a Murut, played a leading part in the most astonishing story I heard in Asia.

He spoke Murut in the accents of the complete backwoodsman. Alan Belcher, Chairman of the B.E.M., translated for me as we sat in the shade outside one of the houses of the Bible School before church on Sunday morning. "I was then a young married man," Panai Raub began, "over twenty-five years ago in Dutch Borneo. I was just the same as all the others, loose morals, drinking, smoking, and adultery."

The Muruts' homeland was over the border, but many had migrated into Sarawak. They were Rajah Brooke's problem tribe. Muruts were so steeped in animism that farming was almost impossible; the start of the season would be endlessly delayed because no one had seen the omen bird; a site cleared by burning the undergrowth and felling the trees would be abandoned unplanted at the bark of a barking deer. A snake as the paddy ripened was a message from the spirits to leave the fields unguarded; monkeys and deer could ruin the crop, rather than have the spirits angered.

Life was devastatingly subject to the spirits. During pregnancy neither a woman nor her husband might eat certain foods and neither might sleep during rain—this in Borneo. Worse, most of such wretched rice as was harvested went into highly intoxicating rice beer which was drunk in constant pagan feasts lasting up to five days. Government officially estimated the whole community, except the dogs, to be drunk a hundred days in a year.

Malnutrition, disease, high death and low birth rates: the rajah decided that if the moral and physical bankruptcy of the Muruts were not to infect other tribes the one course was to draw around them a *cordon sanitaire* and leave them to die out.

As Panai Raub began his story, Muruts were streaming across the wide airstrip to the church.

"We were clearing the undergrowth for the new season's farming when we heard of a wonderful white man they called Tuan Change because he changed wicked natives and said they could have a new life. He was on an island off the coast. 'We will go down and get him here,' said some. 'How can we go?' said others. 'That is where the white men live.' Nothing was done."

Tuan Change was a young American called Prestwood, of the Christian and Missionary Alliance. He must have been a remarkable character to create this impression when a bare year out of the United States before he had even grasped Malay. He died as the result of a river accident shortly after release from Japanese internment.

"When," Panai Raub continued, "I heard 'way up in the hills, in the midst of all that drinking and fear of the spirits, about change and new life I just could not sleep at nights for desire. Two months later when we were felling the big timber we heard that Tuan Change was downstream. We all went to meet him, taking our sick. On the way everyone squabbled as to who should be first to meet him. I got in front. When we arrived we saw a big gathering of Muruts, heads bowed. Prestwood was standing, eyes closed, arms outstretched toward the sky. 'What is this? What are they doing?'

we said. The praying stopped. Prestwood greeted us. Of course, in those days we were all just in loincloths. I sat down right at his feet. It was already late, and Prestwood, who used one of the few educated Muruts as interpreter, said, 'You all go and eat and we will have a meeting this evening.' I said: 'I am not losing my place. I will eat tomorrow.' " Panai Raub laughed loudly at the memory.

"The meeting began. Prestwood unfolded some pictures. We all surged forward. I was right in front and could hear every word. Some of the others could not. He preached on the Resurrection, with amazing effect on the crowd. Right from the beginning it hit me"— and here he became excited as he told—"I was just drinking it in. When I first heard the Word I believed. I have believed from then right until now.

"After that first night we went home. We were at the divide of a river and we traveled one way, he the other." Prestwood went to the United States, married, returned to Borneo, and at Panai Raub's invitation came up to visit them.

The next chapter was told me in a wide canoe on the Trusan by a lay deacon of the Murut Church.

Alan Belcher had taken us by launch in the cool of the morning across the Lawas and by Land-Rover along the new road until it disappeared in a welter of mud and stationary bulldozers; we walked the last two and a quarter miles. A short wait brought the deacon, another deacon driving the outboard motor, his wife, a village head-man and three other men, all Christians. They must needs entertain us in a Chinese shop to cups of tea and rolls of minced venison and rice, steamed in leaves, before taking to the river, and the whole expedition was punctuated by unbounded hospitality.

The deacon wore a trilby and a T-shirt, and his smile was golden because his front teeth were plated with gold. He said, "When news of a man preaching about new life filtered across from Dutch Borneo, we had heard that another white man was preaching the same thing on the Limbang River. And we heard that the Ibans he had settled among were not interested. I was one of those who went to the Limbang to beseech him to come to us."

The year was 1933 and the white man Hudson Southwell. On founding the Borneo Evangelical Mission in 1928, Southwell had

SARAWAK

The Bishop of Borneo and Father Basil

SARAWAK

The Kayan longhouse near Belaga

received permission to settle with his few companions among the Limbang Ibans and had achieved virtually no result.

"Mr. Southwell trekked back with us across the jungle to avoid government officials." The deacon pointed out the spot where the party emerged on to the Trusan. "He found us very willing to hear and he promised to return to live amongst us. We asked him what we should do about rice beer because it made us all so drunk. 'If we don't drink,' we said, 'we can't endure the sun on the farms.' Mr. Southwell suggested that we take a little in a kettle. We tried it but soon turned to excess. After Mr. Southwell had gone we got together and decided never to drink rice beer again. Not long after that, we discovered how to grow coffee."

Southwell returned to the coast and asked permission to settle among the Muruts. The Resident of the division and the district officer were aghast. They refused. Government officials had visited the Muruts once in two years and believed that no European possibly could be risked among such people. Indeed, as far as I could discover the *cordon sanitaire* was officially imposed only after Southwell's visit. The Muruts were abandoned.

Our canoe speeding up the Trusan approached rapids. "The Lord has been good to us," said one of the men. "There is more water than when we came down." Rain in the headwaters the previous night had been filling the river. We were now well into Murut country, and every house was Christian; they do not live in longhouses around here but in small villages.

Panai Raub takes up the story.

"When Mr. Prestwood first preached the Gospel I was so pleased to hear it that I felt I must go and tell relatives the other side of the border. We had been just as big drunkards and as heavily involved in the works of the Devil as they were. I asked Mr. Prestwood if I could go and preach. 'What will you preach?' 'What you did.' He gave me some Sunday-school rolls."

Panai Raub's memory has contracted events. He must have been referring to Prestwood's second, extended visit, nor were the first Murut preaching trips across the border, but to nearby pagan villages. At least two years passed before Panai Raub came into Sarawak. Certainly Prestwood lay at the center of a phenomenal turning among the Indonesian Muruts, and certainly he provoked in them three characteristics which have stayed: an intense desire to be complete, uncompromising Christians, an ability to make decisions without being told, an urge to share their discoveries. Muruts are never people to do things by halves—whether drinking or preaching.

In 1933 or 1934 Panai Raub crossed into Sarawak, one of several native missionaries going in small parties through the Border Range. "The first village I came to, just over the border, a big drinking party was on. They gave me drink. I refused it. 'I do not drink now.' 'Why not?' 'Because I follow the Lord Jesus Christ.' 'Don't you drink if you follow the Lord Jesus Christ? Where did you hear about this Lord Jesus?' 'From Tuan Change.' 'Does he live near the Lord Jesus?' 'Oh, no, the Lord lives in the heavens.' They were very pleased and very keen to hear. Even the old people who had been heavily involved in headhunting and the old worship brought the fetishes and burned them."

Panai Raub visited four or five villages and returned home. His next tour covered a wider area. He went out regularly on trips lasting a month or five weeks.

"When I returned to the first village, they told me they turned out the drink because of what I had told them. I taught as I had been taught. Mr. Prestwood had said nothing about drinking and smoking. I asked him. He said, 'Does evil come?' 'When we drink, we quarrel. When we smoke it leads to seduction.' 'Then as Christians, do not drink or smoke.' Smoking and drinking and the old custom went together—you could not separate them. If a man offered a woman tobacco and she took it, this was the giving and accepting of an invitation to adultery."

When later we went among the Tagals, cousins of the Muruts, Bill Lees was always careful at meals never to pass anything to Anne; in their eyes he would have been guilty of improper advances.

"There was not one house," continued Panai Raub, "among the Muruts which did not want to hear. 'Where *is* this Lord Jesus?' they would ask. 'Where is His house? Where does He live?' The Lord used the Bible pictures a great deal, of the birth, the cross, the resurrection. I was not literate then, and no Scriptures had been translated, only a few simple hymns. I preached from the pictures. His birth for us, His death for us; He is risen, we can be risen with

Him and live evermore. 'Eternal life. *That's* what we want,' they would say. We Muruts had thought that we died and were buried and that was the end of us. When I returned home, those who showed leadership became leaders of the church."

"Why was there such response, Panai Raub?"

"I do not know any reason other than the working of the Spirit in their hearts."

In 1938 the rajah heard that something extraordinary had occurred. He ordered an expedition of inquiry led by Mr. Banks, curator of the Sarawak Museum, and a B.E.M. missionary, Stafford Young. They were up the Trusan from December 12, 1938, to February 4, 1939.

At Tang Lepadan on the Trusan I met Pastor Lawai, a Murut who as a boy of fifteen was Stafford Young's servant and acted as interpreter. "Mr. Banks was a day behind us," he told me. "Mr. Young was surprised at what we discovered. Round here they were not following the Lord fully, though very interested. In the interior some were following fully but some still drinking. The people were pressing to hear the Word of God. They were full of inquiries as to how a Christian should behave, what should be done when they planted and reaped and when there was a death. Those who had broken with the old custom were telling others that there was no need to leave a dead body for weeks in the house until the right omen. Disregard omens. The Lord would undertake. Some had given up adultery.

"At Long Semadoh at the headwaters of the Trusan we met Mr. Banks. Mr. Young talked with him but I do not know what they said."

Mr. Banks is reported to have told Kuching that he was not acceptable to the Muruts because he smoked, carried whisky, and did not possess a Moody and Sankey hymnbook.

In 1939 Lawai came again, this time with two missionaries, Davison of the B.E.M. and an American of the Christian and Missionary Alliance. In the few short months between the expeditions the Muruts had progressed. More praying, less smoking, the end of adultery. Now they were taught to build churches. Davison settled on the Trusan, Lawai with him. "By the time the Japanese came, every village had its church, and some had pastors brought over from the Dutch side." In the early stages of the occupation Davison and Southwell hid in the interior and continued to teach. After the Battle of the Coral Sea the Japanese, less sure of themselves, rounded up remaining Europeans, including Alan Belcher, and the Muruts were threatened with punishment if Southwell and Davison did not surrender. The Muruts besought them to stay and be hidden deeper in the interior. They refused. Davison died during internment.

At one house on the Trusan where we fared sumptuously in a merry atmosphere on biscuits and hot condensed milk followed by rice, chicken, and delicious hot cucumber, our host mentioned that recently the district officer, who must share the sentimental view about old Sarawak customs, had suggested they take up dancing again and the old pagan songs. "No," we said. "Don't you realize these things are wrong? We are not in the headhunting days now!"

The Muruts are neither morose nor sanctimonious, but Christianity colors all their thinking. "God, God, God!" exclaimed a young district officer who had received a distinctly Fabian education, "I want to get away from this Murut country. You hear about nothing but God all day long!"

At the end of the war the Murut church might have dried up and died.

We were walking through the night. The truck to take us from the river had its wheels off; it would have bogged within a mile, as rain had turned part of the road into a morass which continually sucked off my gym shoes. As we trudged the fourteen miles back to Lawas River, carrying our things and the gift of a load of rice, Alan Belcher spoke of the immediate postwar years in the B.E.M.

The Bible School was founded in 1947 at Lawas. The Muruts were past the first stage of recovery as a race but needed establishing. The mission, however, developed factions, misunderstandings and a knack of doing much to achieve little. A medical missionary from China visited Lawas. I met him in Hong Kong, a large, jovial man. He studied the ways of the B.E.M. and told them: "You are a lot of wilderness Christians. The Holy Spirit has already done all that you are trying hard to do." And since they knew their Bibles they saw what he meant. "Slowly we began to draw on the power of the Holy

Spirit," Belcher said, "to learn new ways. The Spirit penetrated our lives. And that made a difference to anything we could do for the Muruts." Breaches in the mission were healed, not without resignations. Fresh standards emerged. Things began to happen.

As for the Muruts, the census shows them a growing people; in British territory about five thousand. And of this total adult population of a tribe which less than thirty years ago was committing collective suicide, no less than one in every twenty is fully occupied in Christian service or training. Adding lay church officials and the like produces the surprising figure of one in every ten Muruts an active Christian worker.

The most significant factor is that nearly half the Murut pastors are missionaries to tribes of other tongues.

THIRTY-TWO ❧ *Spontaneous Expansion*

"We're a jungle outfit. We wouldn't be happy in a city." This remark may indicate why the Borneo Evangelical Mission attracts criticism; local public relations do not receive the attention a more sophisticated mission might allot, and where facts are not given, tales grow.

The mission is punctilious in liaison with government officials at all levels. Dr. Bill Lees, the secretary, has such concern for the tribal people of Borneo, goes for his objective straight as a die like the road the Japs built across the plain from Keningau, has a forthright way of speaking emphasized by a hawk nose and piercing blue eyes, that when we paid a courtesy call on the Chief Secretary of North Borneo I had a slight feeling that the Chief Secretary was on the mat. Mixed with admiration for devotion, hardihood and knowledge of the country is a slight recoil, until officials come under the spell of the charm and tact of Alan Belcher, who to Bill Lees' bulldozer wields a scalpel.

Because the B.E.M. uses planes it is supposed by some to be wealthy. They ought to stay at Lawas. Every effort made for our comfort by Bill and Shirley Lees did not eradicate the feeling that

Lawas was a place to tighten belts. And the general wish to avoid widening the gap between missionaries and tribespeople in the Bible School leads as far as wearing unironed clothes in the compound. Planes do not appear rich to natives; no one in the interior has seen a motorcar or has any standard by which to judge, but a missionary who has four clean shirts in his baggage is parading his wealth.

A small mission working in one country has a limited constituency at home. "We have been through some lean times," they say, "but it is wonderful how gifts arrive just as we need them."

The B.E.M. does not create or serve big institutions. Whatever may be the role of institutions in forwarding missionary aims in the modern world, this criticism springs from a misunderstanding of the function of a missionary society: a mission is not in a country to save taxpayers' money. A government, colonial or national, feels soft toward missions with obvious social activities. And may forget how much is done, especially in a developing country like Borneo, incidental to the primary religious aim. The B.E.M. has a fair claim to have introduced mechanical rice farming in Sarawak; the Bible School abandons desks from July to September for the farm a few miles off. "These are times of terrific change for the tribal people," said Alan Belcher. "If they get an idea a pastor is a 'white collar worker' too dignified to work, it will be bad. Also, if a person is always lazy on *that* job" (pointing to a group at the daily stint on the vegetable plots), "you know he will be no good as a pastor."

And the Mission has played a notable part in opening up the country. Its most enthusiastic allies in the governments of Sarawak and North Borneo are the Directors of Civil Aviation.

The Great Tobacco Legend. Borneo suffers from lack of knowledge in Britain; it is unfortunate that one of the most entertaining writers about Sarawak is not the most accurate. While in the country I read an article in the *Sunday Times* which in all good faith, following the book being reviewed, perpetrated statements about missions anyone on the spot could disprove with ease. But the Great Tobacco Legend circulates in Kuching. "The B.E.M. has told the Muruts," I heard from several people as a recent piece of news, "that they must stop growing tobacco. So now they no longer have a cash crop and the Government is justifiably annoyed."

The facts were different.

In 1957 the Resident was impressed from results in North Borneo that the hilly Murut country would be highly suitable for planting tobacco, which gives a good yield and is light for export. The Muruts would thereby have a cash crop such as the Sea Dayaks' rubber. A district officer was sent up the Trusan to tell the Muruts to start growing tobacco. He met blank refusal: "Lead us not into temptation. If we grow it we shall soon smoke again and be back to our old troubles. You are inviting us to adultery. Why not tell the Muslims to raise pigs as a cash crop?"

The district officer, unsympathetic to missions, returned displeased. When the late Chief Secretary came to Lawas, he sent for Alan Belcher. "I don't want you to fight government over this. Please do not teach them tobacco is wrong." Belcher made plain that smoking had stopped long before the B.E.M. influenced the Muruts. The Chief Secretary asked Belcher to urge them to grow tobacco for others. Belcher declined to attempt to overrule their own decision. He made a countersuggestion. An Indian veterinary officer, Christian, had told him that the Murut country was ideal for cattle.

"Government cannot understand that the Muruts never do things by halves," Belcher comments. "For them it is all or nothing."

"Government cannot understand a Christian conscience," added Bill Lees, "and says the Muruts are an obstinate people."

"It is a constant concern that we should leave behind a church." The tribal churches, the Muruts the largest, have organized themselves on a presbyterian system fashioned on that of the parent church over the border, itself derived from the Christian and Missionary Alliance, a presbyterian mission.

In place of the old drinking feasts annual tribal conferences take place at different churches in rotation; the people listen to convention addresses and the pastors and lay deacons settle affairs. For a week or ten days in December the pastors of all the tribes, their wives, and selected deacons gather at Lawas. They elect the executive and the Ketua, or Moderator. The same man has been elected for several years. They discuss business and problems submitted by the churches. During the year a small committee of the executive functions, and only one missionary is on it.

The support of the pastors by the churches is impressive. Every household tithes its rice and cash, and the annual conference has laid down a stipend scale: "To the pastor we say, look to God. To the church we say, it is your responsibility to support your pastor." The pastors have no legal claim, and some go through hard times and spend their holiday earning wages. If a church falls too far behind, the conference sends a man to rebuke the people; a threat to withdraw the pastor is normally sufficient. "I guess a lot of this is due to mission policy," Belcher remarked, "but a lot of it has been hammered out among themselves." On Christmas Day the Muruts make a collection to support pastors pioneering where no church exists; as soon as a church is formed, support is withdrawn.

Discipline in the tribal churches would delight a Scottish Covenanter, though mixed with mercy. "And the amazing thing in this," I was told: "it all came up through translation." The Ketua and Mrs. Belcher translating St. Matthew had reached our Lord's words on discipline, "If thy brother trespass . . ." "Why don't we do that?" asked the Ketua.

"I suppose because we never taught you."

"Why not?"

"I suppose because it is not done at home."

"It is clear enough." The missionaries were nervous, but the churches having studied the whole of that eighteenth chapter saw that God's judgment leads to God's mercy.

This is preeminently a teaching church. "To teach others also" might be its motto. The Bible School is a cornerstone. Here Kayans and Kenyahs and Dusans, and Kelabits with their distinctive haircut, bright beads, and lobes so stretched that they wrap them round their ears, and their wives go through a four-year course. Muruts still form the bulk of the students yet are accepted only if they are willing when required to go out as missionary pastors. About a dozen couples graduate each year, the supply having at length equaled the demand from churches.

This family concern where cooking, laundering, crêches, and a primary school may be as much a part of a student's life as learning, aims "to train the few rather than the many, that they may teach others and to give them a missionary vision for surrounding tribes. Every lecture is a sermon, every sermon a lecture. Most of the students have a spiritual awakening while they are here. We believe very vigorously that 'the letter killeth, the Spirit giveth life.' "

Into a vigorously expanding church the white missionaries fit almost imperceptibly. One of their principal tasks is translation accompanied by the promotion of literacy, their village schools being later handed on to government. From the moment an untouched tribe is reached, the aim is to discover the language, reduce it to writing, and translate the New Testament; for a start, St. Mark or St. Matthew followed by one or two "letters to young churches." The time taken to complete a New Testament is about fifteen years, and by then the mission reckons to have finished its direct task in that tribe, leaving a responsible, well-taught church. The B.E.M. thus has on hand a series of fifteen-year programs.

The level of a mission's devotional life must be reflected in the quality of its influence. The dominant impression made on a visitor to these tribal churches is not of the initiative of man but of the sovereignty of God.

Adjoining the Murut country over the range dividing Sarawak from North Borneo live the Tagals, their cousins and hereditary headhunting enemies. I was anxious to see the extent of Murut missionary activity among them. Distances in North Borneo are extensive, and apart from one long jeep road down the edge Tagal territory can be covered only on foot, often with three or four days between villages, squelching uphill, slithering down with nothing to see but interminable trees. Bill Lees made the novel suggestion that we should survey from the air. In a flight of an hour and three-quarters we covered two days' driving and seven days' walking.

The Tagals number 18,000. Confusingly, in North Borneo they are known as Muruts and the Muruts as Lun Daye. For clarity I retain the Sarawak terms.

Having had paradise weather when time was precious, I now had to endure more normal uncertainties.

The first attempt was abortive. We waited an hour and a quarter for improvement and took off one morning at 9:47. Eighteen minutes later, from 2,800 feet, we saw the last Murut village, its church and pastor's house, but the hills were angry with storm cloud. Harold climbed to 6,000 feet, and still the cloud. We were above its level at 7,000. It was spreading across the coastal lowlands and stretched inland. "I couldn't get over it," Harold said. "Even if we got over we wouldn't be able to get out of the valley." We took a last look from another angle at 8,900 feet and spiraled quietly down through a hole in the clouds, a delightful sensation, and headed home. Fifty minutes and nothing to show.

We flew up the coast to Jesselton in the early afternoon for courtesy calls on government. Returning we found an opening in the weather, followed the railway through the Crocker Range, and bumped in turbulent air to the Keningau plain and the government airstrip.

Next morning we were flying up the narrow Padas Valley. "Average flying weather," said Bill; "you don't often get it better than this. Shows how you need to know your way around." The valley opened and we saw a few houses near an airstrip, Meligan, the original Tagal missionary center.

I had met Amat Lasong, the first Murut pastor there, a middle-aged broad-shouldered, deep-chested man, very much a peasant with no obvious gifts. The Tagals scattered around had heard about Christianity from the Muruts on the trade route to the coast and as far back as 1947 had asked for a missionary. In 1951 an airstrip was made at Meligan by their labor that they might receive occasional visits; a year later Amat Lasong went as pastor. "To begin with, I was homesick and very afraid. Fighting used to go on between the tribes until the government stopped it. But they wanted me! They had been waiting five years.

"They turned from following omen birds and barking deer. They asked at once to be taught to pray because they were afraid of the spirits. There is a certain palm good for roofing. They believed to cut it down brought death. 'Please don't cut it down. We don't want you to die. We want you to preach us the Gospel!'

" 'God has given everything for use,' I replied, and cut it down. For two months they waited for me or one of my family to fall sick. We did not. The impression on their minds was so strong that, a year after I came, they really did believe. It was then they built a church."

I could see the church, a football field, a school. On the lower hillsides were swaths of lighter green marking the changing annual farms, the deeper the color the more years returned to jungle. Jungle on the edge of the village had been burned off to encourage deer into the grass, to be shot for the pot. Bill pointed to houses away up the hill on the far side. "Do you see that farming area right over there? They walk six hours for church each Sunday. And that one? They walk three. There are more houses here than there used to be because people five to ten days away wanted to hear the Gospel, and migrated here."

Bill had brought his family for two months in 1954 to make a start on the language: Shirley is a linguistics specialist and both have had training. I could see their house where they come back regularly.

Harold flew southeast across a very rough tract of hill country. I detected the line of another valley. "That's the Tomani," cried Bill, "the first time I have seen both valleys at once." Meligan people made visits telling about the Gospel; Tomani people came and listened and asked for a pastor. We were covering in five minutes a two- to three-day walk which involves crossing the Padas, Bill said. "You can either go over on a bamboo raft which has a bore of up to eight inches, because of interior rain. Or a bridge of saplings and creeper between two overhanging trees sixty feet above the water. Hair raising." Amat Lasong went all the way round by the coast.

Government allowed Tomani a pastor in 1956. As the Tagals rebelled during the First World War and after the Second stopped farming and expected the mountainside to open up and take them all to heaven, they were reckoned unstable and their area closed to missions. Each step now must receive official approval.

We could now see Tomani's farming land and a rectangular slice of shadow near the houses. "They don't think they get enough visits," said Bill, "so they have found a strip site. We'll survey it. . . . I say, they have shot ahead! I hadn't realized they had begun. Government haven't sent permission yet. They would have forty fits if they knew how far it had gone."

The new airstrip appeared less inviting from a lower height. "Looks pretty close to this hill here," muttered Harold.

"Looks a bit like a one-way job," said Bill.

"How do I take off from there?" asked Harold.

"Do you want them to swing it a bit down the valley?"

"It's a one-way takeoff down that way. I couldn't get out of that valley. . . . Those trees down there will have to come down."

Bill wrote a note to the pastor, who with his flock waved excitedly. Harold went as low as the ground allowed, and Bill dropped the weighted message through the door. Harold got the Civil Aviation Department over the air.

We climbed again, and flew down the valley. A flame of the forest (or some such tree) stood out, a single blaze of scarlet on the dense green of the hillside. To the right lay very steep country over which Tagals from the next main valley came to the Tomani to listen—a shattering walk, it looked. In a few minutes we were over the river's junction with the Padas, two easy days from the half-built airstrip.

We flew on down the widening valley toward the railway. Three times more I saw settlements where a church has sprung up in the past two years. Bill said: "Notice how the Gospel has spread from the interior toward the coast. Yet people ask what good can come from the interior!"

On that flight I had a distant sight of the mountainous area stretching back into the interior. From Meligan and Tomani and the Padas Valley the Gospel is penetrating far in among remote, backward Tagals.

One Tagal village we did visit—with the first European missionary ever to go there.

We marched in by the tiny church beside a football field to the village house. Watermelon and papaya, as much as we could eat, disappeared in a welter of sucking and pips spat through the floor, disgusting manners for an English country house but in keeping here. They brought cups of coffee; they brought a second round and a third. Every family shared in the hospitality until we were embanked by twenty-seven cups and two large pots.

Bill had warned me that the Tagals generally fed him on little but rice and a noisome substance called Tamba. "It's their specialty. They do it perfectly. Other dishes may be spoiled. Rats cooked with too much fur or python with too many scales." To make Tamba, cut raw pig or fish into small chunks, insert with a little cooked rice and plenty of salt into a sealed bamboo, put in a hole and leave for two months and it is ready to eat. It tastes like gorgonzola stored in mothballs. This village was celebrating the arrival of its first white missionary. With Tamba there was wild pigeon, pork, boiled fish, fried fish, an egg dish picked up from the Chinese as a special delicacy for Europeans, and twenty-seven plates of rice.

They told us how a headman of a village on the Padas, an illiterate, came to visit his married daughter. "He stayed a week and he taught us this way. He had some pictures and he taught us hymns. Now what was it he said?"

A young man in a green striped shirt entered and sat down. "He told us Christ died on the cross and was raised again."

"That is right. And he made it very plain that we should not have anything to do with sin. Specially drinking, smoking, and adultery." (Bill added to the interpretation: "This makes sense when you remember that these are the three great addictions of these people, and lead to other sins.")

"Some of us immediately decided this was the right way. Others wanted to weigh it a while. Some immediately stopped following omens. Some still do." Deacons from another village succeeded the headman. Three men from here went to the Padas and saw a church in action. Then the headman came for two months, and went on deeper into the interior.

It was odd to recall hearing a local government official discussing whether this man should be banned from visiting his daughter. For a year the people had been asking the government to allow them a pastor. Permission was withheld. "Without a pastor we have not always kept regular in holding services."

A Murut trader in our party rebuked them: "Do not rely on earthly leadership. Keep it up whether a pastor or not."

"Would you support a pastor?" asked Bill.

They were insulted. "If we have been asking for one all this time, do you think we do not want one?"

The formal question was put. "Do you want a pastor?" Every hand shot up—literally, two each.

They still wait. The complication is that the village is nominally in the Roman Catholic sphere. A Roman priest came for the first time when the Padas headman's visit was known, and preached. They were not interested. "We do not want a new custom," they told him, "but new life." Administratively the village is linked with another settlement a mile or two away which has accepted Roman ministrations. Despite the geographical separation, government hesitates.

Government officers have undoubted concern for the well-being of their areas, feeling a special responsibility for illiterates such as the Tagals. Demarcations between missions were made to prevent natives being swayed this way and that. The Chief Secretary at Jesselton said, "As the country gets more civilized we realize we cannot keep missions in separate pockets." It is a disturbing comment on the liberty of the subject in a British colony that a request for the pastor of their choice, made repeatedly before a missionary had ever been seen, should not, at the time of writing, receive assent.

In their own context these people have the intelligence levels of any civilized community. The gnome who carried my traveling tin looked in his G string pathetically timid in the town; in the pulpit of his church, in a clean white shirt, he appeared competent and decisive. Another, very much the primitive native when we started, emerged among his own kind as a man whose face portrayed a character of steady dependability. Our hostess was a veritable princess.

And civilization with its materialism, perhaps its communism, is tearing aside the jungle screen.

THIRTY-THREE   *Through the Sulu Sea*

In talk about translation and linguistics I heard reference again and again to the "Wycliffe method." Fifteen hundred miles away I saw the Wycliffe method in action.

If Borneo had cast its spell, Borneo was most reluctant to let us go.

We were in the Dusan country below gaunt Mount Kinabalu, the highest in Southeast Asia, at Ranau, where are a small bazaar, a mission station, a rest house, and a government airstrip. Ranau lies at twenty-five hundred feet, surrounded by mountains.

The agents suddenly announced that the ship for the Philippines would sail late on Monday afternoon, June 22. The B.E.M. do not fly on Sundays except for medical emergency. Ranau to Labuan is only one and a quarter hours' flying time, though we planned to call in at Lawas, and Lawas radio ordered us to be on the airstrip for takeoff at 10:30 on Monday morning. The Piper, Whisky Alpha Yankee, was unserviceable. Captain Cooper would come in the Auster.

The hilltops were in cloud. At 10:15 the Asian radio operator heard the Auster turn back: the pass from Jesselton had a dangerous downdraft and its less powerful engine needed higher clearance than the cloud base allowed. The day worsened. At 4:15 the airstrip closed down. "Ship now sails tomorrow," Ken Cooper's voice crackled over the V.H.F. "Don't worry." He would stay overnight at Jesselton.

Tuesday made a brief, feeble attempt at a fine day. At 9:15 Cooper was expected any minute. "I think I shall get through," he radioed as he flew up toward the pass. . . . "Can't make it. Returning Jesselton. Returning Jesselton." The operator very kindly called Lawas, who reported the ship not sailing until 5:00 P.M.; the Piper, now serviceable, designated elsewhere; weather bad all up the coast.

Lawas called back. "Whisky Alpha Yankee unable to go as designated. Standing by for Pollocks. What is the weather toward Keningau?"

"Totally overcast."

We sat listening to the traffic between the government V.H.F. stations. A party of Dusans took up positions to watch if there might be a landing, the neighborhood's entertainment. Turkeys gobbled at my feet. "Ranau, Ranau, Jesselton, Ranau," came a voice. The operator took up the handset. Jesselton reported the Auster having one try more. Twenty minutes later Cooper announced failure, but almost immediately, at 11:00, Keningau came up with news that Captain Parsons was there in Whisky Alpha Yankee. We fled for a hurried lunch, and at 12:20 he landed.

We circled above the airfield but could not set course to Jesselton over the mountains because thunderstorm cloud rose to 17,000 feet, mixed with thick medium cloud to 25,000. "We shall have to go round. I'll fly up the valley and try to get over. There are two gaps. One may be open." Only part of the valley was clear of low cloud. Harold came down a few hundred feet nearly to the level of Dusan villages perched on the hillsides hemming us in. The turn of the valley showed a barrier of mountain and cloud. Harold was going for the higher pass. As we approached, he could just see over, that the valley on the other side, the Tuaran, was safe to enter, but the gap between the clouds and the pass gave too narrow a margin for the downdraft. The Piper would have been sucked onto the rocks.

Harold extricated himself, banking steeply to port, circled and flew at the lower of the two passes, at 3,800 feet. "This is a very tricky bit, this valley." One small hole invited us on. As the mountain rushed to meet us, the plane bumped severely. We flew between the clouds and the pass with 150 feet to spare, the downdraft pulling hard. The Auster would not have had a chance. We shook in turbulence, but the Lycoming engine lost us little height. "Really dangerous," said Harold as the mountain fell away again. "The most hazardous thing, getting through that gap."

He dropped quickly, for the cloud base over the Tuaran was only 3,000 feet. As the valley widened we had to go down to under 1,600. We were coming out of the mountains.

"There's the sea!" I cried.

"Yes," said Harold in his matter-of-fact Australian voice, "troubles are over. The Lord has been very good to us."

"Superb flying I should say."

"No credit to me. Give Him all the praise."

We were inside the fine new airport building at Jesselton by 1:30 P.M. Calling at Lawas was out of the question, and Harold flew us direct up the coast to Labuan and then ferried our luggage. Weather in the interior looked its worst, and the Cathay Pacific Skymaster from Hong Kong for Kuching, which touched down majestically as Harold scuttled off the runway, was grounded overnight.

Early next morning when the *Ascanius* sailed at last, the hills of Borneo never were more perfect.

Ascanius, Blue-Funnel freighter, Captain Laxman, was a dream ship: the only passengers, sumptuous cabin, shown all over the vessel, perfect weather; and because she was not on a regular run the cost almost nominal.

At Cebu in the southern Philippines, forty-eight hours after leaving Labuan, the master received agent's orders: contrary to expectation he was to call at Manila, after other ports, in a week or ten days. We were tempted to stay, having writing to do, but other factors decided us, and with great reluctance we landed, took a night tourist flight, and at sunrise, nearly an hour earlier than in Borneo, circled over Manila and in across the bay.

If you asked a Filipino, "Are you a Christian?" he would be insulted, 90 per cent of the population being nominally Roman Catholic.

"What do you think I am," he would reply, "an aboriginal?" For despite nearly 350 years of the Spanish church, nothing was done for the tribal people in the mountains until the establishment of American rule.

The Wycliffe Bible Translators' principal Philippine area lay far down in Mindanao, and not knowing that we should be landed in Cebu I had declined their invitation. We were, however, back in the hands of the Overseas Missionary Fellowship, whose tribal workers in Mindoro used this method, and who in Hazel Page, a Canadian, had a highly trained linguist who had worked with Wycliffe in Mexico when unable to go to China because of the war.

To reach Hazel Page involved travel by plane, pony cart, bus, outrigger canoe, and foot. After a few days in Manila, that astonishing city, we hopped from Luzon to Mindoro. The Philippines is a scenic country. Lacking the loveliness of Java, it offers continual picture-postcard scenes formed of volcanoes, lakes, and sea, but the rainy season was beginning and the plane flew too low and the weather was too poor for enjoyment. Seen off at Manila by a Canadian and an Australian, we were met at Calapan by an Englishman, Dr. Jim Broomhall, and taken in a karitela, a high-wheeled pony cart of obvious Spanish descent, to the mission house overlooking a dazzling turquoise bay fringed with coconut palms.

At 3:40 A.M. next morning, accompanied by a Czech, we boarded the one through bus of the day for Mansalay in the south of Oriental Mindoro. I had proposed to travel in the best British Borneo manner, in shorts. "You can't! You must not! This is a former American area, and shorts are a sign of poverty. An Austrian who lived here walked about in shorts, and they all said, 'He is so poor that he can't afford trousers below his knees.' " Not until I was safe among the tribes could the shorts emerge.

A Filipino bus, a long red thing, is designed to carry the greatest number in the briefest space. Retiring age for a conductor must be about twenty-five, for there is no corridor and he must clamber athletically outside while the express bus roars along at fantastic speed. In Luzon on the few main tarmac roads a bus will pass a fast car, and my heart was in my mouth until I saw a Safety Award displayed by the driver's seat. Then I recalled that in this country such a certificate could easily be bought. A local bus in Mindoro is at the other end of the scale. It will stop every few hundred yards through the barrios to pick up bananas or pigs or people. Early on our return journey from Mansalay the bus developed engine trouble. The noise became violent when the driver engaged a rival in a leap frog race for passengers. We fell far behind, and at a shady bus station fifteen miles before Calapan the end obviously was near. They must fill up with water, grind on half a mile, and with an expiring groan deposit us on a shadeless, airless stretch of road.

The outward journey was smoother. At Bongabon the Czech left and a Swiss, Nick Wehren, joined us, seen off by a German. The road degenerated after we had negotiated a series of river beds in the rain. Six and a half hours later, ninety-two miles from Calapan, we reached the little fishing village of Mansalay and at a tiny house of nipa palm, right on the beach, were welcomed by a Dutch girl, Elly van der Linden, Hazel Page's partner in translation.

Mindoro is shaped somewhat like a fried egg, the white the coastal plain, home of the "Christianos," or lowlanders, the raised yellow in the middle the mountainous home of the Mangyan or animist tribes. Of the six main tribes of Mindoro, each with a different language, we were to visit the Hanunoo, numbering some five or six thousand, one of the more advanced. In certain tribes it was impossible to bring in visitors such as ourselves. The people would have fled. The lowlanders despise and exploit the Mangyan; the Mangyan hate and fear the "Christianos."

Next morning Elly van der Linden, Nick Wehren, Anne, and I went to sea in a beautiful pea-green boat, a typical Filipino canoe, twenty feet long with outriggers, a frame of bamboos that ride the waves. The blue of the coral sea blended with the mountains, but wind and approaching rain stirred the water to prevent us seeing the underwater gardens.

We rounded a headland, crossed a bay, disembarked at a cluster of fishing huts, and set off across muddy fields into the hills. My pack was the heaviest of our tour. The path rose, and despite sticks I slipped on a banana leaf and went down like any old gentleman. We crossed a stream and in a shower ascended what can best be described as a staircase without stairs. There were banisters of creepers and roots.

As the gradient slackened we entered a clearing. Sitting on a fence to see if the first shoots of newly planted rice had appeared was a young woman in sleeveless, shapeless blouse of red and white over a short tight dirty skirt, a headband of white and red beads and lips to match—not lipstick but betel juice; her teeth were blackened stumps.

Hanging on to the hillside were the few bamboo huts of Tarubong. A cleaner but scarcely larger hut stood to the left—the missionaries' own house. We turned the corner to the entrance. At that exact moment, round the opposite corner, having come from a village several hours off, walked Hazel Page.

THIRTY-FOUR   🌿   *In Search of Words*

The first task was to fetch water from the trickle of a stream at the bottom of a steep path, carrying it up in bamboos slung on our backs with a strap round the forehead.

The village consists of six couples and their children, and most of them were sitting on the porch when we returned. Elly, a delightful companion on the trail, is never happier than when dangling grubby tribal babies, attending sore eyes or listening to troubles. Immemorial custom demands that if anyone eats all present must have a share, and since tins of meat, fish, or cheese carried up on foot are too precious to distribute in morsels lunch had to wait. Gone was the largesse of Borneo longhouses. These people exist on rice, roots, and a sour banana boiled and eaten with salt.

I was prepared for hunger. Then we heard of the Providential

Cow. I am sorry that a poor tribal woman, and a Believer, should lose her cow. If it must break a leg, it was providentially timed.

After lunch Elly took us down to the stream, up as steeply beyond and through the trees another two or three hundred feet to a hamlet where dwelt a shaman, or witch doctor. He was out but we called on friends. In a murky room twenty feet square, a fire at the far end, were two men, a granny, a younger woman, seven children, two skinny dogs, and three kittens. A meal was in progress. "Will you eat?" they called. We declined. Later they brought a tray of sour bananas. We ate little, knowing that between seasons food is scarce. "I am hungry," one of the men said. "We have no rice left. The new crop is just planted."

This man wore a G string, a torn blue shirt over a filthy vest, and round his neck were cheap beads. We sat on the veranda overlooking the distant sea and the headland, the steepness of these hills above the plain, here very narrow, giving the villages the effect of hanging over the sea. Granny pounded her betel, the younger woman admired herself in a cracked mirror, and the man brought out a small bamboo tobacco box and began to read aloud.

The Hanunoo and their neighbors are distinctive in having a primitive script, a pre-Islamic Indic script, a mystery to savants, which is a syllabary of forty-eight characters like shorthand signs, incised on bamboo and rubbed with charcoal for clarity. Translation into Hanunoo involves mastering and adapting this primitive script; an American scholar had made a beginning, but Hazel and Elly have got further.

"It is a love song," the man said. "This is a very old language. I learned it from my father. He learned it from his. . . . Will these Americanos you have brought stay long enough to learn Hanunoo? I could talk direct to them then." He asked Elly to take down the song.

She was delighted and said to us: "It has given me several new words. I am always listening for words I haven't heard to add to my card index."

A nest of very small bees hung above the entrance. "And don't they give good honey—my!" said Elly. Pigs, chickens wandered below, and the flies were a plague.

"I have accepted the Lord," said the man, "and my young sister has. We all have here. The shaman really believes, but he goes on with his witchcraft. I have stopped. I could not make it work."

Elly said that she doubted any of them truly believed. They did not show deep interest and had not discarded the chattels of witchcraft. The trouble was that they had not the New Testament in their tongue. "Very difficult for them to study the Word because they haven't got it. I hope to start translating Mark before I go on furlough next spring. We hope to get it finished in two years."

Back at Tarubong, while our share of the Providential Cow stewed, I read in the latest copy of *The Bible Translator*, a journal of the United Bible Societies, an article about Wycliffe by Kenneth Pike, one of its leaders.

The Wycliffe Bible Translators and the Summer Institute of Linguistics were founded as the result of the experiences of Cameron Townsend, an American. As a young man he abandoned his work as colporteur among the Indians of Central America when he discovered that most of them could not speak the language of the Scriptures he was selling. In the jungles of Guatemala, in addition to normal mission work, he applied himself to learn, analyze, and reduce to writing the local language—without technical training a remarkable achievement. Invalided home, he had an urgent concern for the tribes of Central and South America whose languages no one knew.

In 1934 he and a friend founded a training school of linguistics in Arkansas. Here missionaries pooled knowledge that recruits might learn principles which their elders had laboriously discovered on the field. Townsend's aim was nothing less than the Bible in every language, however few might speak it, "the small tribes hidden away, lost to civilized view." Wycliffe believes that every man needs at least a part of the Scriptures in his mother tongue, even when knowing a trade language, if he is to be a strong Christian. "The growing leadership of a growing church needs the Epistles to give guidance as they mold their culture to Christian basic truth." "Two thousand tongues to go" became Wycliffe's slogan.

Wycliffe translators and literacy promoters work in remote parts of North and South America, in New Guinea, in Vietnam. In Manila the Secretary for Education had in his office a map of their Philippines locations, and spoke of them warmly. Beyond this direct activity is the far wider influence of their summer schools in the United States, England, and Australia, to which numerous missions send recruits to learn and missionaries to teach, under Wycliffe direction.

My head swam at the technical details, but I absorbed enough to realize that the approach is to get at the princples behind language rather than to master any one language as a schoolboy learns Latin or French.

Hazel Page said she had "tasted" twenty languages. In Mindoro, Hanunoo is her third, for the O.M.F. operate over the whole island. "I want to go for *details,* details of sounds and so on. To listen, and not just to be told what to learn. Wycliffe's strong point is to listen to what is going on right now, what they say as they cook and mend things and tell the children what to do. And then use that, the everyday speech, as an instrument to get the message of salvation across. People who are not Wycliffe-trained wait for those who have learned long before to come and tell them the grammar and syntax and give reasons. That's no good if it is an unknown language. If you're Wycliffe trained you are more anxious to figure it out yourself."

The whole village gathered that night in the headman's house, the men against the far wall, the women nearer the door. The matriarch leaned against a wooden pillar. "You must come into the light," she called to youths. "We must be able to see you." Hurricane lamps lit shadowy brown bodies and muddy feet, and touched a red headband there, a red blouse here, and gold in the one safe place—their teeth. Baskets, red cloth, a large sheaf knife, a cradle of creeper hung from the roof. A woman fed her baby; a black cat washed its paws; dogs slept.

Hazel and Elly had notebooks at the ready. Hymns were sung to chant-like tunes rather uncertainly, one after another. A woman who swayed as they sung saw her child beat time. She remarked, "He is *bouncing*." Instantly the word was in both notebooks. The fifth or sixth hymn caused difficulty. "I cannot *sing-the-tune*," grunted a toothless old man sitting hunched in a coat. Down went the word. After hymns a tribesman prayed and Elly read a Scripture portion in Tagalog, the trade language, and gave a quarter of an hour's talk in Hanunoo. Some discussion followed on whether a Christian (or a Believer, as they say, to distinguish from "Christianos," synonymous with lowlander) should chew betel. A woman, fast asleep, woke up at the yap of a puppy playing with her baby. The closing prayer, by another tribesman, continued at least four minutes, and the two ladies, alert even when at prayer, noted new words.

The next day I watched Hazel at work with an informant.

After a comfortable night on the floor of the hut which seemed suspended between the stars and the twinkling lights of the fishing boats, we had left Elly at Tarubong and trekked five hours up and down until we reached Binli where Hazel had another little house.

Hazel Page, whose home is in British Columbia, looks younger than her years and taller than her inches, has fair hair and a fresh complexion which the sun affected little. She is an untiring walker. "She is very Spartan," we had been warned, but there was nothing Spartan in her manner. She was, as Elly had said, "a good sport."

She sat on the veranda of a bamboo house a little way down the hill from her own. The best informant was out of the village, and this man was willing but unskillful. She read to him in Tagalog the Feeding of the Five Thousand from Mark. "Now tell it back to me in Hanunoo, freely in your own words." As she was still learning syntax, not translating, Hazel did not want word for word but the gist. The informant was anxious to understand, and insisted on rendering it verse by verse. Hazel scribbled in her orange notebook. "No, No," she said at the end of the first verse, crossing out what she had written, "it says, 'there were many coming and going and they had no leisure to eat,' but you have said, 'there were no people and no food.'" She explained it again, and he got it right.

They plodded on, a time-consuming process. He was clearly enjoying it, absently stroking his little daughter's hair as she leaned against him. Now and again Hazel questioned him on a word. If it was new to her she added it to her list. With her usual informant Hazel could go faster, and she has prepared and mimeographed a Hanunoo version of the Parable of the Sower, using the ancient script. When he is fully trained and Hazel and Elly feel that their grasp of Hanunoo is firm, the exact translation will start. The translator must make certain the informant understands the meaning of each verse, and between them they decide on the best words to use. "When a Gospel is roughed out I call in several people, foreigners and local, to go through it together and discuss it with me and the informant. The whole business is almost always a great spiritual experience for the informant," she said as we climbed back to her hut; and she added with expressive mixed metaphor, "They grow like a house on fire."

"Kanmi Ama, kami kanmu anak . . . Our Father, we your children ask you to keep us on the way and safe from all evil. Bring us safe today." Agin stood beside the doorway in the sunrise before we set off on the longest leg of the trip, to Sinariri.

Agin was fairly sure of the trail because he had gone part of that way in search of a bride six years ago. His hair, piled on the head in the fashion of a young lady of the Regency and tied with a natty pink band which flopped over his forehead, could drop to his waist. He wore a pink T-shirt and bright pink flaps fore and aft. He had been a believer two years.

Agin carried my pack, and the gradients made me glad to be free at last. Hazel had things at Sinariri and could travel light too. Agin yodeled with *joie de vivre* as we marched out through the undergrowth and climbed slowly to a high plateau of coggan grass, fresh green on the distant hills but tall and coarse and inclined to make a rash on arms and legs. We passed several small villages. We met a man with a steel-tipped hunting spear. He gave Agin betel nut, and next meeting Agin must make a present to him. Half an hour later we reached this man's village which has a bad reputation. The girls sleep in a little house on stilts. A man serenades with a wooden guitar. If a suitor is favored, he comes and passes the night. Marriage need not follow.

Agin checked the trail. We drank from our bottles, took salt tablets, and walked on sucking malted milk, much to be recommended. The path sometimes was marked by tribal signs such as a stick stuck in the cleft of another for direction; a rotted banana leaf in a cleft stick meant: "Who is stealing my bananas? I'm keeping a good lookout." And another sign, "Please do not burn this grass."

Nearing a valley the path abandoned all pretense and we jumped from rocks, slipped on mud, and clambered with close concentration up and down precipitous slopes. Hazel found wild raspberries and tomatoes and we saw papayas, but the ripe ones had been eaten by wasps. We reached a spring where a one-eyed Hanunoo gentleman wearing a G string and a U.S. Army identification disk politely stepped aside. The trail tumbled into the valley and at the bottom flowed a river, though Borneo would have scorned it.

We splashed up it and forked on to one of the dry beds. A man carrying bows and arrows and a fish basket, accompanied by two women as nearly naked as himself, came from the opposite direction. "Where are you all going?" asked the man.

"To Sinariri," said Agin. "I am accompanying them. Where have you come from?" The questions went back and forth.

Hazel asked, "Have you ever heard of Jesus Christ?"

"No."

"You tell them, Agin."

Agin launched a sermon, waggling his finger. "For example," he began, "we have families and the father and mother look after the children and the children call the father 'Father.' God is our Father and wants to look after us but we can't call Him Father because our hearts are black. So they must be washed." He spoke of Christ's death. "Ever heard this before?" he concluded.

"Never. If it is so, it is good. How did you hear of this?"

"These people have lived with us and told us from God's book."

"Why cannot those two speak Hanunoo?" The conversation drifted inevitably because we were strangers.

Before we left the river the ladies, hungry as they were, kindly allowed me to go upstream to a place just deep enough for a quick buffalo wallow, and after that we scrambled up a rock path and into a forest, emerging, exactly at midday, beside a small house in a clearing. A gruff old man crouched on the veranda pounding betel, his pregnant daughter and a grandchild beside him. We squatted down hopefully. The old man having concluded he had nothing good enough for Americanos sat still. "They will pay," said Agin encouragingly. The old man spat juice, and the daughter brought water in a coconut shell and a reed tray of sweet bananas, two kinds, a pleasant relief, as I had feared tapioca roots. He refused payment when he had done. Hazel gave him the mimeographed Parable of the Sower, and he began to read to himself in audible voice. A bloated leech fell out of my sock.

One steep valley more to be crossed, and seven hours after leaving Binli we walked past the miserable spring that was Sinariri's water supply and wash place; when the villagers scratch too much they journey to the river below. We entered the village to the delight of those who were at home. A man climbed a palm and brought us each a young green coconut. He made a hole and you drank the milk. He cut it in half and handed you a piece of the husk as a spoon; the flesh was soft and delicious. They brought us sugar cane. You cut sections, sucked out the sugar and dropped the cane through the floor, where it was instantly eaten by pigs.

We hoped for rice, for they were busy round the fire in the other room, as dirty as the one we sat in. After long delay the woman appeared with fresh boiled sour bananas and salt. "We have run out of rice and the pigs destroyed our root crop." Spoken with smiles of hospitality, even this dismal speech yielded a word of some new shade of meaning. Out came the notebook.

A pitch lamp guttered feebly in the doorway. The pitch from a forest tree is dried in fiber, wrapped in banana leaf to lessen the rate of burning, and placed in the cleft of a long stick supported by two smaller ones in the manner of a primitive arquebus. One leaf burns for about half an hour, and smells slightly of incense.

We were on the long windowledge, the only seat in the house. I was munching sugar cane, thinking of the baby white elephant of Myitkyina who had a similar partiality, and brushing away the innumerable insects. Agin and Hazel chatted. "When I first believed," he said, "I was not afraid at all. Now I find I am. Afraid of the lowlanders, afraid of people laughing at me, and getting angry at them. I think it is because I am not feeding on God's Word enough." As they had no Hanunoo Bible, Hazel had been giving them a little teaching nightly. When work in the fields became heavy they said they were too tired. "Now I am losing strength," said Agin.

The elderly headman, Ii, entered and sat in the shadows against a pillar. Hazel said: "Ii, I have told my friends you are a Believer."

"Yes, I am." Turning to Agin, whom he had not met before, Ii said, "Are you trusting the Lord too?"

"Yes."

"What good do you find comes from trusting the Lord?"

"People do not boast any more," replied Agin, "do not lie, do not fool around with women."

"How about the Romanos, is it the same?"

"No," said Agin. "Romanos are allowed to swear, steal, lie, anything so long as you go to church and tell the priest. The priest wants your money. Now these people," pointing at Hazel, "they have never asked for money. They don't tell lies about us. If they promise something they do it. That's why we follow them. We don't really follow *them,* it is Jesus we follow but they told us about Him."

"What is this about Romanos? What do you say about them?"

"I do not want to seem to be dictating to you. You are my elder. But I think Romanos chase after money. And they despise us Hanunoos. No matter what we say, if we tell the truth or tell about the Lord, Romanos ridicule us, say we are uncivilized. But I tell them the Gospel anyway, even if when they hear the Word it does not always enter their ears. Some listen and believe but not all will believe."

Hazel said, "That's exactly what Jesus told us in the Bible, that not all will believe."

"I never knew that," said Ii. "I knew I would go to heaven but I never knew that."

Agin described film slides and posters he had seen at one of the coastal bases of the mission. Most of the men of the village had entered and sat along the far windowledge intently listening in the dim light, as Anglo-Saxons in Augustine's day must have listened.

"Oh, I wish people could see these pictures," cried old Ii. "I am sure they would believe."

Banyan, one of Ii's sons, a fine believer, a happy character who had shown us how to use bow and arrow and how to wait for your quarry with one leg resting on the other, asked Agin, "Is it true that if a person whose heart is full of wild animals dies without trusting the Lord, the Devil takes his soul?"

"Yes, there were pictures of a man like that."

"What did he look like, this man with a heart full of wild animals?"

"Like a lowlander! He wore trousers!"

This was rather below the belt. In another tribe an American missionary leaving for furlough was seriously told to ask the President of the United States to send planes to bomb the lowlanders.

Banyan was concerned to learn that men could die without hope of heaven: "There are many in the world that do not know about this. They should know."

Agin replied: "We should show everybody this and many would believe. If they could see these pictures they would know God's *grace*. God is not *partial*."

And he used two Hanunoo words Hazel had never heard. For grace she had always used *pakuan*, a gift. He had used *pabur*. Back at Mansalay, in his smart town suit of short white collarless jacket beautifully embroidered over a vest and G string spotlessly white, Agin explained the difference. You used *pakuan*, he said, when the gift could be seen and touched, when you actually handed it. But *pabur* implied an attitude of grace and favor when the gift was not visible. "I will give you a bag. I have not got it here."

"I have nothing to pay you for it."

"It is a gift to you—*pabur duy*, yours because I feel friendly to you, yours though it is not yet in your hands." Hazel looked up *pabur* in the American scholar's proto-dictionary. It was Spanish derived: the meaning he gave was no stronger than "favor." Before accepting it as the best word for the "grace of God," Hazel would need to test it on others, for Agin might have used *pabur* in a sense not generally accepted by his people.

"God is not *partial*," he had also said. She had taken down his word without knowing what he meant. "It is simple," he explained. "If I build myself a nice house and then build a rotten one for you, that is being *partial*. God is not *partial*. He is not doing one thing to the good and another to sinners. Salvation is a gift for all who will take it."

THIRTY-FIVE ✒ *Manila Calling*

Agin's strictures on the Romanos in the Philippine lowlands were only too accurate. Unbiased Roman Catholics share with Protestants an unsavory opinion of the Christianos of the countryside, friendly and cheerful as they are to meet. Compelled to become Christians by the Spanish, their old animism is close under the surface. Every cottage has a shrine to the Virgin or a saint; the pagan spirit under another name. "It is the idol that is everything, not the idea behind it. Again and again we have been told that," said an Englishman. A Jesuit, Father Bernard, readily admitted this animistic substratum.

The Filipino rustic is as terrified of the dark, of ghoulies and ghosties and gibbety beasties and things that go bump in the night, as any medieval Cornishman. Indeed, there is a close parallel with the elfs and gnomes of pre-Reformation England; not until a Christianized people has the Bible widely in the vernacular will it say, "Farewell, rewards and fairies."

In the Philippines relationship between church and state is like that of France, not Spain. The Spanish domination, the tyranny of the friars, the moderate freethinking of José Ritzal, martyr of the Revolution, cured Filipinos of subservience to the political control of the Roman Church. Fifty years of American rule imbued them with a tremendous sense of the rights of man—freedom of worship, thought and expression. This liberty sometimes produces odd results. A fine new bridge in Manila is still unopened because the government cannot remove slum dwellers squatting on land needed for the approach.

Church and state are kept well separated. "Must the President be a Roman Catholic?" I asked the Secretary of Education, José Romero, former Ambassador in London, in his cramped office noisy with typists.

"Why should he?" he replied. "We have no state religion. It might, of course, be as difficult for a Protestant to be elected as for a Roman Catholic to be elected President of the United States." All good causes, such as the Bible Society, display presidential messages of congratulation or good wishes.

Unfortunately America was unable to transplant its high standards of public life. "Graft in my country is awful," said a leading journalist entertaining us to breakfast at the Manila Hotel. "If only President Magsaysay had not been killed. He was incorruptible. He was leading the nation to honesty."

"Please leave your Firearms and other Deadly Weapons here"—the notice is at the entrance to public buildings, gas stations, factories. It is symbolic of an attitude. I doubt actual violence, apart from election times, is normal—except on the roads. Bangkok traffic could not light a candle to Manila. To step off the sidewalk at a major intersection, even at traffic lights, and dodge the jeepneys, buses, and automobiles on the pavement might in sound and fury be an exercise at a battle school. Hard to forgive is the persistent honking in the early hours; you do not "hoot"; that is a word to create merriment in a city where everyone speaks American.

Eight hundred thousand Protestants beside the fifteen millions, at least, who are reckoned in the census as Roman Catholics may not appear an impressive figure. Not one Filipino Protestant existed before the end of Spanish rule in 1898; and vast numbers of Romanos make no pretense of personal religion beyond churchgoing. "There is not much changing from one to the other," a prominent Catholic layman said. "The attitude is, 'What was good enough for my father is good enough for me.'" He may have been complacent. Much dissatisfaction is felt at the preponderance of foreign priests, including many Spanish, and the religion taught in most Filipino churches and in all but the leading Catholic institutions grates on the intelligence of modern youth. It is mechanical. It is morbid, dwelling on sins rather than on salvation, on death rather than on resurrection, on works more than on faith.

"Three different people," an American missionary told me, "two Filipinos and a Chinese, said the very same words to me within a week: 'I was brought up in a Catholic school but I couldn't swallow that stuff.'"

The Filipino passion for liberty is a fertile field for every shade of opinion, from pseudo-Christian cults such as Jehovah's Witnesses to most of the major Protestant denominations, some of whom have united. "Missions just fall over one another in this country," said a missionary leader. The Filipinos have developed several sects of their own. The Manalistas, claiming two million adherents, call themselves "The Church of Christ"—with effrontery, since they deny His Divinity. They follow Felix Manalo, former Catholic, former Protestant, former Seventh-day Adventist. I tried to visit his cathedral but was turned back by an armed sentry. His teachings include the belief that he is the "angel ascending from the east" in the Apocalypse, the other four angels being Lloyd George, Clemenceau, President Wilson, and Orlando of Italy. Their churches are ornate outside, luxurious within. One is air-conditioned.

An Anglican is bound to be interested in the Philippine Independent Church, known as the Aglipayans from their founder; for it springs from a genuine attempt, following the Philippine Revolution, to make a church which should be Catholic without being Roman. "Bishop Aglipay's great desire was to build a replica of the Church of England," said the Supreme Bishop, His Eminence the Most Reverend Isabelo de los Reyes, Jr., whom I went to see in his pocket cathedral in a working-class district of Manila. "Our dream today is to be a church of the Anglican Communion."

Proclamation of an Independent Church in 1902 brought enthusiastic support which failed to survive immediate difficulties. Roman church buildings taken over on the claim that they had been erected by forced labor and thus belonged to the people were lost after a legal battle. Aglipay became politically suspect to the American authorities. He was befriended by Governor Taft, but Taft was a Unitarian and converted him; doctrinally the church split. Bishop Aglipay died in 1940, and his successor, Fonacier, who collaborated with the Japanese "while our children were still fighting in Bataan," was removed from office after the war and the resulting legal wrangle was settled only in 1955.

"When I became head of the church," said the Supreme Bishop, "I found a sort of haze. Some were Unitarian, some were Trinitarian, some nothing at all, just Christians, and we were losing ground." In Bishop Norman Binsted of the Episcopal Church, de los Reyes found sympathy. Largely through Episcopal help the Philippine Independent Church is on the road to recovery—"smaller, but united, and stronger."

Admiration for courage and faith cannot blind an observer to the restricted limits of Aglipayan influence. They are more impressive from a distance, or as a brave idea, despite forty bishops, twenty-three dioceses, and a claim of three million members. The teaching is symbolized by the contrasts I saw as I passed through the tiny procathedral to the Supreme Council chamber: a large statue of the cross-bearing Christ which had been dressed in a scarlet robe and a wig; a plaster of Christ with the sacred heart exposed; an image of the Virgin; a poster of the American Bible Society.

The car turned into Dewey Boulevard with its breeze and the distant view of Corregidor and Bataan across the almost landlocked bay, sped by the Ritzal Monument, the docks, the ruins of the old Spanish city destroyed in the war, through a slum district and on to the northern highway, as narrow and crowded as the Great North Road at its worst. Ten miles out we took a rough lane to Christian Radio City—the Far Eastern Broadcasting Company, the famous D.Z.A.S. whose trail I had been crossing all over Asia.

Christian Radio City was a small compound all set about with antennae and wire. Robert A. Reynolds, the director, took me into his modest but sensibly air-conditioned office, and sitting at a desk in front of a large Trans World Airlines map of the world told me of the founding of F.E.B.C. by three Americans in 1945 with total assets of $1,000. Fortunately failing to get permission to build missionary radio stations in China, one of the three came to the Philippines in July, 1946. "We went on the air in 1948 with one medium-wave 1,000-watt transmitter. Now we have eleven—two medium- and nine short-wave, an average of one transmitter added every year." The cost of installation, organization, and maintenance of equipment and program is met entirely by gifts, chiefly from North America.

Reynolds, a small man with gray, thinning hair and a youngish face, rather solemn in his manner, took me across to a National Geographic map of the Eastern Hemisphere dotted with colored pins. "Last autumn we did a six-weeks test of our new 50,000-watt short-wave transmitter which is primarily intended for India. We were on three hours every evening and had 600 letters as a result. The pins show where it was heard." They were thick in Asia, sprinkled quite widely in Africa, and as far as the South Atlantic; two or three were in England, Sweden, and Belgium. "South India reported

MINDORO

Hazel Page and an informant at Binli

MINDORO

Agin preaches the Good News to wayfarers

HONG KONG COLONY
Street Scene on Cheung Chau Island

HONG KONG COLONY
Temple on Cheung Chau Island

JAPAN
Torii to a Shinto shrine at Nikko

reception clearer than Radio Ceylon, and Zanzibar said the signal was louder than the local station. Since December, 1958, we have broadcast a regular schedule for India, 2 hours and 45 minutes a day, organized by the Evangelical Radio Fellowship of India." He stubbed a finger on to Okinawa, midway between the Philippines and Japan. "Here our new 100,000-watt transmitter is being set up. In Red China they are not allowed to have short-wave receivers, so to reach them we had to have a really powerful medium wave." It came on the air three months later, in October, 1959. "It should be heard clearly all over China and in parts of Russia. The Communists will be hard put to prevent listening. The harassed Church in China may soon look to Okinawa as a main source of inspiration."

Crossing to a big studio fitted up rather like a chapel, I was shown a board giving the daily schedules. "The Call of the Orient" is divided into three services—the Philippine Service, Manila's Fine Music Station, and the Overseas Service, the last being on the air almost round the clock.

Dale Golding, General Program Director, explained that the terms of license from the Philippine Government obliged F.E.B.C. to broadcast 50 per cent secular programs. "When we went on the air in 1948 there were many commercial stations making a lot of money but *not* serving the public. To get a license we had to agree to put across public instruction, news, good music, and so on. We feel it a tremendous advantage, as we gain many, many listeners." The Overseas Service schedule had 75 per cent religious material, the different language programs being organized by missionaries working in the various countries. British missionaries were less adept at producing programs than were Americans. "They do not get the opportunities at home as we do."

None of the D.Z.A.S. staff is amateur. Dale Golding held a radio degree from a university in Texas and had worked at a Christian radio station in Iowa. "All my training was geared to coming here." The chief announcer, from Seattle, who also covers local news, organizes and sings on musical programs, took five years of voice training in London. "My aim was Christian service, but I wanted to do something different from the usual run."

Dale Golding and I sat beside a baby grand in the studio of the Manila Fine Music Station where the walls had prints of famous composers and a chart of studio signals. On the highly sensitive microphone by Phillips of Holland glowed a red light; the Filipino engineer at the controls across the glass partition was testing our voices. Through another glass an engineer recorded a Russian on holiday from Korea who, in the studio beyond, was making programs in Russian for later release.

Golding took me out past a Coca-Cola dispenser to the Traffic Room. It looked like a paperback bookshop. "Over there are Burmese tapes, Cambodian, and Chinese dialects. To the right are Indian languages, Nepali, Tibetan."

"Roughly how many tapes are here?"

"I can tell you almost exactly: 11,567, I think, and 3,500 records. That is, 5,500 hours. At present we are programing 32 different languages, including 8 major Filipino dialects and 22 major languages of the Orient."

Most of the Overseas Service was "canned," except for the announcer who was "live." The work was done on a missionary basis—men on the spot recording their programs without charge to D.Z.A.S., who broadcast without asking payment for time. My mind switched to North India, to the Tibetan pastor who was supposed to record tapes for Manila but was absorbed in the Nationalist Revolt; to Thailand, where the Manoram Christian Hospital and the Presbyterian Hospital at Chiengmai used the Manila program as the principal evangelistic service in the wards.

"The only way *not* to have the bulk 'canned,'" Golding continued, "would be a team of nationals here. That would be limiting, and besides, we feel the people who make the broadcasts need to be actually involved in work in their countries. On the other hand, we had a young Indonesian here for a year and three months, and he created great interest back in his own country. Had 1,500 letters last Christmas and New Year when he offered a Gospel Calendar. We're still getting letters for him, and that presents a translation problem. We hope to get a Cambodian, and later a Russian, and we had a Jap for a bit. We aim, and desire, to have nationals from many countries: to supplement not to supplant the tapes."

I had been at D.Z.A.S. for nearly three hours. Mr. Reynolds reappeared and took me over to a workshop, the home of yet another original enterprise: the Portable Missionary, or P.M. D.Z.A.S. buys portable wirelesses and lends them to Christians all over the Philippines on the promise of use as "portable missionaries." A large round notice is sent to display outside home or shop: "D.Z.A.S. P.M. Club Everybody welcome!" In remote areas especially hundreds of people not owning a wireless could gather round a P.M. and listen in to Christian broadcasts. In 1948 a clumsy wooden receiver was used—I saw a few of them. "Retired missionaries," the Filipino technician remarked. A compact Dutch transistor model it now is. "Dutch are better for this size than United States models. Japanese would be cheaper, but our problem is dependability." Each set costs U.S. $35, and remains the property of D.Z.A.S., being returned for repairs. About a thousand were out, the number growing yearly but limited by funds with which to buy them. The scheme was necessarily confined to the Philippines, but could be adopted elsewhere if supporters in other Asian countries set up the necessary organization.

In the compound we examined the antennae, and I stretched my neck at a tower which had been picked up, if that is a phrase for 308 feet of metal frame, for a song from a local cable company which did not know what to do with it. The interior of the transmitting shed looked Martian.

Back at the office I listened to stories of the influence of D.Z.A.S. I asked about Tibet. "Yes," said Reynolds, "we've heard of many traders coming out of Tibet and hunting up a missionary. They have heard the Gospel from us and want to know more. Then there was the missionary in North Thailand who went where no missionary had been before and was asked by a man if he had a Bible. Of course he wanted to know why, and the man said, 'Radio Manila says everyone should have a Bible. I've never seen one.' But we can't tell you very much about influence overseas. The evidence doesn't normally come back here. We can tell you a lot about the Philippines." He rang for his Filipino public-relations officer, Max Atienza.

Atienza had plenty to tell. Of a barrio nearby where people listened, and wrote to say so. Atienza went over, preached, and now there was a small Protestant church. Of an Aglipayan priest who said: "My people now study the Bible—that is new. They sing now, all of them. Because we listen in."

"We have evidence," said Atienza, "of Roman priests telling

their people that they must not listen. Many go on just the same. And we know that priests listen to our broadcasts." The strongest evidence of general interest was the Bible School of the Air. 330,000 have enrolled. "That works out at one in every eight people of the Philippines."

After lunch Reynolds drove me ten miles farther into the country to see the new 50,000-watt transmitter bought, with the 100,000-watt at Okinawa, from the United States Government for a mere $30,500. The story of how a new member of the staff, in San Francisco Bay for the voyage to Manila, noticed a huge Voice of America installation for sale, how the money was raised and the heavy equipment moved to the Far East, was nothing short of miraculous, and a sterling endorsement of the faith of those behind the enterprise.

. I looked at the antennae in the paddy fields and walked about the transmitting building. These smart gray cubicles of machinery, so silent to the bystander, were almost ceaselessly sending sound to the far corners of Asia, an unfathomable Christian influence.

four

Farthest East

THIRTY-SIX

Pearl of the Orient

A home of your own. In Hong Kong after nearly a year of constant travel we had the luxury of a flat. Two flats, rather, a week at each while the family was on holiday, in the shadow of the Nine Dragons, the hills from which Kowloon takes its name, and both on the far side of Boundary Street, a reminder that in less than forty years, except for four square miles of the Peninsula and Hong Kong Island itself, the whole reverts to China. The flats were under the approach to the International Airport, and all day, but mercifully not at night, a succession of Britannias, Electras, and Skymasters flew out and came in from the corners of Asia and the world. The Comets generally used the harbor approach to the man-made peninsula of the new runway, a mountain removed and cast into the sea.

That the first flat should be lent by David Adeney who spends his time traveling the universities of the East as an officer of the International Fellowship of Evangelical Students, and the second by Bryce Gray, a Londoner, of the staff of the Christian Witness Press, was symbolic of Hong Kong as a center, like Singapore, of missionary activity for all the Far East. Our actual host, originator of this kindly scheme for our comfort, was the head of the Christian Witness Press, Ron Roberts, an Australian. The posters, leaflets, books, and the *Lighthouse* magazine of the press I had met constantly in different languages in jungle, mountain, and city. Ron Roberts gave me a complimentary copy of the latest production, a thirty-five-page picture comic in the lurid style beloved of Chinese children, as violent as the immoral rubbish they hire from street stalls and pore over for hours, but with a Christian story and message.

A home of your own. By that very fact our attention was focused on the appalling problem of Hong Kong—refugees.

The superb setting of Victoria Harbour, the loveliness of the Peak, the outer islands and the New Territories, the magnificence of skyscrapers and huge office blocks, the ceaseless shuttle of the ferries passing freighters, liners, and American warships may blind the tourist to the shacks festooned on the hills, to the rooftop and bedspace slums.

At the end of Oxford Road, where the second flat was, a track led off to a piece of waste ground. Squeezed between vegetable gardens and a hill stood hundreds of shacks housing at least a thousand people, less cramped than in many squatter sites because after a fire they were forbidden to rebuild until fire lanes had been marked.

Near the other flat in College Road ran a narrow alley arched with laundry and old clothes. We went to photograph a woman who had squatted there with her family eight years since flight from Kwangtung. Her entire home consisted of a shelter like those seen in London beside holes in the road. Her view was a high brick wall, her kitchen the public alleyway, its closeness such that Anne had difficulty in focusing the woman, her two grandchildren, and what passed for the door. Two coolies were moving sand from a dump a few feet off, and every time they needed to pass Anne had to step up the alley and stand back in a recess.

Off Waterloo Road from bus or taxi I had often noticed a dump of boxes and a knot of people on a covered pavement. I presumed it a street hawkers' pitch. A woman missionary took us visiting. "Eighty to one hundred people are living in this section of the street," she remarked as we said goodbye to a woman making cheap paper bags, and moved six inches to the next "home." "They were cleared once but they've all come back again." There were cooking pots on one side of the pavement, trunks, boxes, a stick or two of furniture on the other. Traffic passed continually. Water could be obtained from a stream across the main road or from rain in the gutter, and latrines were on the other side of a big crossroads with traffic lights.

Over by the lights, into a doorway, up dark and littered stairs and out onto a small rooftop. Seventy to eighty cheerful Chinese, including children, here had homes. Most were of carton paper, which was surprisingly waterproof; some were of wood, some looked like rabbit hutches, others like dog kennels, and some were only shoulder high. All water had to be brought up the steep stairs. "The old ladies earn money by carrying for those out of work," I was told. "Quite a few of these huts blew away last typhoon season."

Farther down the same street the missionary took us into another doorway, up a short flight of dark stairs into a room, about the size of a medium-length classroom, shared by twenty or thirty families, each "flat" being roughly equivalent to half a ping-pong table. We called on a woman who had fled from Shanghai and had lived in this bedspace flat for eleven years. The raised floor was bed, sitting space, everything, covered with a red reed mat. A little shelf held four small cups. Clothes from a hook draped two Thermos bottles. A clock and a photograph of her late husband in marine uniform told of former prosperity, and above were washing lines. The next flats were curtained off, and she was fortunate in a "ground floor" with no other bedspace above, and having only herself and her granddaughter; her son and grandson came home occasionally and one of them slept underneath the bed. At the back the communal kitchen for all thirty families was also washplace and latrine: the lids on the wooden pails did not entirely shut off the stench.

These bedspace rooms were not as crowded as some; when two houses nearby burned down, five hundred Chinese were made homeless. "Think of the fug when the door is shut at night," said the missionary. I asked about sexual promiscuity. "They are very good on the whole. There are prostitute streets, of course. And there might be a prostitute or two here, but they are always known." On the next floor an old man, flat-chested and gaunt in his black pajamas, sat by the window, hands shaking in a perpetual nervous dance; opposite, a woman minded a baby for wages, and in the murk by the door a man made matchsticks by the light of a weak oil lamp, though it was midmorning. Going to the roof we found a couple with a child apparently of nine months but in fact of two years; his sores were nauseating. "Malnutrition," said our guide, producing a tin of condensed milk. "The woman is subnormal. The man sells soft lime on the streets." The wall of their home was a filthy abutment of roof.

None of these slum dwellers looked morose or savage. They were grateful to be out of Red China, at the price of existing in little more than coffin space, while all around in the same room neighbors ate, slept, quarreled, lay sick, and died.

Indignation must be directed to the right quarter. Hong Kong is not to blame. The old slums of London could be laid at England's door; the refugees of Germany were the result of making war. Hong Kong's refugees are her responsibility only because she did not refuse asylum to hundreds of thousands fleeing from Red China, until forced to close the gates except on a quota system.

Indignation must relate to facts. Someone gave me a sentimental booklet by a missionary contrasting in shocked tones handsome offices and stacked shops with the squatters' poverty. The dazzling shoppers' paradise is a key to the solution. Only through prosperity can the colony afford to continue rehousing squatters. The booklet insinuated, in the manner of Charles Kingsley's *Two Years Ago,* that the tourist who bought a tailor-made suit at Hong Kong's low prices was wicked to encourage sweated labor. It is only by suits being cut, jade earrings fashioned, more Hong Kong goods exported that wages can rise, as at last they have begun very slightly to rise. Sweating is inevitable with a labor reserve of such magnitude and a tradition of piecework. Nearly every person can earn a little; few can earn enough.

I came to Hong Kong expecting to describe missions and voluntary relief agencies as the principal actors in the solution of the refugee problem. I had my casting wrong. I saw soon, and every day strengthened the conviction, that the real hero of this drama is the Hong Kong Government. It is a saga not of dedicated missionaries, despite the value of their contribution, but of ordinary British expatriates and their Chinese colleagues. They are supported by British and Chinese businessmen. "Our chaps are jolly good about it on the whole," I was told; "so are some of the Chinese, some very definitely so. A lot of their effort is a matter of 'face,' of course. And there are the thoroughly selfish ones too." Government is not the least complacent, and what it has already achieved is remarkable.

Chinese birth rate is proverbial; the sea door from China cannot be tight shut, and thus the population rises every month. "To keep pace with the birth rate alone, we have got to build the equivalent of a city the size of York every year." The Colony—Hong Kong Island, Kowloon, the New Territories covers 391 mountainous square miles; not until I had sailed in under hills green above red cliffs like South Devon, and driven or walked or viewed the Hong Kong Cotswolds, Cheviots, South and North Downs, Snowdon, did I realize how mountainous. Of the 391 square miles as little as 62 are usable; at present 50 square miles are in agriculture and 12 for housing, commerce and industry.

Into this must be packed a population larger than that of New Zealand. Over 2½ million are crammed between the mountains and the sea. It is believed that about ¾ million are uninvited guests or their subsequent progeny. "Don't forget," said the bishop, "that nearly every family has one or more relatives from other parts of China living with it. They do not swell the official refugee figures."

"Not every squatter is a refugee," the Colonial Secretariat pointed out; "many are pre-1949 inhabitants who have been elbowed out by richer immigrants or fallen on hard times."

Government deputed the usual resettlement officer to show me what had been done for refugees, a young man who was, I discovered, a convinced and active Christian. He conducted me from a squatter area to the first resettlement site where in the early 1950's, when it became clear that refugees were not returning to China nor the United Nations taking responsibility, the government built cottage lines as on a tea estate in Ceylon or Malaya. This attempt to empty a reservoir with a teaspoon was abandoned after the disastrous fire of Christmas night, 1953, a fire which made 80,000 squatters homeless and provoked the bold decision to keep the cleared site vacant and build there permanent two-story blocks. Seven months later another large fire made plain that even these were not a sufficient use of land. Once more public funds were dedicated to the uninvited guests. Hence the great six- or seven-story *massifs* rising ugly but practicable, fifteen or twenty together on more and more sites, some by superlative engineering feats, carved out of hillsides or reclaimed.

From the top of one of the twenty-seven blocks at Shek Kip Mei, site of the Christmas Day fire, the noise of Chinese was as breakers on the seashore: 63,000 people live in the settlement, 2,500 or more in each H-shaped block. Superficially like workers' flats on the slum-cleared area of a British city, they differ in that the crossbar of each story contains communal water taps, lavatories, and laundering space, and that each small room may be the home of five adults, or of two adults and six children. "Mere concrete boxes," sentimentalists say; the phrase suggests a bleak cubicle far different from the gay confusion of Chinese decoration and furniture. It is crowded. "They would crowd in more if we did not stop them," said the resettlement officer. This is emergency housing at a rent which can be afforded.

The rooftops of these blocks have an importance of their own. The Communists, having created Hong Kong's problem, do all they can to play on the poverty and overcrowding. Government realized that social and spiritual needs must be met, if for no deeper motive, and keeping some of the rooftops for recreational space it gave the rest to churches, missions, or other voluntary agencies. Rooftop primary schools, vocational classes, and clubs are scattered freely in the resettlement areas: a ready-made field for religious and social workers in which magnificent work is done.

There must be more missionaries per square mile in Hong Kong than anywhere else on earth. The list of organizations in the resettlement areas, in relief, in the slums and among the squatters, in schools, hospitals, orphanages, and old folks' homes, is imposing. Added to that are the normal missionary affairs of a great city with a predominantly non-Christian population.

Relief money pours in, much from America, and is welcome despite its importance being secondary, the real burden falling on the Colonial Government. Charity and sentiment will not solve the problem. "Why can't everybody get together and give enough to finish it off?" said a woman in the ship going on to Japan. Money is not enough.

Across Asia I often felt critical of governmental attitude to missionaries. In Hong Kong this was reversed.

I went to see the head of one of the relief organizations, impressive to watch in action. I liked him, admired his crusading zeal, and he happened to do me a personal kindness.

Emphasizing his belief that the relief of distress was an important Christian ministry to be done professionally with technical competence, not as a religious sideline, he described the clinical method by which a man's need is discovered and relief arranged irrespective of creed. He swung into a blistering attack on the Hong Kong Government. He complained of lack of coordination between government and the voluntary agencies; he was scathing in accusation of unimaginative policy. The multistory buildings were "horrible." Government was creating ghastly slums for the future; the tuberculosis rate, already high, must rise; Europeans never would have stood for such overcrowding, only the poor, patient Chinese. "How would you like to live in a concrete cubicle with only one tap between two hundred persons?" Government ought to have built satellite cottage cities out in the New Territories—he knew a nice flat valley just waiting for one.

Anne and I had been invited to dinner the following evening by Colonel John Clague, to whom we had a private introduction. Head of a Hong Kong business house, Clague had first come to the Colony as a soldier in the war, had escaped from a prison camp and served with guerrillas in Kwangtung before rejoining British forces. He was now a member of the Legislative Council and had been on the Resettlement Committee from its start.

I told him of my interview of yesterday. He said: "We do not like two hundred persons per tap or latrine any more than he does. The multistory blocks are a temporary expedient. The first job is to get the squatters off the streets." Government reckoned that this would take another five years. Overcrowding could then be eased. The blocks were designed "so that they could be converted at a later date into orthodox self-contained flats." The words come from a government publication I read afterward, wondering why the relief missionary had not read it. So much for future slums.

Clague gave me an insight into the rackets and ramps, the pressure on Chinese officials which endangered the scheme, rendering essential the building of accommodation that should not be attractive enough to the wrong people. I was impressed with his approach to these problems and his interest not only in resettlement but in the promotion of better housing. We discussed relief, and he commented, "America's best way of helping the refugees is not to tax Hong Kong exports!"

The next morning I was flown round the Colony in an R.A.F. Auster of the Hong Kong Defense Force. The flight had been postponed two days because of heavy rains. We crossed the Dragon's Back, Stanley Peninsula, and the south coast of the island to Aberdeen, around mountainous Lan Tao, by Castle Peak Harbour into the New Territories and back across Kowloon by Boundary Street. Two facts were irrefutable: the extraordinary difficulty of finding flat or accessible land for new housing or for new industries, for no Chinese will move from the city to a rural resettlement if no means of livelihood is at hand; and the extent of reclamation in progress.

The third day I went to the principal planning officer of the government. The relief missionary's case, already tattered, was left in shreds. Instead of an unimaginative government content to cram its squatters into concrete slums, I saw plans for the next ten years. "Money, on the whole, is not the limiting factor," said the officer. "In other words, if we decide on a thing we can generally get ahead with it right away. The limiting factor is land." He had no need to say more after that flight. "The answer is Reclamation." He marked on my map places to be reclaimed by 1965, and those designated for reclamation by 1970. Great new reservoirs were to be built by enclosing and draining arms of the sea. Goverment aimed to resettle at the rate of 140,000 a year. By 1965, 3,000 acres would be reclaimed, and built over at the density of a mere 700 persons per acre instead of the 2,000 in the present resettlement. The type of dwelling had not been decided; it might be a cottage type as in the original experiment.

The idealistic missionary might have justification in his plea for a satellite city in the "nice flat valley" in the New Territories. "That valley," said the planning officer, "is one of the most historical places in the Colony. They used to say the best rice in all China grew there. The Emperor always had his rice from that valley brought overland the whole way to Peking." Was it right to dispossess hereditary farmers by a wave of the hand to house uninvited refugees? The plan was to reclaim the inlet below the valley and build there, in the belief that the farmers would then sell out as a profitable investment.

No government is perfect. Notwithstanding defects of personality at any level, departmental rivalries or mixed motives, Hong Kong proves that a government in the East may still be actuated by Christian principles.

THIRTY-SEVEN ❧ *Approach to Japan*

No road to China. Negotiations for a visit to Red China had broken down before we left England. As for Formosa, I was warned that an Englishman might be refused permits for travel away from main centers, nor could I expect to meet national leaders.

And so, a year and a day after leaving Liverpool we approached Japan, followed Commodore Perry's course into Tokyo Bay, passed a fishing fleet of strange striped sails such as he saw, and steamed under factory chimneys belching orange smoke to dock at Yokohama.

Owing to causes beyond my control we arrived in Japan without knowing our itinerary. One clear intention I had: to avoid the tourist areas, the show-piece "cherry blossom" Japan—not that it was cherry-blossom time—until I had encountered the ordinary workaday life of the Japanese. If ever there was a country that hides its true face from the casual globe-trotter blinkered in a package tour, it is Japan.

I locked the last suitcase and came out of our cabin. Hurrying toward me was a man I had known at Cambridge, followed by another whom I took to be Arthur Kennedy, who was to look after us in Tokyo. "Michael!" I said, as we shook hands, "I had no idea you were in Tokyo."

"I arrived this morning—to take you back up north." Mike worked at Hakodate on the near tip of Hokkaido, the northern island which is under snow three months of the year: as humdrum a place as could be wished.

We took a taxi that evening through built-up streets stretching

the sixteen miles from Yokohama to Tokyo, the most heavily populated city in the world, which must also be the worst lighted, for
brilliant displays of neon lights outclassing Piccadilly Circus are no
substitute for street lamps. The taxi, mindful of the reputation of
Tokyo taxis, quickly reduced us to nervous debility. I clung to
Luther's dictum, "I am immortal until my work is done."

The Kennedys lived in an outlying district, Ealing or Croydon,
as it were. Like every Japanese house the exterior was drab, and
like most it was built of timber. The interior was not fully Japanese,
but as I removed my shoes in the porch and put on slippers provided by my host I had that sense of entering a different and older
culture under the thin veneer of the West.

Most of our time in Japan was spent in houses of Japanese or
semi-Japanese interiors, similar without regard to class, wealth, or
district, of which the basis is *tatami,* yellow mats made of the fine
long stems of a weed on a foundation of rice straw and, beneath that
by law, a layer of D.D.T. powder sprinkled twice a year. Sliding
doors of decorated paper partition off other rooms or the cupboards,
in one of which are kept the thick quilts to be laid on the floor at
night as mattresses. In completely Japanese homes everything is
done on the floor, on cushions at low tables or desks. Because slippers must be worn in the passages, no shoes on the *tatami,* wooden
clogs in the bathroom and straw sandals in the lavatory, life in a
Japanese house is pernickety. I always seemed to be changing foot-
gear.

Two afternoons later we left for the center of Tokyo in one of the
endless procession of electric trains which speed down endless suburban tracks through innumerable stations—300 trains an hour at
certain junctions. We strap hanged. And the enigma of Japan was
forced upon me. The politeness of railway officials could not be
exceeded; the orderliness of the rush-hour crowd on the platform
was admirable. Came a train, and the assault, the unsmiling, relent-
less shove, left me gasping.

The train ran through the unbroken belt of villages that is
Greater Tokyo, mile upon mile of dingy one-story wooden dwellings,
all much the same, relieved here and there by concrete structures at
the centers, until we reached the area of the great department
stores, the office blocks, a brief sight of the Imperial Palace grounds,
and the tallest tower on earth—Tokyo Television.

We left Tokyo in a saloon carriage of spotlessly clean upholstered seats in pairs, all facing one way for extra privacy but able to be swiveled round if four wished to travel in company. Efficiency was everywhere: circulating fans, a red light to show when the toilet was occupied, fresh iced water available, polite detailed announcements over the P.A. before reaching a stop, waitresses deftly dispensing fruit juice tins, cleaners swiftly removing litter with long tongs. For all this, Japanese trains too much reminded me of English in wartime. They are crowded; they are so smutty the cleanliness fails to survive ten miles; they smell of bad coal. Unlike English trains in wartime they ran dead to time. The most important junction will not detain a Japanese express more than two minutes, and when they are scheduled to arrive at 1100 hours they arrive at 1100 hours, not 1059 or 1101.

Men sat with transistor wirelesses attached to their ears by plugs. Others curled up: in any Japanese railway carriage at least half will be asleep, nor will a passenger searching for a seat in a crowded train remove trespassing legs. Little boxes of cold rice, seaweed, dried squid, and other delights were opened and disposed of with short chopsticks. A woman undressed her upper half completely and put on a kimono. Men prepared for sleep by removing most of their clothing.

In these couchettes we slept well, and awoke to a countryside typical of Northern Honshu in August: a landscape garden of hummocky pine-clad hills, green rice fields flecked with silver paper to scare birds, thatched wooden houses which were mostly drab but occasionally of a Worcestershire black and white, a dirt road, trucks churning dust, cart horses in the fields. And always grid lines or electricity wires. When the train entered the famous apple country near Aomori, I marveled at the patience behind the protective paper wrapped round every apple on every tree.

Aomori, a port bombed flat in the war, since rebuilt, was like any other small port in Japan, dingy despite a fine setting of hills and bay. The ferry steamed out under an umbrella of black smoke to the strains of *Auld Lang Syne* from the P.A., in a shower of colored streamers from passengers' friends. As clean and efficient as a Swiss lake steamer the ship replaced one lost with all hands in a typhoon two years before; they had such trouble identifying the bodies that we were ordered to write out name and address before going on board.

The population pressure again forced itself on my consciousness. Here was a cross section of Japan. Western-dressed young women carrying babies strapped to their backs under "happy coats," some of the older in kimonos which must be duller colored the more aged the wearer; schoolboys in shirtsleeves or the usual black cap and uniform resembling that of a British naval officer in late Victorian days; schoolgirls in sailor suits complete with the three white lines for Nelson's victories. The schoolboys practice their English, solemnly announcing "I am a boy," the first line of the primer; the schoolgirls giggle and stare. Their elders whisk camera to eye, intent on the oddity of skin, eyes and hair, for few Japanese may go overseas. Several members of the United States Security Forces were on board, but the novelty of a foreigner appears never to wane.

The crossing to Hokkaido took four hours. I had always supposed Mike to work in a remote, even desolate corner. As we neared Hakodate a helicopter hovered and flew away. When the ferry turned the headland on which a fort used to stand, now a television tower, I might have been approaching Barrow-in-Furness or Sunderland: a pall of smoke; cranes, railway yards, a large ship on the stocks, tall chimneys, a cable car for tourists up the hill, and colored advertisement balloons floating over a department store.

We traveled nearly three thousand miles in Japan, and never ceased to wonder.

I suspect that Japanese efficiencies do not appear so impressive to an American, but I could wish for the adoption of several in England. Public telephoning is easy. Nearly every shop has a red hand set on the counter, with a coin slot. Restaurant windows display priced models of the dishes; occasional attempts on this line in England are repulsive. In Japan they are temptingly realistic. A railway-station name board gives the next and last stop (in characters, phonetic script and English). A provincial department store has exciting electric toys—an elephant blowing bubbles was my favorite—and gadgets. The Sony transistor radio is world famous. Fire alarms, fire precautions, the fire service are the best of any nation, and need to be.

The Japanese have a passion for information: maps, plans, the temperature, endless announcements; for photography, mostly of themselves draped round ancient monuments; for sport; whenever

I saw one of the nine television channels a baseball match was on, except during the autumn tournament of the wrestling called *sumo*. They have a passion for classical music and for education, as befits a nation highly cultured when England was emerging from the Dark Ages: literacy is nearly 100 per cent, and more than 228 universities are recognized. The competition for a place is as fierce as the struggle a graduate has in finding a post.

Japanese roads are bad, except for a few major routes. Japanese sewage is worse. The ordinary house has no flush toilet and no drain, merely a tub under a hole, and in the streets you may see municipal night-soil removers using long hooks to pull out and lift the tubs, emptying the brown stinking stream into a cart or lorry. It is disposed of for agriculture, and the excuse that sewers might crack in one of the frequent earth tremors strikes me as lame. The hole and the tub are tucked in a corner behind wooden doors, but unless a Westerner has installed flush and a cesspit, the house is never quite free. Another small point of breakdown: I lost my glasses and was astonished to discover that this highly industrialized country of myopics with an alarming road-accident rate has no triplex unbreakable glass, only plastic which, they admit, scratches easily.

I reached Japan with a total misconception of the position and strength of Japanese Christianity. A misconception widely shared, I believe, in Britain.

Accounts in the immediate postwar years of vast evangelistic meetings, of huge demand for Bibles, of missionaries flocking in; the Japanese bishops at Lambeth, the Archbishop of Canterbury's visit and the great welcome accorded him; the centenary celebrations; all this made me expect a flourishing settled church, predominantly Japanese in leadership and thrust, a minority but powerful, steadily reducing the non-Christian percentage of the population.

I found a Church microscopic.

Out of a population numbering 91 million, Christians of all kinds total somewhat over 600,000, or between half and three-quarters of one per cent; in India Christians form 2.2 per cent of the population. Japanese Protestants are two-thirds of the total, a lead which Roman Catholics are believed to have shortened in recent years. The indirect influence of Christianity must always be considerable. And an Oriental nation which imbibed and adapted Westernization with the speed and thoroughness of Japan inevitably swallowed a large slice of the Christian heritage of the West. The Japanese frankly ascribe to Christian initiative their progress in the emancipation and education of women, although the recent outlawing of prostitution owed more to women members of the Diet than to direct Christian advocacy. Japan's greatest leaders of social reform, such as Kagawa, have been Christian. This tradition is maintained. "Everyone in the flooded district," reported the *Japan Times* after the Great Typhoon, "lavished praise and gratitude on the Christians who rushed to their aid when they needed it most."

Direct influence is negligible.

When Christianity was first brought in the sixteenth century by the redoubtable Francis Xavier, swift progress, entangled with the politics of warring feudal lords and complicated by the custom that a man must adhere to his lord's religion, was followed by brutal repression on the decision of the Shogun, hereditary ruler of Japan in the name of Emperors kept powerless in seclusion, that the Jesuits were precursors of Portuguese or Spanish conquest. Dutch merchants played no creditable part in the intrigue, but had Dutch or English Protestants of the early seventeenth century sent missionaries they might have been admitted. None came. Japan closed its door tight against the West, except for the trickle of trade permitted the Dutch under ignominious terms. Christianity was outlawed and Christians were ruthlessly exterminated.

The centenary celebrations of Protestantism's arrival in 1859 continued during our visit. The first few missionaries, English and American, had a forbidding task. Christianity remained proscribed until 1872, four years after the Meiji Restoration had broken the Shogunate and set Japan on her Western road. A later suggestion that as a political expediency she be made Christian in the manner of Constantine's Edict mercifully came to nought. The 1880's saw such remarkable progress that to read contemporary mission literature is to sense an expectation that Christianity might soon become dominant. The spirit of Japan frustrated this hope.

After some fifty years of freedom the churches were maturing, despite a tendency toward fragmentation and an inevitable inoculation of the loose theological thinking of the 1920's and 1930's, when they ran into the appalling tensions of the militarist tyranny and the Pacific war. The government imposed on Protestantism the Nihon Kirisuto Kyodan, a United Church. Those who resisted, including two-thirds of the Anglican-Episcopals (Nippon Seikokai), several smaller groups, and individuals of the major collaborating churches, were persecuted and imprisoned. Some died, in prison or after release. A Japanese vicar in Tokyo offered me a novel view of the origin of the Kyodan. "The militarists," he said, "intended taking large numbers of Christians to Manchuria and there executing them. Moderates in our ministry of education thought out this scheme of merging Protestants into one group, Catholics being the other; they could then assure the militarists that Christians were under control and mass execution unnecessary."

"A very Japanese way of meeting the problem," commented the Englishman with me.

As for persecution, Bishop Michael Yashiro of Kobe, Presiding Bishop, one of those who refused to join the Kyodan, firmly put me in my place. The Bishop of Kobe is, on a Japanese scale, of Johnsonian proportions, a mountain of a man. Illustrating his point with a doodle, he said: "Missionary societies are too fond of talking about 'the period of persecution,' 'the period of opportunity.' That is the wrong way to look at it. The truth is that a Christian can *turn persecution into fun*. Opportunity is there all the time."

Some denominations regarded the Kyodan as providential, and remained in it when freedom returned. Christians as a whole, within and without the present Kyodan, whether they collaborated or not, look back on the militarist period as one of shameful compromise. "Yet it was very difficult for any of us to *do* anything," said a pastor whose own record is unblemished. "The Church was small and insignificant." In Hitler's Germany the Confessing Church could hope to awake an echo in the German conscience. The Japanese had no Christian conscience.

"Defeat was the Providence of God." I heard this again and again from Japanese Christians. Shinto was toppled from its exclusive position as a state religion binding on the adherents of all others. Complete freedom of thought, worship, and propagation was introduced by the Allied Occupation and has remained; no restriction of any kind is placed on national Christians or on the entry of foreign missionaries. More than India, far more than Burma or Indonesia, Japan is a nation true to the United Nation's conception of freedom of religion.

"MacArthur was God's gift for that time," said an English missionary with service before and after the war. "The Japanese greatly loved him, aloof as he was. I do not think," he added, "that the British with their reserve could ever have succeeded as did the Americans with their friendliness." For all its mistakes, the predominantly American Occupation must rank as the most enlightened and successful in history.

General MacArthur appealed for missionaries. They flocked in, Scandinavian, Australian, British; very many American and Canadian. Former missionaries returned. Excellent men and women joined them, prepared to give unstintingly in the hour of Japan's need. Others were arrogant: "We'll show these old-timers how to do it." Most of the new were handicapped by knowing no Japanese, and a few, to this day, consider a grasp of the language unnecessary, with painful results.

The Japanese in their poverty and distress, and in the tremendous fresh wind of freedom, showed inquisitiveness. Motives were mixed. "They would invite us to church and have coffee and cakes," recalled a young schoolmaster, now a Christian. "Lots of us went just for the coffee and cakes. My friends would say to me: 'Let's go to church. We can get coffee.'"

"Many came to our center," said a missionary of long experience who returned to work among students in Tokyo, "because we had light and paper, somewhere they could read and work. Some were genuine seekers." The demand for Bibles undoubtedly was inflated because they made good cigarette paper.

Japanese preachers and foreign evangelists using interpreters, attracted enormous crowds. Anchorless, feeling national guilt or national failure: "The Japanese gods have failed. The American God was victorious. Let us try the American God": they swept forward when the preacher asked for decisions.

What went wrong? There has been growth: official government figures give an increase in Christian membership of over 158,000 be-

tween 1952 and 1955. Allowing for normal birth rate in Christian
families, the growth is infinitesimal in proportion to population, and
belies the apparent promise of those crowds sweeping forward.

"It was all in their front," said a ticket collector, a postwar Christian, now deacon of a church in northern Honshu and a delightfully
spiritual man. It was, he said, a superficial desire for conformity
"rather than heart interest." Genuine converts became lasting Christians, but the mass of "the Deciders" are no more seen.

"The Church took the opportunity as far as it could," said an
elderly pastor in Kobe whose opinion I respect. "It gave what it
could but it had not much to give. There was no real linking of the
Deciders, no building up." That the Japanese Church was not prepared to absorb people is the considered opinion of many. One further
disadvantage: the Bible was largely unintelligible to the younger
generation. The new translation of 1955 has not received unqualified
approval but is a great advance on its predecessor.

Some blame for the general situation must fall on the American
approach. I have no wish to seem impertinent, and I respect deeply
those who endure a spiritual climate so uncongenial, but in a country
where the trappings of life differ little between peasant and prince, it
was easy in the days of the defeat for a missionary unconsciously to
cause affront by an apparently too high standard of living. "There
were some splendid missionaries," said a man who then lived in
Kyushu, the southernmost island, "but some of the others lived in
such luxury, and we had nothing. We saw them in large cars, comfortably off. I began to feel, 'You go back to your own country.' I
felt a resentment against those preaching the Gospel. I had the impression you have to be rich to be a Christian."

Apart from those of obscure semi-Christian beliefs such as Mor-
mons, the good fight of the majority has been impeded by two types
of missionary. One is the shallow thinker, secure in an ostrich hole of
clichés, often with little or no knowledge of the Japanese. This is
the kind who forms his own little church, content with a prolifera-
tion of sects. There are 2,400 foreign missionaries in Japan and 112
societies; of these, more than one-half have less than 10 members
and 97 have less than 30 members. It is true that among those listed
as very small will be great societies who have in Japan a few representatives working with mainly indigenized churches; and there is

no doubt of the admirable contribution of certain reputable and old established interdenominational missions. Nor is God necessarily with the big battalions. But the number of fractional churches in Japan is disturbing.

The second damaging type is the profound theologian of one "school" or another, who confuses the Japanese with theological systems not plainly drawn from the whole heritage of Christian truth, or who leaves his hearers with a tattered Bible. Japan has been an echo board for transatlantic theological quarrels, to its confusion. The Nippon Seikokai is less affected. I was asking the Presiding Bishop whether in the Seikokai, the Incarnation, the Atonement, or the Resurrection was most stressed. "But we're Church of England!" he cried. "We don't belong to one or other school. We have no Barth or Brunner. It is all there in Anglicanism."

The Korean War stressed another trend which has had adverse effect: the implied identification of Christianity with the American way of life. The Japanese were already inclined toward this error, and they have not been adequately disabused. The mid-nineteenth century British missionary never was free of an unspoken conviction that Christianity was synonymous with the Empire, and his attitude to finance, education, and leadership in native churches was benevolently imperialist. In the mid-twentieth century Christian imperialism flies another flag. If missionaries only were concerned, the harm could have been slight. They returned in the wake of a Christion Occupation. Church and administration appeared interwoven.

A foreigner resident in Tokyo before, during, and after the war, whose church affiliation, Protestant or Roman Catholic, I never discovered, pointed to the Achilles heel of the Allied undertaking: "We said their old gods were bad but we have not given better. The result is, we have left the Japanese with nothing but extreme egoism— nothing but shove. It was impossible to do what we set out to do without the Christian foundation. We were attempting to create what was essentially a Christian society without giving the Christian basis, because we had ourselves drifted away from it."

THIRTY-EIGHT   *Enigma*

"Well, what is your verdict? What do you think of us?" asked Iemasa Tokugawa, former Prince, grandson of the last of the Shoguns. I dissembled. I was touched that a man of such venerable eminence, a Minister to Canada and Ambassador to Turkey, should trouble to call on me, and with exquisite courtesy and charm, typically Japanese, should lay himself out on my behalf. I dissembled.

If every missionary had been perfect and every church, sect, group paragons of Christian wisdom and ministry, the additional gains of the past fifteen years would have been trifling. The seat of the trouble lies elsewhere.

The Japanese way—their age-old traditions, structure of society, customs and outlook—is antipathetic to the way of Christ.

"The longer I live in Japan, the less I feel I know them." This remark of an English missionary sums up the enigma of Japan. At first the contrasts astonish. The Japanese are polite and they are pushing, friendly and uncivil, artistic and unfeeling, gentle, especially with children, and harsh. And there is the behavior in war.

When astonishment is replaced by discernment, the contrasts begin to fall into pattern. Even a visitor may peep into the Japanese mind, for this most logical race is the prisoner of so complete a structure that its members behave true to pattern.

The bows, return bows, and return-return bows, pleasing to watch, are part of an elaborate individual saving of face interwoven with mutual obligations. Whenever a relationship, whether of hospitality or of service, exists, the Japanese are exceedingly polite and efficient. To see the airline office girl bowing as the passengers enter the bus, to enjoy the blend of friendliness and helpfulness of the staff of International House, or the service of a maid at a *Ryokan*, the Japanese-style hotel, to have the privilege of being received in a home, all this made me glad to be in Japan. Courtesy may take odd forms. Waiting for a train, Anne and I were being rude about the Japanese bath. A young lady shared the seat. "I had better stop," said Anne, "she may know English."

"No, no," said the girl with a charming smile. "It is all right. I do not understand English."

When they think themselves free of obligations, when "face" is of no import, politeness vanishes. I lost count of the times I was elbowed aside in booking-office queues or at exit barriers, or bruised by the angular backloads of old women boarding buses.

The Japanese is spotlessly clean in person and generally in his home, and every evening the householder throws water over the street outside. Face would be lost by dirt or by failure to maintain community obligations. Away from home the Japanese are litterbugs. A railway carriage quickly becomes a slum. Climbing Mount Fuji is like walking up a municipal ash heap because on the endless volcanic ash is the most complete collection of thrown-away empty tins I have seen.

The individual counts for nothing. There is no sense of personality, only relationship. A man has no importance for himself, only for his place in the family or community. And thus there is no compassion. A kind deed will be rooted in obligation or in displaying superiority. Homes are bleak, except for the small child who is idolized; indeed the Japanese have no word for "home," only for "house," and the man seeking color in life goes out of his house. Gambling arcades are frequent and full. To the numerous hot springs businessmen take not wives but mistresses. The train through the mountains had stopped at a hot spring where a man took the one vacant seat, and his middle-aged woman in brown kimono straphanged. "How do you *know*?" I said when my companion murmured "mistress."

"The way they are being so chatty. If it was the wife there would be less chat." I looked at her face, and had little doubt. The Japanese have no word for sin, only words for vice and crime. A preacher who, dilating on St. Paul's Epistle to the Romans, tells his audience, "You have all sinned," may seem to be offensively implying that they are all convicted criminals who have done time.

"The great national sin of this country," said Bishop Yashiro, "is pride."

"The great national failings," said an Englishwoman who first came to Japan in 1916, "are pride and jealousy. Pride rather than arrogance." They are insular, unbelievably insular. A student asked a friend of mine, in all seriousness, whether London buses carry signboards in Japanese as well as English.

The great changes since 1945 have opened a gulf between the old and the young, who have broken with many traditions. The differences are raucous but superficial. And any conscious transference of loyalty has been to communism. Saiji Hasegawa, a leading Japanese publisher, said that the dominant factor among the young is communism: "They look to Marx, Russia and China, not to the United States. Tibet made no difference. Japan's prosperity is due to United States trade, but this makes no difference either."

It is common knowledge that the teachers in Japan are largely left wing. In this are the seeds of disaster. Japan's nationalist militarism has gone. Her postwar desire to be the Switzerland of the East was genuine, though much harping on the atomic bombs has dulled the sense of guilt, and the older generation is now firmly aligned to the West. The young are not. As I was told, "The Communists may be small, but they are noisy and well organized, have a great purpose and know how to fight."

An equally sharp division appears to lie between city and country. I was more at home among the country people with their apple cheeks, long blouses, aprons and wooden clogs or cloven-hoof boots. The women especially would smile. With Mike in Hokkaido we entered a third-class carriage full of men and women returning from carrying goods to a distant market, a long journey done daily. A large friendly woman, a cake seller, recognized Mike because she had once played with his small son in the same train. She gossiped like any English villager. I was wedged next to an equally bulky woman asleep under a newspaper. The cake seller tapped Mike's arm. "You listen to this. That lady in the corner there is a seller of eggs and she weighs seventy kilos." She made an expressive gesture. "Very big in the bosom too!"

These divisions are more apparent than real. The same instincts move country and town. As for the gulf between old and young, it is as hard to get a Japanese self-assessment as to ask a cockney to define sportsmanship; foreigners who know Japan best believe that the fundamentals are unaltered. "There have been great changes in Britain since the war," said a professional man recently returned to

Japan after many years' absence, "but the British character has not really changed. And the same here."

"We are not a religious people." To wander round Nikko, one of the show places and to me more beautiful than the older and larger temples and shrines of Kyoto, is to gain some awareness of the odd mingling of faiths and philosophies. Confucianism, altered to the Japanese taste, for conduct of life; Buddhism for burial and life after death, a Buddhism introduced from China, absorbed and adapted. The Japanese visits the Buddhist temple and pays his respects to the idol. He passes through the *torii*, a distinctive square open gateway, to the Shinto shrine, tugs the rope to pull the bell, claps his hands, throws money in the box, and departs.

Shinto, the religion which is proclaimed as indigenous to Japan, is the ancient animism of numberless gods and devils, blended with the exaltation of great forebears and of the spirit of Japan. No longer a state religion, its exponents still consider that, as the Nikko guidebook claims, Shinto "stands above all religions so any Japanese should believe in it even if they are Buddhists or Christians." In the Buddhist temple are the ancestor tablets. At a quiet and lovely temple in Hirosaki, the religious and cultural center of Aomori Prefecture, a black-robed priest opened one of a row of red-lacquered family shrines, identical with the shrine in the home. Inside stood the tablet inscribed with gold leaf, and a photograph of the dead, a young soldier killed in the war, waiting for the family to worship him and report to him.

At the Meiji Shrine homage is paid to the spirit of the great Emperor who opened Japan to the West, and at the war shrines to the dead, by death made divine. The Sun goddess, founder of Japan, is worshiped at the greatest Shinto shrine of all, at Ise. Shinto is stronger than it was immediately after the war when the gods had failed. The statistics of "worshipers" are inflated by the hundreds of thousands of Japanese tourists and schoolchildren on excursion. At Nikko I counted forty motor coaches in the car park on a Sunday afternoon. The line between devotion and diversion is drawn thin.

Custom rather than religion, sentiment rather than belief: the Japanese spirit is irreligious because it is essentially pragmatic, not speculative.

In Tokyo I was invited to the house of the Chief Justice of the Supreme Court, Kotaro Tanaka. The Chief Justice, a former Minister of Education, and professor at Tokyo University, who was an opponent of the militarists, is a Roman Catholic and has the face of a Japanese St. Francis. In a long discussion he emphasized that "in Japan behavior counts more than belief—this militates against acceptance of Christianity." He spoke of the conflict of Christianity with the Japanese tradition, and above all of their lack of absolute values. From his experience in education and law he described how his non-Christian countrymen do not consider whether an action is morally right or wrong, good or evil, but whether the results will be favorable or adverse.

The Chief Justice has stated, "I dare say that in no other country of the world have foreign missionaries been confronted with greater difficulties in propagating their faiths than in Japan." He was principally referring to the period between 1859 and 1945. His words remain pertinent.

The Japanese rejects Christianity as foreign because it was not born in Japan. "Why must we accept Jewish Scriptures and believe that someone born a Jew was the only Son of God?" He rejects because Christianity will not conform, will not trim its doctrines to suit traditional Japanese outlook. Defeat has not cured the assumption that Japan is a nation more exalted than any. Christianity stands for an internationalism alien to the Japanese mind; it preaches that individuals matter, that love and obligation extend limitlessly. The Japanese is prepared to accept Christ as another god in the pantheon, but will not tolerate the First Commandment.

I felt no affinity with the Japanese, no bond of sympathy. They threw up a barrier I had sensed with no other race in Asia. Oppression of spirit was strong. The weight of heathendom which had not burdened me as it burdens better men, in lands where the symbols of heathendom are far more evident, here seemed overwhelming, and my admiration for those in Christian work in Japan increased daily. I was not surprised to learn of the high incidence of nervous disorders among missionaries, caused not only by the extreme difficulty of language and written characters. I wished to escape. I found myself beginning to dislike the Japanese.

The very deserved rebuke came from a man, not a missionary, of thirty years' residence who had asked us to lunch. Analyzing the Japanese character during the meat course, during the pudding he had been describing hours of wartime interrogation from the *Kempei*. "Remember, as I remembered then," he said, "that these people had no Greece, no Rome, no Christ, no Renaissance, no Reformation." He thumped the table. "There is only one thing to do with the Japanese, and that is to love them."

"There have been and are," said a forthright missionary, "individual Christians who have lived tremendous lives of self-sacrifice. But that spirit has not been captured by the whole Church."

Too many characteristics in conflict with Christ have not been shed. Pride. "You can't tell a Japanese Christian what to do. You have to whisper from behind a bush." The same might be said of Christians of most races in Asia, and of many Englishmen. Lack of consideration for individuals is more peculiarly Japanese. The Japanese have a word which means "not interfering in the affairs of others": from a passing bus I saw a girl fall off her bicycle and struggle to replace an awkward load. No one stepped forward. In the Church this attitude may extend to a deficiency in pastoral care.

Buddhism has left a legacy. Having gathered his little coterie of disciples, the Buddhist teacher has no desire to expand it; and the disciple's loyalty is to the master rather than to the teaching. The normal Christian congregation in Japan is a similar small group: I heard of a pastor, with theology as soundly reformed as that of Calvin or Knox, whose attitude was, "My faith is for me and my Christians. Other people have their own faiths." And as for the disciples, missionaries sometimes complain that on taking over a station from a colleague they lose church members.

Bishop Vile, Assistant Bishop of Tokyo, a senior American missionary told me that in the Seikokai was "little evangelistic drive. I am anxious to get laymen moving." A recent conference of diocesan evangelism officers concluded that the laity were "not pulling their weight." Bishop Vile considered this a matter of considerable gravity, concerning which Christians in the West should pray. He added that in his opinion nonepiscopal Christians "have better private prayer lives. Our people are rather inclined to depend too much on corporate prayer, and that is not the first thing."

Dr. Matsushita, President of St. Paul's University in Tokyo, commented that "it is comparatively easy to be a Christian but not an aggressive Christian. When a man becomes Christian the attitude of his friends is indifference, tolerant amusement, or friendly opposition. There is no aggressive opposition. It might be better if there were. Our young people are content to keep their faith and not to attempt to spread it."

Undoubtedly one of the strongest temptations of Christians is compromise, for syncretism is a Japanese tendency. Sects such as the Tenrikyo, which was founded by a woman in the nineteenth century and which might be termed Shinto's Christian Science, have strong followings who propagate their beliefs vigorously. For the Christian, now that he is no longer bidden by militarists to worship the Emperor, the temptation is to fail to discern between religion and culture, to accept idolatry as part of the Japanese scene and, as an Englishman might watch morris dancing, attend the Shinto festivals forgetful that this is a betrayal of the uniqueness of Christ. I asked a middle-aged pastor his reason for Christianity's small strength in Japan. "Because of the many churches that do not preach against idolatry," he replied. "Compromise and expediency" was the diagnosis of the missionary interpreting. "There are two ways ahead," added the Japanese. "Either compromise, and let your so-called believers hang on to old beliefs. Or trust the Holy Spirit to break through."

"If you are thinking of committing suicide here, please think again." This notice, in red characters, by a way over a railway track where trains pass every two minutes, is symbolic of the hopelessness which easily grips the Japanese in debt, business troubles, examination failure. This hopelessness is a road Christ takes into the citadel of Japanese heathendom.

There are other roads. The mass meeting under certain conditions may yet prove of lasting influence: the tent campaign, the English Bible class for students where study of the English Bible often leads to serious study of the Word of God. Even the Japanese public bath, a faint parallel to the English pub, is a useful source of contacts in a small town. In Borneo a missionary took off his rain-soaked shirt and went on teaching the little group of even more naked tribesmen. After a few minutes he dived into his pack. "I had better put on another shirt or you will put me down as preaching the Gospel in string pants!" In the steamy leisure of a Japanese men's bath house I was delighted to see the Gospel propagated in a state entirely Adamic.

These ways into the citadel cannot replace humdrum persistency. "One hundred and fifty visits yielded one contact," I was told in Hakodate. "The hardest part is to drive yourself out to house-to-house visiting. Sometimes you feel, Is it worth while? The proportion of returns may be very small. I expected it to be humdrum. It was even more humdrum than I expected." Only intense devotion and patience, so far as human elements are concerned, yields chips from the granite. Nor is that all. "Rather than just doing a lot of talking," said an elderly Japanese, "the very life of the Christian should do a lot of shouting."

THIRTY-NINE ❧ *The Morning Sun*

Ega San is a Hairy Ainu. The Ainu were the aboriginals of Japan, now confined to Hokkaido, and almost entirely assimilated. Only a third, including Ega, are still pure-blooded. A white race of Caucasian origin, their presence in Japan is an anthropologist's puzzle.

When I saw old Ega he certainly seemed hairy. His grizzled head was cut close as a schoolboy's but black hair ran riot on his forearms and down his fingers and peeped over his collar, in a manner thoroughly un-Japanese. He had deeper-set eyes and a face oval instead of round. His home was messy. And the walls were hung with family pictures and Bible patriarchs, such a forest of whisker that it was hard to tell who was who. He was voluble and mercurial; I laughed with him more than in all my talks with Japanese.

He was retailing his life history. He seized my writing pad, my glasses, a book or two, Anne's knitting, everything on the table and, laughing, laid them in a line. I was mystified until the translation came through: "These are bear pelts! This is how the Ainu were cheated by the Shamoo [Japanese]. They hunt bears. They bring the pelts for sale. Twelve pelts. 'Ah,' says the Japanese, 'you bring pelts. I count.' He points at the first: 'Beginning, one, two, three, four, five, six, seven, eight, nine, ten, end—that is ten. I pay you for ten pelts.' And the silly Ainu did not know he was cheated. When I was growing up I raged against the Shamoo. I wanted revenge. My race were poor and cheated, always cheated, and this because they were illiterate and drunk. I determined to be a schoolmaster, and never to drink. My one aim was revenge."

He became literate in Japanese and in Ainu. Ainu had been reduced to writing, roman letters being used, by an English clergyman of the Church Missionary Society called Bachelor, who came to Hakodate at the age of twenty-four in 1877. Hearing about the Ainu, then still in the forests hunting and carving, he devoted his life to them. He retired when forced from Japan in 1941 at the age of eighty-eight, with a beard that would have done credit to an Ainu, and died in Sussex at ninety-one.

Ega taught in a small Hokkaido town. His resolution to temperance wilted under pressure from Japanese colleagues. "I became as hard a drinker as any of them. One night in 1917 I had been on a round of the teachers' houses getting really drunk. My pupils were helping me home. I was asked into yet another teacher's house. A stranger was there, a Japanese, who had been sent by Mr. Bachelor to preach. 'You are an Ainu, aren't you?' he said. 'Have you heard about God?'" Ega, who could not have been more than tipsy, replied that he knew scores of gods.

"But about the one God?"

"No."

"There is only one sun, isn't there, for the whole world? Not one for Japan, one for China? So, there is one God for the world."

"As he talked," continued Ega, "and told me of God, and Christ, and judgment and the cross, I saw that I would perish through drunkenness like all the Ainu. I believed then and there. I returned home and I apologized to my wife for being out every night and for all the wrong I had done. She was even happier than I was and determined to believe with me. We were baptized a month later by Mr. Bachelor."

To go to church on Sunday from his town he had a round walk of fifteen miles, "but it seemed no distance because I loved the Lord."

He still hated the Japanese until he heard a story, so involved that I lost its thread, which convinced him that in God's eyes hatred was no better than murder. Having taken up teaching from a false motive, he resigned, and spent two years with Bachelor preaching among the Ainu. He went to Tokyo to the Bible School of the Holiness Church, leaving the Anglicans but looking always on Bachelor as his hero. He saw him off to England in 1941, and wept bitterly. Listening to his tale I was defeated by garrulity and guffaws, but in 1931 Ega seems to have been back teaching in the Hokkaido coastal town where we met. On the militarists' order that pupils and teachers must bow daily to the Emperor's photograph, Ega was faced with the struggle of conscience common to every Japanese Christian. "I went to the higher school authority and said it was wrong. He said I must do it or leave. I bowed for a time." In 1936 Ega left teaching for evangelism with the Holiness Church, down south in Kyushu, until on the outbreak of war he had to return to Hokkaido, and worked in the town office.

A few Christians lived in his town. All had lapsed by 1941 except one, who came to Ega's house every Sunday for service, two but not three "gathered together in My name." Ega said he did not do much for his faith, but I was told that this denial might be mere modesty. When members of the Overseas Missionary Fellowship came to live in his town in 1953, he and his friend remained the only Christians. Ega is now a mainstay of the modest but growing church.

On September 23, 1923, at 11:58 A.M., occurred the Great Tokyo Earthquake. One of the survivors was Shotaro Kogo, then aged eighteen.

"The two things I most hated," he told me, "were rats and Christianity." His father was a contractor, reasonably affluent, and next door to their home in the Honjo district of Tokyo was a church and pastor's house of the Japan Evangelistic Band. The family belonged to the Nichi Ren, a militant Buddhist sect, and refused every invitation to church. If Kogo saw the pastor coming, he would cross to the other side of the street.

After the earthquake came fire. Gas and water mains had burst, electric wires fused. "Near our house was a wide-open space where a military uniforms factory had been. Everybody around fled to it, fifty thousand people with their belongings filling the place. Gradually the fire enclosed us. The heat was terrible. There was a tremendous rush of air, sucking up men, horses, chairs, tables, even a large notice board buckled up and went whistling into the air.

"As the fire closed in, all began to pray to the gods they had been worshiping. I looked up. The sky began to redden, and smoke passed over. I felt at that moment that there must be something behind the universe. 'O God, please help!' I cried. 'Even if my life is cut down to another fifteen years, please help!' There was no hope because the water mains were burst. It had started to rain, then stopped. The fire roared nearer. People fled this way and that, and were caught and burned. On those who stayed, sparks ignited the thick hair oil people used in those days, and set them on fire. Father went back to the house to rescue things, and was burned to death. Mother was knocked down by lumber. The fire caught my younger brother in the back. I should have tried to rescue, but rather than help others my desire was to help myself.

"My younger sister and a neighbor's girl clung to me. We found a small ditch which had two meters of water. We jumped in. Others jumped on top, frantic. I lost the girls; they slipped under. All I thought was: I am free now. I can escape. The fire swept right over us, but there were bodies above me and I was untouched." Somehow he extricated himself and ran where the fire had not gone. "All around, people were being hit by flying things. The fire finished them off. It was a real miracle I was saved. Just as I approached a wall I was hit in the eye." The wall was nine foot high, but he was a gymnast and, half blinded as he was, scaled it. He thought then that he was the only one of the fifty thousand to escape.

Kogo ran to a brook, blood streaming from his eye. Survivors had made a bridge of boats, and he crossed. He found a watermelon, but one bite making him sleepy he stopped eating, for he knew the fire might come. Desperately thirsty, he refused more than a mouthful because that too made him sleepy. People helped him cross the wider Sumida River to safety. A nurse, without medicine, bandaged his eye, the splinter still in it, and he fell asleep covered with blood on the roadside.

When he awoke he became one of the hundreds of thousands of shocked, wounded survivors struggling toward medical aid. He could hardly see. For a time he clung to a woman telephone supervisor and four of her girls, and they reached Ueno Park. Becoming separated, he knew he was dying. "A young laborer, a poor man, picked me up and put me on his back. I feel he was like an angel from heaven. He took me to a rescue center manned by medical students." Kogo's life hung on a thread. "That night great numbers committed suicide in Ueno Park. I greatly rejoiced I had been saved." He was taken to one of the few undestroyed hospitals; though the doctor expected him to go blind, his right eye survived. He has a glass eye for the left.

After a month he learned that his younger sister survived. Nothing was left of their home, "no friends, no neighbors, only a bit of the old bath."

Two years later he was a maker of compasses in Nagoya. He had no lack of money; but, "I just could not understand the problems of life. Why must man suffer? No parents, no home. I took to drink. It is better to die. I got a train. I was drunk. I was going to throw myself from the train over a precipice. The thought came, What if there is a future life? Fear gripped me. Difficult to live, impossible to die."

Some time afterward he returned to Tokyo. A friend who was a Christian found him lodgings in the home of a member of a Japan Evangelistic Band church. One day a visiting pastor came to call. It was the man who many years earlier had been his next-door neighbor and special aversion. Kogo went to the church with him. "The first words I remember hearing in a Christian service were, 'The Lord is my Shepherd.' I found a former member of that next-door church in this one. What struck me as noteworthy was that having lived next to the J.E.B. in childhood, now after the earthquake I met them again."

He went to a week of meetings on Christian holiness. He could not understand, was annoyed, and refused to continue. Some friends urged him, and he went again, in a bad temper. "I could not follow what the preacher was talking about until the story of the Prodigal Son. This went home. I thought I was righteous, but that night I realized I had been lying. Many past sins came before me, such as deserting my mother and brother in the earthquake fire. At the close of the meeting, when all the Christians began to pray, each on his own but aloud, I burst forth in prayer and confessed my sins to God. The preacher had urged us to believe in the cross of Christ. During the closing hymn I had assurance of sins forgiven. I just wanted to dance with joy. That was Sunday, February 21, 1926. Next Sunday I was doing evangelistic work."

He served as a Sunday-school teacher, went to Bible school, and became an evangelist. During the war he worked steadily in a country district. He is now dean of a Bible school, but his love is to evangelize. I met him in a little country town through the hills behind Kobe, where he was holding a tent campaign.

Walking one day with a missionary, we saw a working woman in typical blue apron, white blouse, cloven-hoof boots, and baby strapped to her back. I was pleased when she invited us to her cottage. I had heard about her husband.

By trade a soya-bean curdler, he showed us the process next morning. Bean curd with rice is a favorite and succulent Japanese dish. Some months earlier, at the time when Anne and I had been nearing Borneo, he was a sot; in his own words, "utterly dependent on drinking, doing no work at all but just going crazy with drink." He would come home at night drunk, rout out wife and children from bed, and beat them. He tossed his children into the gutter. Once when his wife was pregnant he knocked her down and kicked her. He was always in debt.

On May 8, 1959, after assaulting a policeman and spending the night in jail, he was wandering about the town with a hangover, hating himself, unable to pay his debts, considering suicide. He walked up a side street toward the church, which was merely the front room of the missionaries' little house. He knew nothing of Christianity. He thought vaguely as he saw the Gospel posters that through faith he might be able to stop drinking and become a true man. He entered and spoke to a Swiss girl. She said at once: "The Lord Jesus loves drunkards. The Lord Jesus can save drunkards." These words struck home as no phrases about sin or judgment would have done. He came again and again in the following week to hear more from one or other of the women.

He bought a Bible on May 14th, and on his way back called on an elderly Christian. "I asked him: 'What does this mean? I can see the

Lord Jesus just a foot before me, like a vision, crucified.' 'It's grace,' he said. 'The door of your heart has opened.' I went home. At two o'clock I went out for work as usual on my motor bicycle. Without particularly noticing anything, I had just come to the entrance of the primary school. The Lord Jesus, dressed in white and hanging on the cross, appeared before me clearly. At that moment the tears streamed from my eyes. Like flood waters bursting through a dam came the realization. 'Ah, I'm a sinner, a fool; how sinful I have been!' Like a revolving water wheel all my evil deeds passed before me, and I cried out aloud, weeping. I must have wept like that for ten minutes, I think."

It was typically Japanese that no passer-by ventured to ask if anything was the matter. He said, "I cried: 'Ah, this is my Saviour, truly my Saviour. Here, in this world, He was crucified in my place. Truly I have been a great sinner.' I rocked to and fro in a distress so deep I could not remain still. 'I must lay my face against His cross, at His feet and beseech His forgiveness,' I said.

"That same evening a friend who belongs to a new faith religion of Japan came to see me. He urged me to join his religion. I was embarrassed. But finally taking out my Bible, I said, 'I have believed this teaching.' After a lot more talk I said, 'We are traveling on parallel lines that can never meet.'

"Again before I slept I saw the Lord's form, on the wall there before me. And after that I saw the Lord high and lifted up, with a multitude standing at his feet and the morning sun rising behind Him. Then I realized clearly that Jesus is the only God of all the earth." In the middle of the night his wife found him in their mean living room, bare even of *tatami* so poor they were because of his drunkenness, weeping and praying. "She was amazed to see me in such a state of mind.

"Since then I have burned the idols in my home, and I was able to stop the priest who used to come twice a month from visiting us any more." The bean curdler wanted at first to make a fresh start elsewhere, but felt that he must stay where his unsavory past was known and that men should see what God could do to a drunkard. Spiritually he has grown fast. The little local church is cautious: he has still to stand the test of years, and they recall that what grows quickly may wither quickly. His wife, now awaiting baptism, tells her friends, "You have no idea how wonderful it is to have an ordinary human being for a husband instead of a sot," and wonders why she had never discovered Christ for herself earlier. "I could have had peace all the time."

When walking back from baptism the bean curdler said to the missionary, "I am like a starving man who was grubbing on the rubbish heap to look for a ten-yen piece to stave off hunger. Instead, I have found a treasure I can never exhaust."

FORTY ✳ *Typhoon*

On September 22, 1959, we went to Kobe for the final episode of our Asian tour. After that there would be nothing but the journey back to Tokyo and on to Karuizawa, in the hills ninety miles northwest, where we had rented a log cabin to spend the autumn writing before sailing at the beginning of December for the United States and home.

We flew, intending to return by train and enjoy the unsurpassed scenery of the Tokaido trunk line. It was our first flight in Japan, and gave fine views of the summit of Mount Fuji wreathed in cloud, and an impression of a delicate but highly developed countryside. The stewardess kept us informed about the landmarks. At one point she corrected herself, and thus I distinctly remember the coast line of Ise Bay, "and up there at its head, Nagoya." The plane being early at Osaka, we circled the city three times, as if to emphasize the immensity of Japan's industrial might—factories, bridges, roads, railway lines, and children in their thousands ranked on the playgrounds for gym at schools across the city.

From Osaka Airport our last host of the tour, Mr. William Bee, Field Secretary of the Japan Evangelistic Band, took us by complicated suburban electric lines, three changes, twenty-five miles to Suma in the suburbs of Kobe, the great shipbuilding center and now first port of Japan, set on a fine position on a narrow strip between mountains and the Inland Sea.

Four days later we awoke to a sultry but sunny morning. When I went down by bus to meet the presiding bishop, it had turned overcast and sticky. "Pretyphoon weather," said Mrs. Bee. By the time

I emerged from seeing the bishop, rain had begun and the wind freshened. Back at Suma, Mr. Bee welcomed me with, "They say it is the worst typhoon of the season, and coming straight at Osaka." There would be no going out that night, and this meant disappointment: we could not visit the famous Mission Hall which has been called "the most strategic in the Far East" because it is in the Prostitutes' Street in the heart of Kobe's amusement area. No one would be out; too much danger from falling tiles or collapsing buildings. It was our only opportunity, for the next day we were to return to Tokyo.

A typhoon's punch is in its "eye" where the winds swirl at a fantastic speed. The "eye" is comparatively small in diameter, but travels irresistibly for a long distance, carving through a country.

We tried a short walk in the driving rain after lunch. The wind, coming from the east, blew us along the beach where the waves were beginning to boil. Turning back, heads well down, we could just move. Ships were making for the open sea to ride out the storm. Trains had slowed down; road traffic was thinning. "If the gusts get too strong and frequent, come back at once," we were told; "a typhoon arrives with a rush, and then the tiles fly." Our host and his neighbors were boarding up their windows. The whole world was going to ground.

After tea the view from the windows was of nearly deserted streets; and on the hillside tall pines dancing madly and slender firs almost touching the very ground in wild homage to the storm, a salute of the condemned before they should be torn out by their roots. The electric light flickered off and on, breaking finally at five-thirty.

Half an hour later the seven of us in the house sat down to a meal by candlelight. In the middle of a lively conversation above the noise outside, at six-fifteen Mr. Bee left his place. "Forgive me, friends, but the wind has changed. The rain is pouring in the other side. I must shut that window." It was at that moment that Typhoon Vera smashed into the peninsula near Ise at 161 miles per hour, roared past Nagoya City, about sixty-five miles east of us, and charged into Central Japan while tidal waves swept up Ise Bay and over the seawalls: 5,276 persons were killed or drowned or washed out to sea; 10,000 were injured.

At Kobe by bedtime it was certain that the "eye" had missed us; rain lashed windows, trees still swayed, trains had stopped; the gusts were at longer intervals, and weaker. No one then knew that it was the worst typhoon in Japan's recorded history, destroying 39,000 houses, washing away 1,875 bridges, sinking 276 vessels and damaging over 2,000. The Australian liner *Changsha* ran aground. Damage to public works amounted to over £80 million, to agriculture, fishery, and forests, £45 million. A tree one thousand years old fell on a building of the Grand Shrine at Ise.

Next morning we were due to leave Osaka by the crack express at 9:00 A.M., and Mr. Bee accompanied us from Suma Station at about 7:30. Apart from a bric-à-brac of branches the only signs of the typhoon were small trees uprooted from the pavement: they could be replanted. Local trains were running, but at Osaka Central the express was not in the platform. Mr. Bee went to reconnoiter. "No trains to Tokyo," he reported. Nineteen lines of the Japan National Railway had been cut. The express might run the next day or the day after; seats were limited and the chances of obtaining two, even should the line be restored, were remote. The only hope was by air.

We hurried to the travel office outside the big station, joined the crowd jostling for air tickets, and thanks to Mr. Bee's command of the language were half-promised seats on a plane for 2:00 P.M. The railway Fare Adjustments Office instantly refunded our tickets, a forcible contrast to the seven or more months' delay on Indian Railways.

Expectation was dashed twice. Tickets for an extra plane finally were handed to us at 1:00 P.M. Not until then did the faithful Mr. Bee leave us.

We had reached Osaka from Kobe about 8:45 A.M. After two postponements, we were dispatched to the airport at 10:15 P.M. A wait of thirteen and a half hours. Plenty of time to cast my mind back over thirteen and a half months of tour.

I have been decisively convinced that missions and the Christian churches are a weighty factor in world affairs. They helped very largely to make Asia what it is, since missions were foremost in the promotion of intellectual and social progress, without which the birth of many modern Asian nations would have been retarded. And they are an even weightier factor today. Asia is on the march. The direction of that march matters to the world.

A man of experience said to me: "It is true that when the people of Asia are as highly developed as the people of the West, she will dominate the world. She will never reach that stage until there is a much higher level of moral integrity and righteousness." I disagree. This tour has continually touched, without entering, the lair of the Dragon—Red China. In Nepal, Indian Tibet, the Kachin and Shan States of Burma, Laos, Hong Kong, I was close to the borders of China, and throughout East Asia expatriate Chinese, looking more to Peking than Formosa, were in the scene. Red China shows how fast and dangerously an Asian nation may develop when urged by a perverted purpose and a false morality.

The sure bulwark is a right foundation; most of Asia's millions have not got it. "Democracy can only work in a Christian background," said an Englishman during the last days of my tour. "That's why it has failed in Asia."

"The big burden of Asia is fatalism," said an American right at the start. "People's wealth consists not in what they possess but what they produce. These fields and factories are not producing what they might. There is no right incentive."

That American, Dr. W. A. Zoerner, a Presbyterian in Lahore with whom we stayed on our way through to Nepal, was a man of great knowledge of India and Pakistan. We had discussed the present close interaction of West and East; a truth since impressed more forcibly on me as we traveled, by the opening of the regular jet services between the Far East and London, the Far East and United States, making the very word "overseas" more redundant. Dr. Zoerner and I were agreed that if the West did not help the East to a firm spiritual foundation, in a generation it might be too late. I told him how our local postman, saying goodbye, had exclaimed, "If we don't help those people now, we are sitting on our own children!"

"Ah," said Dr. Zoerner, "the approach of Enlightened Self-Interest: the motive behind United States aid to underdeveloped countries. It has no place in a *Christian* ideology." He conceded that a low motive was better than no motive, and that if men and women awake to the stark reality that their own future is threatened they may develop a less selfish concern as knowledge grows.

"I am so concerned at the home situation," went on Dr. Zoerner. "Many of our people think they can discharge their Christian obligation to the overseas mission of the church simply by contributing money. They do not follow through with personal involvement in what is going on. The result has been that they are not well informed. They contribute their own imagination, and have no idea how people live, or what missionaries do."

Undoubtedly the Western churches are not mobilized. In Borneo I saw the Report of the Lambeth Conference which had ended as we left England. An apt paragraph ran: "To think of missionary activity (whether to the islands of the far seas or to the unevangelized masses of England or America) as a kind of 'optional extra' to be undertaken by those who are enthusiastic for that sort of thing, is to make complete nonsense of the Gospel." The English Christian community gives what is left over from its own concerns, of money, energy, prayer, to the world outside. The way of blessing is to reverse this order.

There are many people of Asia wide open to the Gospel, political difficulties being as nothing to the appetite for truth of the ordinary man and woman. One of the surprises of the tour has been the emptiness of non-Christian faiths as they confront the modern Asian. Resistance comes from custom, indifference, fear, and not because the traditional religions offer a satisfying answer to the riddles of existence or a compelling purpose in life. If the Christian nations, as nations and not as a sprinkling of individuals, set to the task of evangelism, the consequences would be startling.

We reached Osaka airport at 10:50. Extra planes were on and it was as busy as at midday. Television newsreels showed bodies and wounded being removed from the typhoon area, parts of Nagoya under water, hundreds of people clinging to the roofs of houses, United States Security Forces and the Japanese Self-Defense Force swinging into action.

Our Skymaster came in, and the flight ahead took off immediately. At 11:40 we entered the plane. Still delay, for one passenger was missing, and we did not fly until midnight, passing high above

Nagoya in the darkness. The last of the typhoon winds puffed us to Tokyo at exceptional speed.

A tour of Asia that had begun overland because we could not get through by air ended by air because we could not get through by land.

APPENDIX

Log of the Tour

Total Miles Traveled

(Excluding local travel, i.e., out and back to a center within a day)

Liverpool (Aug. 16, 1958) until departure from Yokohama (Dec. 6, 1959)	33,040
Yokohama to England via the United States (approx.)	12,000
	45,040

Methods of Transport, Asian Tour

	miles
Sea	12,177
Air	5,370
Rail	12,000
Road	2,748
Water (canoe, launch)	508
Foot	237
	33,040

Distances Within Countries

	miles
Pakistan	777
Nepal	297
India	5,583
Ceylon	486
Burma	1,880
Thailand and Laos	2,357
Malaya and Singapore	766
Indonesia	1,309
Sarawak and North Borneo	1,443
Philippines	1,041
Japan	2,919